# A Chronology of Stanford University and its Founders

1824 - 2000

Karen Bartholomew
Claude Brinegar
Roxanne Nilan

Stanford Historical Society
2001

Stanford Historical Society
P.O. Box 20028
Stanford, CA 94309
650 725-3332
Stanhist@sulmail.stanford.edu

**BOOK DESIGN:** Karen Bartholomew
with assistance of Becky Fischbach

**PHOTOGRAPHS:** Stanford University Archives, Stanford News Service, Hoover Institution Archives

**COVER DESIGN:** Joanna McClean

**COVER PHOTOGRAPHS:**

*1. Horse-in-motion study. Eadweard Muybridge, 1870s.*

*2. Arched entrance of the Center for Integrated Systems.*

*3. Leland Stanford Jr. at age 14.*

*4. Women pose at site of the future Memorial Church, 1894.*

*5. Track team, 1895.*

*6. Rodin sculpture watches over class in Memorial Court, 1986. By Ed Souza.*

*7. Flag-bearing students lead procession into Frost Amphitheater for baccalaureate, 1993. By L.A. Cicero.*

*8. BACKGROUND: Perspective drawing of design for the university by Shepley, Rutan & Coolidge and Frederick Law Olmsted. Probably 1888.*



May 2001

ISBN: 0-9664249-1-3

# Contents

In honor of

THE STANFORD HISTORICAL SOCIETY'S
25TH ANNIVERSARY

In memory of

PETER C. ALLEN
ROSAMOND C. BACON
DONALD C. CARLSON
FREDERIC O. GLOVER
ROBERT M. MINTO
DOROTHY F. REGNERY
JAMES T. WATKINS IV
H. DONALD WINBIGLER

# Errata

## *Stanford Chronology*

Compiled by the authors
February 2006

Page 14 (1888): In the **Mausoleum** entry, the name of the designer of the nearby Arizona Garden should be spelled Rudolph, not Rudolf, Ulrich.

Page 33 (1900): In the entry on the **Stanford family statue,** the sculptor's name should be Larkin Mead, not Meade.

Page 33 (1900): In the entry on **Tax exempt status,** George Crothers' middle initial should be E (Edward), not C.

Page 35 (1902): In the entry **Hail, Stanford, Hail,** the location of the concert by the Mormon Tabernacle choir is listed as Memorial Church. It was actually Assembly Hall, now known as Building 120.

Page 36 (1902): In the entry on **Memorial Arch,** the carver's name should be spelled Schmid, not Schmidt, and the title of the frieze should be listed as "The Progress of Civilization in America." Schmid designed, modeled, and carved the frieze based on a written description by Augustus Saint Gaudens.

Page 37 (1903): The **Salviati mosaics** entry states that in February 1903 Mauricio Camerino brought the first designs for Memorial Church mosaic decoration from Venice. However, the installation was well under way by November 1901, according to the *Stanford Alumnus* magazine. Much of the church's interior decoration had been completed before its January 1903 dedication, although some mosaic installation remained undone, including the scene for the large space opposite the Garden of Eden. Also note that Maurizio is the preferred spelling of Camerino's first name.

Page 38 (1903): The entry **Durand arrives** should be listed under fall 1904 rather than 1903.

Page 39 (1904): The entry on **Japanese students** should be listed under spring 1903 rather than 1904.

Page 39 (1904): In the entry **First world record,** Norman Dole's world record should be 12 feet, 1 and 8/25ths inches.

Page 40 (1905): In the entry **Jane Stanford dies,** we state: "At that time, small amounts of strychnine routinely were used in some medicines, including Mrs. Stanford's prescription." This should read: "At that time, small amounts of strychnine routinely were used in some medicines, including remedies Mrs. Stanford was known to have taken."

Page 41 (1905): In the entry **Rugby replaces football,** the year the University of California returned to American-rules football should be 1915, not 1912.

Page 43 (1908): The October 1908 entry on **The Toonerville Trolley** should be listed under October 1909. The trolley operated until fall 1929.

Page 49-50 (1917): In the entry **Stanford ambulance units,** the name of an alumnus killed in World War I should be James Grant Fergusson, not Ferguson.

Page 51 (1918): In the **Flu epidemic** entry, it should be noted that the influenza pandemic of 1918 was in the fall, not spring. An early wave of flu hit military camps in the United States in spring 1918, but the epidemic did not start at Stanford until September.

Page 58 (1928): The November 7 entry **Hoover elected president** should be dated November 6.

Page 59 (1930): The entry **Golf Course opens** lists William Bell as sole designer of the Stanford Golf Course and says he also designed the Pebble Beach links. In fact, William P. Bell developed the concept of incorporating San Francisquito Creek into the Stanford course; however, George C. Thomas Jr. is responsible for most of the design. Bell managed the construction and reported to Thomas, who was ill and never visited the completed course. Bell did not design Pebble Beach, but he planned many courses in Southern California and elsewhere.

Page 71 (1945): In the entry **Stegner arrives,** it should be noted that Wallace Stegner started the Creative Writing Program in 1946, a year after he joined the English faculty.

Page 77 (1953): The November 17 entry **Med Center plans,** regarding the decision to relocate the Medical School from San Francisco to campus, should be dated July 15.

Page 81 (1958): In the entry **First overseas campus,** the correct year for launching Stanford in Austria should be 1965 and Stanford in Britain 1966.

Page 88 (1964): In the entry ***Paleoparadoxia* at SLAC,** the fossil skeleton should be described as a marine mammal, not an amphibian.

Page 153 (1952): In the entry on **Felix Bloch,** "their core" should read "their cores."

Dedication page: Donald C. Carlson should be listed as **Donald T. Carlson**

*Please contact the Stanford Historical Society with additional suggestions and corrections.*
*Email:* ***Stanfordhist@stanford.edu***

# Preface

"One of [our goals] would be a substantial chronology. . . . [This] chronology might logically lead to an encyclopedia of Stanford history, perhaps with a who's who. Then at least people would know the difference between the Vow Boys and the Wow Boys, and perhaps the geniuses who put the huge footprints up and down Hoover Tower would finally come forward so we could record their names for posterity."

— Prof. James T. Watkins IV, 1976

The above prophetic words of Prof. Watkins, the first president of the Stanford Historical Society, have inspired the authors to undertake what he called for 25 years ago: A Chronology of Stanford University and its Founders.

We see this chronology as a linking of the key — and perhaps even some of the not-so-key but nevertheless interesting — events that have occurred since the birth of Leland Stanford, 177 years ago, and the development of the world-class university that Stanford is today.

The chronology endeavors to put these events in the right order, with the right dates, and with enough history to make them understandable. We hope the outcome is interesting to the casual reader and useful to the researcher.

But a word of caution. While we have worked hard to be accurate — relying on original sources insofar as possible — undoubtedly some corrections are in order. Discerning readers are invited to call them to our attention. Please write to Chronology Editor, Stanford Historical Society, P.O. Box 20028, Stanford, CA 94309 (email: stanhist@sulmail.stanford.edu).

We wish to thank all those who have helped us — especially Spyros Andreopoulos, James Axline, Robert W. Beyers, Jean Marie Deken, Stewart Gillmor, Margaret Kimball, Norman Tutorow, and Warren G. Wonka. Also, we are grateful for the assistance of the University Archives and Stanford News Service.

Errors and misinterpretations are, of course, solely the responsibility of the authors.

— *K.B., C.B., R.N.*

P.S. Answers to the rhetorical questions asked by Prof. Watkins can be found on pages 62, 67, and 74.

*The Stanford family: Leland, Jane Lathrop, and Leland Jr. in 1883.*

# Early Years

## 1824

March 9 **LELAND STANFORD BORN:** Amasa Leland Stanford is born in Watervliet township in New York's Mohawk Valley. He does not use the name Amasa. He is the fourth son of eight children (six sons survive into adulthood) of Josiah Stanford and Elizabeth Phillips. A farmer and innkeeper along the Albany-Schenectady turnpike, Josiah is also a contractor who supplies wood to local railroad projects. Leland's grandfather, Lyman Stanford, had moved from Massachusetts to the Albany region in 1799.

## 1828

August 25 **JANE LATHROP BORN:** Jane Eliza[beth] Lathrop is born in Albany, New York, the third in a family of seven children (one dies in infancy) of prominent merchant Dyer Lathrop and his wife, Jane Ann Shields. As are most girls of her generation and social status, Jane is strictly reared and educated at home, although she briefly attends the Albany Female Academy.

## 1841

May **LELAND STANFORD EDUCATION:** At 17, Leland Stanford sets out to prepare for a professional career. He studies at Clinton and Cazenovia preparatory academies in upstate New York. In 1844-45, he attends Cazenovia Seminary, a well-respected Methodist academy near Syracuse, where he develops a strong interest in philosophy and debate. Unusual for its day, Cazenovia is coeducational; 40 years later, Stanford remembers the benefits of this experience and insists, over his wife's initial objections, that the new university at Palo Alto also be coeducational.

## 1845

**LELAND STANFORD STUDIES LAW:** Leland Stanford returns to Albany to study law at the office of Wheaton, Doolittle and Hadley. (Typically, those who aspire to practice law read legal texts while working in an established law office.) Three years later, Stanford passes the New York bar and is offered a position at the firm, which he declines.

## 1848

Fall **LELAND STANFORD'S LAW CAREER:** Stanford establishes his first practice in the new state of Wisconsin. He opens a law office with Wesley Pierce in Port Washington, a small but rapidly growing community on the shore of Lake Michigan. A confirmed Whig (the party of Daniel Webster, Henry Clay, and Abraham Lincoln), Stanford runs unsuccessfully for district attorney in a largely Democratic county, but is elected Port Washington village trustee in 1851 and serves as president *pro tem* of the town council for nine months.

## 1850

September 30 **STANFORD MARRIAGE:** Leland Stanford marries Jane Lathrop (whom he calls "Jennie") in Albany, New York. They had met years before in Albany. They make their first home together in Port Washington.

## 1852

March 16 **PORT WASHINGTON FIRE:** Disappointed in

*Leland Stanford in front of the Stanford Bros. store in the California gold fields, 1852.*

*Jane Lathrop and Leland Stanford pose for daguerreotype portraits in 1850.*

Port Washington and its prospects, the Stanfords decide to join Leland's brothers in Gold Rush California when a major fire burns much of Port Washington, including Stanford's law office and extensive library. Port Washington's future is dubious as real estate prices fall, business falters, and the county seat is moved elsewhere. Before leaving the East, Leland and Jane return to Albany to visit their parents.

June **West to California:** Leland leaves New York for California (via Nicaragua), arriving in San Francisco July 12 after 38 days at sea. He joins his brothers in Sacramento. Josiah Stanford first arrived in 1849, and DeWitt and Charles in 1851; Phillip and young Thomas Welton join them in trading ventures early in 1852. Jane Stanford bows to strenuous objections of both sets of parents, and remains at her parents' home in Albany rather than accompany her husband. During the next three years, Leland forges a new career in business selling supplies at his store near Cold Springs (El Dorado County) and in the gold fields nearby, and in 1853, at Michigan City in Placer County. He is elected justice of the peace at Michigan City.

# 1855

June **Reunited:** Informed of his father-in-law's death in May, Stanford sells his store and returns to Jane in Albany. The couple decide to make Sacramento their home. They journey west by steamer from New York to San Francisco across Central America, perhaps by the newly completed railroad, arriving in Sacramento in November.

# 1856

April 30 **California Republican Party formed:** The first state Republican party convention is held. Leland Stanford is among founders of the state's fledgling Republican Party. Republican candidates make slow progress in a state dominated by Southern Democrats and nativists of the American Party (or "Know-Nothings") and a population desperate to avoid the divisive issue of slavery. Despite some local gains in Sacramento and San Francisco by 1859, Republicans have little chance of winning state-wide elections until the firing on Fort Sumter in 1861 shatters local Democratic unity.

Fall **Sacramento:** After buying the Stanford Brothers firm in Sacramento from brothers Josiah and Phillip, Leland builds a substantial new fireproof building at 64 Front Street at the corner of L Street. The Stanfords live in a modest but comfortable frame house on Second Street between O and P streets and immerse themselves in the bustling business and social life of California's state capital.

# 1860

February **Stanford's early political career:** At

Jane Stanford, right, and her sister, Anna Maria, play billiards with young Leland looking on.

Jane Stanford proudly holds her 3-month old son, Leland.

Recently elected Gov. Leland Stanford.

The Stanfords on the porch of their Sacramento home in the 1860s. The house will take on a new look in 1871 (above left) when it is raised and a new first floor added.

the state Republican convention, Stanford is elected a delegate to the national convention in Chicago, but he stays home to deal with business concerns. Like many California Republicans, he supports nomination of fellow New Yorker William Seward, but Stanford later stumps the state for national party nominee Abraham Lincoln in the 1860 campaign. He earns a reputation as a tenacious campaigner under daunting conditions (Stanford had run unsuccessfully for state treasurer in 1857 and for governor in 1859 when Democrats swept state elections). On June 19, 1861, Stanford is nominated again by his party for governor. On Sept. 4, the 37-year old Stanford wins election on a pro-Union and pro-railroad ticket.

# 1861

June 28 **CENTRAL PACIFIC RAILROAD CHARTERED:** During the same month as California's turbulent political party conventions, the Central Pacific Railroad is chartered in Sacramento in an upstairs room of the Huntington and Hopkins hardware store. Theodore Judah persuades a handful of Sacramento businessmen to finance his survey and begin construction, arguing that federal and state support will follow. Stanford, known as a reliable businessman with influence in the Lincoln administration, is elected president of the company, and Judah chief engineer. While none of these men, including Judah, has experience with large-scale construction projects, they do have experience with California's economic and political climate, considerable business acumen, and the capacity for sustained, if risky, effort. Although not California's first railroad, the Central Pacific will take over most competing local rail lines by 1868.

July 11 **SACRAMENTO RESIDENCE:** Leland and Jane Stanford purchase a two-story house at the southeast corner of 8th and N streets for the substantial sum of $8,000. The house serves as Gov. Stanford's office and residence. In 1871, the house is extensively remodeled into a 44-room mansion with a stylish Mansard roof; the structure is raised a story, major additions are added, and extensive interior and exterior renovations are made. In 1872, former Secretary of State William Seward is a guest. In 1880, President Rutherford B. Hayes, the first chief executive to come to California while in office, visits, accompanied by Gen. William T. Sherman and Secretary of War Alexander Ramsey. After the Stanfords move to San Francisco in 1874, the house remains fully furnished but unoccupied except for occasional visits until April 18, 1900, when Mrs. Stanford gives the house and an endowment to the Roman Catholic Diocese of Sacramento. The "Stanford-Lathrop House" serves as an orphanage, then a home for girls, and later as a settlement house.

# 1862

January 10 **GOV. LELAND STANFORD:** Leland Stanford begins his two-year term as governor (terms are changed to

Central Pacific construction crews working near Summit Tunnel, within a few hundred feet of Donner Pass. The 1,659-foot tunnel takes a year of digging and blasting before the breakthrough.

A Central Pacific train crosses the recently built Long Ravine Bridge in the Sierra foothills.

Gov. Stanford locomotive, CP No. 1, near Folsom.

four years in 1863) with a narrowly divided legislature, an empty treasury, a large state debt, and badly organized governmental infrastructure. Although a movement to take California out of the Union is more emotional than practical, rumors of pro-Southern conspiracies persist. A small Republican majority in the legislature leads to a number of significant reforms in the state's civil rights codes during the war years, but public sentiment in California strongly opposes any changes granting equal rights to either blacks or non-citizens. (After the war, the 13th, 14th, and 15th amendments to the federal Constitution are not ratified by California voters.) Stanford does not actively seek renomination (although he may have expected to be so named), and a joint convention of Republicans and Union Democrats chooses Frederick F. Lowe, another Republican.

# 1863

October **CENTRAL PACIFIC CONSTRUCTION:** The Central Pacific begins laying track after Stanford successfully lobbies for state and county subsidies, and Judah successfully seeks federal support. It will take two years to reach Colfax, in the Sierra foothills, only 56 miles from Sacramento. After many problems surmounting the Sierra Nevada further slow construction, the line reaches the California-Nevada border in 1868 and then races across Nevada to Promontory, Utah. The great profits of the Central Pacific associates are made not as company directors but as chief investors in companies constructing the line: Charles Crocker & Co., hired to build to the Nevada border; and the Contract & Finance Co., which lays the tracks across Nevada and Utah. Over the next two decades, Stanford and his colleagues gain control of a western transportation empire that includes rail, stage, and steamship lines.

November **GOV. STANFORD LOCOMOTIVE:** The first locomotive of the Central Pacific Railroad, the Gov. Stanford, goes into service. Built in 1862 by Richard Norris & Son of Philadelphia, the CP No. 1 locomotive is a 56,000-pound standard American-type engine (wheel arrangement 4-4-0). Broken down, it was put aboard a San Francisco-bound clipper ship in Boston on May 18, 1863. Arriving in October, it is reassembled in Sacramento. Contrary to legend, it is not the first engine to cross the Sierra, nor does it pull Leland Stanford's train to the Gold Spike ceremony. But it is at the head of the Central Pacific's first excursion, first scheduled passenger train, and first revenue freight train. After two years of mainline service, it is relegated to yard-switching and fire-fighting duty as more powerful engines are purchased. The Gov. Stanford is retired in January 1895, and given to Jane Stanford in early 1899.

# 1868

May 14 **LELAND JUNIOR BORN:** Leland DeWitt Stanford, the only child of Jane and Leland Stanford, is born at the Stanford residence in Sacramento. Jane Stanford is 39, Le-

Stanford holds ceremonial sledgehammer at Promontory, Utah, in 1869. The Last Spike, made of solid gold, and the hammer are on display in the Stanford Museum.

The Stanfords' Nob Hill residence on California Street (above), and its library.

land Stanford, 44. The boy later chooses to use the name Leland Stanford Jr.

# 1869

May 10 **LAST SPIKE CEREMONY:** Central Pacific Railroad President Leland Stanford drives the gold spike at Promontory, Utah, to connect ceremonially the Central Pacific and Union Pacific railroads, North America's first transcontinental railroad. Of four ceremonial spikes used, two — Nevada's Comstock silver spike and the gold, or "Last Spike" — are currently on display at the Stanford Museum.

# 1870

January **WINE-MAKING AT WARM SPRINGS AND PALO ALTO FARM:** Josiah Stanford begins operating the Warm Springs ranch, owned by brother Leland, and the next year begins experimenting with wine-making. The Stanfords see a promising industry in California wine-making, and believe moderate wine-drinking discourages immoderate use of hard liquor. Leland Stanford had purchased Warm Springs, a health resort and winery near Mission San Jose, in late 1869. By 1876, the ranch produces some 50,000 gallons of wine a year, as well as fruits, grain, and cattle. In 1886, Josiah is given title to the property, and following his death in 1890, his son Josiah Winslow Stanford will further develop both the winery and ranching operations. After a series of owners in the early 20th century, a portion of the original property becomes the Weibel Winery in 1945; much of the Warm Springs site is developed for residences and a park in the early 1990s. Leland also builds a winery at the Palo Alto Farm, where table wine is produced throughout the 1880s and 1890s.

# 1872

May **FIRST HORSE-IN-MOTION EXPERIMENTS:** Leland Stanford hires San Francisco photographer Eadweard Muybridge to provide photographic evidence that a trotter moving at top speed has all four feet off the ground at one point in its stride. Muybridge makes his first attempt at Union Park race course in Sacramento, capturing with his lens Stanford's record-setting Occident trotting at full speed. These "horse in motion" experiments will continue a decade later at the Palo Alto Stock Farm. Muybridge's highly acclaimed comprehensive study of Yosemite is completed this year, as is his commission to document the Stanfords' newly remodeled Sacramento mansion. Muybridge will also photograph the Stanfords' new San Francisco residence and capture his famous seven-part panoramic view of the city from the mansion's roof in 1876.

# 1876

July **PALO ALTO FARM:** Leland Stanford acquires May-

*Paddocks and key buildings of Stanford's Palo Alto Stock Farm, circa 1890. The prominent barn is nearly all that remains.*

field Grange, the former Gordon Estate (generally the area of the current Stanford Shopping Center) near Menlo Park, about 35 miles south of San Francisco. Over the next decade, he will expand these 650 acres through acquisition of adjourning farms to more than 8,000 acres of orchard, vineyard, grazing land, stables, and training tracks. On this, his favorite family property, Leland Stanford continues experiments with the breeding and training of trotting and thoroughbred horses. The name Palo Alto is taken from the landmark tree known as *El Palo Alto,* or "The Tall Tree," a tall redwood tree on the banks of San Francisquito Creek, near the San Francisco-San Jose country road (later, El Camino Real).

Summer **ELECTIONEER:** After attending the Centennial Exposition in Philadelphia, the Stanfords go to New York where, against advice, Leland Stanford purchases the horse Electioneer for $12,000. In nine years at Stony Ford, Electioneer had not produced any progeny of significance, so he had been largely ignored. Although not a winning trotter himself, in the next 14 years at the Palo Alto Stock Farm, Electioneer sires 166 colts that can trot the mile in less than 2½ minutes, including nine of the farm's 13 world-record champions. The many victories of Electioneer's progeny earn high regard for Stanford's Palo Alto Stock Farm.

Fall **STANFORDS MOVE INTO THEIR NOB HILL MANSION:** The Stanfords move into their newly completed $2 million, 50-room residence in San Francisco on California Street between Powell and Mason, sharing a city-block with Mr. and Mrs. Mark Hopkins. When the Central Pacific Railroad offices move to San Francisco in 1873, the Stanfords begin their move from Sacramento. While still using the Sacramento residence, they live in a hotel and then rent a house at 711 Pine street while building their mansion. The Nob Hill mansion is designed by S.C. and C.L. Bugbee. Noted for its extensive use of bay windows on the exterior, its interior features a circular main hall that rises two additional stories above a large, black-on-white mosaic of zodiac signs to an amber-glassed dome. Principal public rooms open out onto this 70-foot sunlit space, including a Pompeiian reception room, ballroom, picture gallery, and dining room. Private family rooms include a family sitting room, library, billiard room, supper room, and bedrooms. The residence also is noted for its detailed woodwork, frescoes, and hardwood finishes designed by Pottier, Stymus and Garbaldi of New York.

# 1878

April **PALO ALTO STOCK FARM:** Charles Marvin, a talented trotting-horse trainer and driver, begins work at the Palo Alto Stock Farm, eventually becoming superintendent. The trotting department grows to employ 150 workers, and includes a blacksmith shop, a wheelwright shop, a feed mill, approximately 50 paddocks, eight tracks, an office building with sleeping quarters for 40 men upstairs, a dining hall, a harness shop, a superintendent's house, and

*The stock farm's eucalyptus-lined Governor's Avenue, circa 1890.*

*Camera setup for horse-in-motion experiments at the farm (top). Leland Jr. rides his pony for Eadweard Muybridge's cameras.*

*Prized breeding stallion Electioneer poses for the well-dressed photographer.*

a school. At its height, the Stock Farm boards 600 horses. Construction of most stock farm buildings, including the Red Barn (the horse barn, not the red brick winery building), probably occurs between 1878 and 1880. The eucalyptus-lined road from the house to the stables that stock farm workers dub the "Governor's Avenue" is planted, and the reservoir now known as Lagunita ("little lake") is built to irrigate the farm.

July **SECOND HORSE-IN-MOTION EXPERIMENTS:** Eadweard Muybridge publishes the first series of photographs of horses in motion, finally proving to Stanford's satisfaction that at one point in its fastest gait, a trotter has all four feet off the ground. Stanford and Muybridge had revived their Sacramento studies at the Palo Alto Stock Farm in 1877. With the help of John D. Isaacs, a Central Pacific mechanical engineer, Muybridge experiments with split-second shutter speeds and a series of 24 cameras spaced 12 inches apart, electrically tripped in rapid succession. In 1879, Muybridge will project "motion pictures" in San Francisco, and possibly at the Stanfords' Palo Alto home, using his "zoöpraxiscope" (which rotates a series of still images on glass disks in rapid succession to give the impression of motion). After a falling out with Stanford regarding copyright in 1882, Muybridge continues the study of animals and humans in motion at the University of Pennsylvania. In May 1929, identical plaques are placed in Memorial Court and at the stock farm site honoring the role Muybridge and Stanford played in the early development of moving pictures. The ceremony is attended by movie producer Louis B. Mayer and other representatives of the Academy of Motion Picture Arts and Sciences. In 1983, the site of the Muybridge-Stanford experiments is made a California State Landmark.

# 1880

May 22 **FIRST GRAND TOUR:** On his first European grand tour (1880-1881), Leland Jr. visits many historical sites and acquires historical objects for his growing collection of natural history curiosities and local artifacts from the American West. On their return, these objects are meticulously cataloged by Leland Jr. and Mrs. Stanford, and displayed in "Leland's Museum" in two rooms of the Nob Hill mansion. As the Stanfords travel though Western and Eastern Europe, Leland and his mother also gather contemporary European crafts (including Italian glassware, French porcelain, and small genre paintings). They are rejoined by Mr. Stanford in June 1881. While in Paris, Mr. and Mrs. Stanford sit for their portraits by noted society painters Meissonier and Bonnat. These paintings are currently on display in the Stanford Museum.

November 20 **HORSE BREEDING AND TRAINING:** Fred Crocker (sired by Electioneer) is the first Palo Alto Stock Farm horse to break a world record for 2-year-olds. Leland Stanford's trotters set 19 world records during the next 15 years. (In its peak year alone, 1891, Stanford horses set seven world records.) The Palo Alto Stock Farm is consid-

*Trotters in harness at the mile-long training track near the paddocks.*

Car Stanford, *commissioned in 1882 by Jane Stanford as a birthday gift for her husband.*

ered by many to be one of the largest and most advanced of its kind in the world. Stanford uses the farm to test his controversial theories about horse breeding and training; he believes that speed and stamina are not a result of chance, but are hereditary qualities that can be cultivated. He also develops the "Palo Alto system" for training colts as soon as they are weaned and driving horses at full speed for short runs instead of the standard practice of longer distances at slower speeds.

# 1881

September **VINA RANCH:** Leland Stanford begins purchasing land in Tehama and Butte Counties along the upper Sacramento River. Over next four years, he makes more than 50 land purchases to build Vina Ranch to more than 53,000 acres. Adding to vines originally planted in the 1840s and a winery built in the 1850s, Stanford greatly increases acreage planted, as well as cellar capacity and production. He installs state-of-the-art equipment and brings skilled winery workers from France. Vina is considered the largest winery in the world. Despite the effort and cost, soil and climate defeat Stanford's hopes to produce a dry wine rivaling French wines, so he turns to sweet wines and brandy. Although most of Vina's acreage is devoted to fruit and grain production, as well as grazing and stock raising, this Stanford "dream ranch" is never a profitable venture. Most of the land is sold by 1919, and is privately owned today.

*A portion of Peter Coutts' extensive Ayreshire Farm, acquired by Stanford in 1882, is seen in a contemporary bird's-eye-view.*

# 1882

September 14 **STANFORD APPOINTED UC REGENT:** Leland Stanford receives an interim appointment to the Board of Regents of the University of California by Republican Governor George C. Perkins. Stanford attends one regents' meeting, but without explanation (though possibly due to ill health) withdraws his name. He maintains good relations with the University at Berkeley, later inviting one UC president (Horace Davis) to serve on Stanford's Board of Trustees, and another (Martin Kellogg) to take part in its opening day celebrations. He also later confers with former UC President Daniel Coit Gilman.

October ***CAR STANFORD:*** An elegant, 70-foot-long private railroad car, commissioned by Jane Stanford as a birthday gift for her husband and named *Car Stanford,* is completed. It includes a lavishly-appointed parlor, dining room and sleeping rooms, a well-equipped kitchen, hot water system, and up-to-date Westinghouse air-brakes.

November 7 **PETER COUTTS:** Leland Stanford expands his Palo Alto Farm by purchasing the adjacent dairy farm owned by Jean-Baptiste Paulin Caperon. Known as "The Frenchman," Caperon was a wealthy French political expatriate who used the name of his deceased cousin Peter Coutts when, in 1874, he bought land in the area very roughly bounded today by Page Mill Road and Galvez Street, El Camino and Interstate 280. Leland Stanford uses Caperon's "Ayreshire Farm" as a "running" farm for breed-

*A dapper 14-year-old Leland Jr. is photographed at a New York studio before leaving for Europe.*

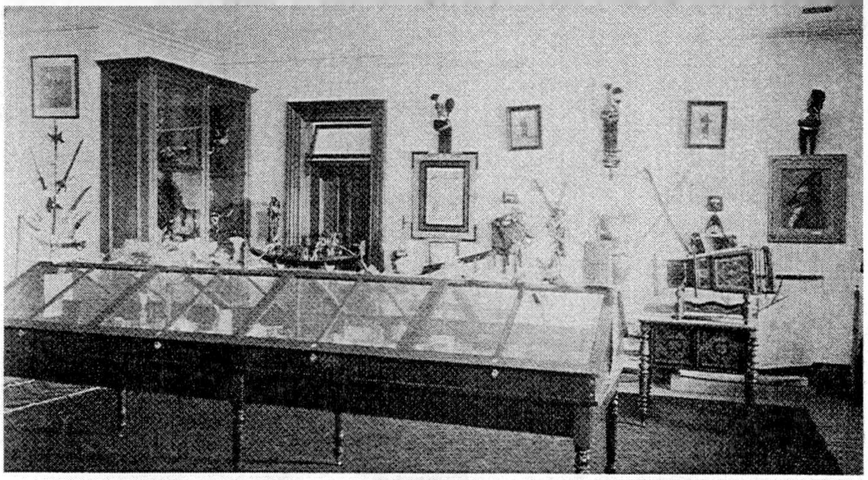

*Leland Jr.'s "museum," cataloged by the boy and his mother, is displayed in the San Francisco mansion.*

*Leland Jr.'s drawing of himself as photographer on the cover of an album of photographs he took in 1883.*

ing English thoroughbreds but the operation never rivals the original "trotting" department. Several of Caperon's structures still stand: his residence, now called Escondité Cottage; the Buttery or Dairy House, which is now a lounge at Rains Houses; Tower House or the Frenchman's Library on Escondido Road, which housed Caperon's collection of rare books and documents and is now boarded up; and Frenchman's Tower on Old Page Mill Road, which serves no purpose other than as a property marker. Caperon had planned to construct a chateau in the area where Hanna House now stands on Frenchman's Road, but he returned to France before starting the project, leaving behind a brick bridge and a nearby artificial lake, now filled with rubble from the 1906 earthquake. Many local legends grow up about The Frenchman, some from the creative imagination of the university's first president, David Starr Jordan.

# 1883

May 26 **Second family tour of Europe:** The Stanfords sail from New York to begin their second lengthy trip (1883-1884) to Europe. Nearly as tall as his father, 15-year-old Leland Jr. is encouraged to indulge his lively intellect and strong interest in art and archeology with visits to archeological sites and museums. Studying the Cypriot collection at New York's Metropolitan Museum the previous year, Leland Jr. had discussed public "art education" with its lively director, Louis di Cesnola, who also provided letters of introduction to some of Europe's most important museum builders. In Paris, Leland Jr. spends hours in the Louvre's Egyptian wing, and learns the rudiments of hieroglyphics from the museum's famed Egyptologist, Georges Daressy. In addition to his studies of French and German, and his practical introduction to the world of museum management and scholarship, Leland Jr. is introduced to the complexity, and duplicity, of the antiquities marketplace through visits to dealers and auction houses. Leland's collection is growing rich in Egyptian, Greek, and Roman antiquities, pre-historic European artifacts, and arms and armor from around the world. It also includes the beginnings of North American, Pacific Island, and African art collections. In January 1884, Leland Jr. meets Heinrich Schliemann, the Homeric scholar famous for his excavation of Troy. By the time the family reaches Naples, Leland Jr. has developed a high fever.

# 1884

March 13 **Leland Jr. dies:** Leland Stanford Jr. dies at the Bristol Hotel in Florence, Italy, of typhoid fever, a virtually untreatable disease that at the time seemed almost random in its victims. Although the family had returned to the more hospitable climate in Florence and doctors decreed Leland's fever a mild case, the boy dies three weeks after arriving, only two months short of his 16th birthday. As they progress slowly home from Italy with their son's body, his grieving parents set in motion various memorial projects,

*Miss Lily Ransome and her charges at the Stanford Free Kindergarten in Mayfield in 1887.*

*Calligraphed cover of the university's Founding Grant, 1885.*

*Marble memorial tablet, marking the site of Leland Jr.'s original mausoleum.*

including a museum initially planned for San Francisco, and an educational institution at their Palo Alto Farm.

May 4 **CONSULTING KEY EDUCATORS:** Arriving in New York from Europe, the Stanfords are detained on the East Coast by railroad business. Over the next seven months, Leland and Jane Stanford take time to visit the presidents of Cornell, Harvard, and MIT to discuss the possibility of founding a university in California in memory of Leland Jr. Although particularly impressed with the type of education offered by Cornell and MIT, and by curriculum reforms undertaken by Charles Eliot at Harvard, the Stanfords plan at the outset to create an educational institution of their own rather than donate funds to an existing institution.

November **LELAND JR.'S RETURN:** The Stanfords return to California, bringing with them, in a special funeral car, a velvet-covered casket with their son's body. After a simple memorial ceremony, the casket is taken to a small mausoleum located near the Palo Alto Farm house. A Dec. 13, 1884, newspaper article describes the structure as stone and brick laid in concrete, located about 100 yards from the house. The ceiling is richly frescoed with a scene of angels bearing the boy upward, and the sarcophagus is covered with slabs of white Carrara marble. The memorial service is held at Grace Church, San Francisco, the following Sunday, while additional memorial services are offered at a number of churches throughout the state. Hundreds of poems, letters, and telegrams of condolence are sent to the Stanfords. After his casket is moved to the family mausoleum in 1893, the original tomb is resealed. In 1898, it is dismantled and the marble slabs are mounted as a permanent memorial on a two-tier sandstone base to mark the site. Jane Stanford has the two sides inscribed with four stanzas of a poem, *Haunted Ground,* by Felicia Dorothea (Browne) Hemans. One hundred years later, the university moves the marker from the site to make way for a senior housing complex.

# 1885

January 28 **LELAND STANFORD ELECTED SENATOR:** Leland Stanford is elected U.S. senator from California by the state legislature. Stanford's candidacy is aided by early news of his plans for the new university. The Stanfords take up residence at 1701 K Street, on Farragut Square, in Washington, D.C.

March 9 **ENABLING ACT:** To permit the founding of Stanford's proposed university, California's Democratic Gov. George Stoneman signs legislation allowing establishment of charitable and educational trusts in perpetuity, and to allow the founder of such a trust greater control over the proposed institution during his lifetime than previously has been permitted. (Prior state law limited the life of trusts to 50 years, after which the state legislature could specify any terms and conditions for reinstatement or dissolution.) The Enabling Act is signed into law on Leland

Harper's Weekly *view of proposed quadrangle, April 21, 1888 (left). The rectangle is reoriented 90 degrees and church location changed by the time architects prepare their final 1888 plan (below).*

*Frederick Law Olmsted*

Stanford's 61st birthday.

Spring **EDUCATIONAL PHILANTHROPIES:** With an interest in children's education prompted by her son's death, Jane Stanford donates funds to the Golden Gate Kindergarten Association and to the Silver Street kindergartens (still experimental in the 1880s). She supports five of 11 Golden Gate kindergartens, including at least one named for Leland Jr., and as honorary president encourages other society women to take a more active role in charities for child care and education. A Stanford Free Kindergarten is established in Mayfield by 1887. Mrs. Stanford also promotes Sunday schools, a school on the Palo Alto Farm, and a night school for stock farm employees. In 1899, she converts her parents' home in Albany, New York, into a shelter for working women and their children, and turns over the Sacramento mansion to a Catholic charity.

November 11 **FOUNDING GRANT:** Leland and Jane Stanford sign the Grant Founding and Endowing The Leland Stanford Junior University, commonly referred to as the Founding Grant, in the library at their home in San Francisco. The grant outlines the university's purpose: "to qualify its students for personal success, and direct usefulness in life," while encouraging them to exercise an influence in behalf of humanity and civilization. It provides for the university's initial endowment; defines its scope, responsibilities, and organization; and names its 24 trustees and formulates their duties. Unlike most private universities elsewhere, it is to be coeducational and nonsectarian, and open to all students regardless of social position or economic status. The grant articulates the Stanfords' faith in American democratic government, individualism, and the work ethic. Woven throughout is the fundamental assumption that through education, the public can best govern itself, and that an educated people will make a greater contribution to American society. Three large tracts of land — Gridley Farm, Vina Ranch, and the Palo Alto Farm — provide the underpinnings of the University's future endowment. The campus is to be built on the Palo Alto Farm. One New York editor later remarks that there is as much need for a new university in California as for "an asylum for decayed ship captains in Switzerland."

November 14 **FIRST BOARD OF TRUSTEES:** In the library of their San Francisco residence, the Stanfords present the Founding Grant to the individuals named as trustees. The board is made up of Stanford's friends and business associates and includes some of California's most successful businessmen and lawmakers. Judge Lorenzo Sawyer is elected first chairman of the board. In the Founding Grant, the Stanfords retain control over the trust properties and the construction and operation of the university until the death of the surviving founder. After the presentation, the Stanfords leave for Washington for the next congressional session and for further consultations with potential architects and faculty. The board does not formally meet until they come together again at Jane's request in 1897. They assume oversight of university affairs when requested to do so by Mrs. Stanford in 1903.

*Jane and Leland Stanford at 1887 cornerstone ceremony hastily arranged by architect Charles Coolidge (standing to right of stonemason in white overalls). Engraved silver trowel used at the ceremony is preserved in the University Archives.*

*Cornerstone and its capstone, installed in 1887, can be seen today on Building 60.*

# 1886

August **GEN. WALKER OF MIT ADVISES:** President Francis A. Walker of the Massachusetts Institute of Technology arrives at the Palo Alto Farm to serve as a consultant on the university's administration and academic organization. In 1885, Walker had declined the Stanfords' offer of the presidency of the new university (at a salary substantially above his present salary) because he felt he had much yet to do at MIT, and because he feared that neither he nor his family would be happy in so different an environment. Agreeing to return as a consultant, Walker arrives for an extended visit to the Palo Alto Farm, which coincides with the first visit of Frederick Law Olmsted (who had been recommended by Walker). In his extensive November report, Walker recommends 13 one-story buildings of stone, uniform in structure; suggests the order of their construction; and outlines an organization of departments and university administration. Walker's philosophy and practicality impresses the Stanfords, although they reject his recommendation that they wait several years before admitting women.

September 26 **OLMSTED-STANFORD PLAN:** Landscape architect Frederick Law Olmsted presents to Leland Stanford what is believed to be his first drawing of the proposed university. Olmsted, who had arrived at Palo Alto in August, had accepted Leland Stanford's commission to plan the overall layout of the university, including buildings and general and site-specific landscaping. Olmsted initially selects a foothills site for the campus and recommends an informal layout reminiscent of his natural designs for Central Park and other university campuses. Stanford, however, rejects this plan, insisting that the flatlan are more appropriate for the grand memorial he has mind. He also prefers a quadrangle plan, along the lin suggested by Walker, rather than the many smaller sing buildings recommended by Olmsted. The new site is chosen days later. Stanford wants a distinctly California sty for the buildings. Olmsted remains concerned about the Stanfords' preference for a New England-style landscapi of trees and turf, which requires too much water for California's arid climate.

Fall **ARCHITECTURAL PLANS:** The Boston firm of Shepley, Rutan, and Coolidge, recommended by Walker ar Olmsted, is selected as architects of the university. The 2 year-old Charles Allerton Coolidge is assigned responsibility. Coolidge, George Shepley, and Charles Rutan, you associates of famous architect Henry Hobson Richards (who had died the previous spring), are influenced by Richardson's Romanesque designs. The Stanford project their first major commission. In March 1887, Coolidge ar Rutan bring to Palo Alto the next set of Olmsted plans a their own plan and model for 12 one-story buildings, pl a church, all facing a large central courtyard. The inn quadrangle buildings are staked out by surveyors. Aga the Stanfords make significant changes: rather than pr senting a lateral view from the wooded area of the ma soleum into the foothills, they wish the vista to end

*Surveyors at work while the Inner Quad takes shape (above left). Stonemasons carve capitals before placing them atop arcade columns (left).*

Memorial Church and envision a large memorial arch at he quadrangle's entrance. The quadrangle is rotated 90 legrees.

## 1887

April **RAILROAD INVESTIGATED:** After a decade of growng anti-railroad public sentiment, President Grover Clevend appoints a Pacific Railway Commission to investigate he financial affairs of all Pacific railroads that had reeived federal funding. Leland Stanford and other railroad fficials testify in controversial public hearings. Governnent officials fear that the railroads have no intention of epaying extensive loans made in construction bonds, due n 1895 and 1897. As early as 1873, when illegal operations f the *Crédit Mobilier* (the limited liability corporation ised to construct the Union Pacific) are investigated, calls ire made expand the investigation to the Central Pacific's Contract & Finance Co. Suspicions had been further raised by the incorporation of the Southern Pacific Company in February 1885 which, in turn, leases two dozen rail lines, ncluding the Central Pacific Railroad.

May 14 **CORNERSTONE LAID:** The university's cornertone is laid at what is now Building 60, next to the future ite of the church, on the 19th anniversary of Leland Jr.'s birth. Several hundred local residents and guests attend he ceremony organized by Coolidge, with music provided by the Menlo Park Presbyterian Church. Construction begins soon after, with landscape plans temporarily postponed except for the area set aside for a family mausoleum. It will take another four years just to complete the Inner Quad. By the time the Outer Quad is completed in 1905, the Quadrangle occupies about 17 acres.

December **PALO ALTO RESIDENCE:** Having given up plans for a costly new residence in the wake of their son's death, the Stanfords instead begin extensive remodeling of the Palo Alto farm residence, which takes place through much of 1888. The Stanfords add a new brick wing between the original house and servants' wing, and move the library and dining room to the new wing. It is furnished with European antiques selected by the Stanfords on their recent overseas trip. Lawns and gardens surround the residence. After her husband's death there in 1893, Mrs. Stanford continues to use the Palo Alto house often until her death in 1905. Initially she suggests to the Board of Trustees that after her death they rent the house "to some responsible person for a summer hotel," but in 1902 she formally recommends that the trustees turn the house over to the university for use by the president. She again reconsiders in 1905 and recommends that, due to the expense in maintaining the structure, it be used for academic purposes. Badly damaged in the 1906 earthquake (only the original servants' wing survives), the remaining house wing is used by the Tichenor family from 1916 to 1919. It is leased by the Stanford Home for Convalescent Children (Con Home) from 1920 to 1965. It is then demolished to make way for the Stanford Children's Hospital.

*Construction of the Stanford Family Mausoleum progresses in early 1888. At Mrs. Stanford's bidding, the all-too-feminine sphinxes are moved to the rear and replaced.*

*Wooden memorial marks stock farm horse cemetery after an 1888 fire.*

*The mausoleum can be seen in the far distance in this circa 1891 view of the Arizona garden.*

*Front of Palo Alto Farm residence, after extensive remodeling in 1888.*

# 1888

April **PALO ALTO FARM FIRE:** Fire, believed to be arson, destroys the stock farm stable in which some of Stanford's most prized horses are boarded. The fire kills nine horses in the 12-stall barn. The valuable colt Palo Alto is saved, and goes on to set a world record for stallions in 1891. But Palo Alto dies of pneumonia in 1892 when he is boarded in a "fire-proof" brick stable Leland Stanford orders as a replacement for the burned stable. Palo Alto and 14 of the stock farm's other most valuable horses are buried in an oak grove not far from the white brick barn. A white wooden shaft initially marks the site, but that is replaced in 1926 with a bronze horse statue university trustee Timothy Hopkins provided from his Menlo Park estate, Sherwood Lodge.

Summer **MAUSOLEUM:** The family crypt, designed to hold Leland Jr.'s remains and those of his parents, is completed. The exterior of the 25- by 40-foot vault is made of Vermont granite. Two granite slabs forming the roof weigh 30 tons each. Two feminine Greek sphinxes are placed on either side of the doorway, but these allegedly so displease Mrs. Stanford that around 1900 she has them moved to the rear of the building and more masculine Egyptian sphinxes take their place at the front door. The interior is lined with polished Carrara marble. Three sarcophagi, cut in Italy from solid blocks of marble, will hold the coffins. The area surrounding the mausoleum site had been graded and landscaped in the early 1880s for construction o grand summer home. The nearby Arizona, or cactus, g den, designed by Rudolf Ulrich and laid out between 18 and 1883, is part of a larger overall plan to include an arti cial lake and a great parkland of trees. The actual site the mausoleum and its approach roads is selected by Fre erick Law Olmsted, who wishes to avoid damaging t large oak growing at the site. By February 1891, additior landscaping for the surrounding area, including pin olives, and shrubbery, is completed. In 1899, Jane Sta ford's younger brother Henry Lathrop is buried neart memorialized by a marble Angel of Grief.

July **DORMITORY PROTOTYPE:** While traveling throu Switzerland to Italy on their third European tour, Lela and Jane Stanford visit the Hotel-Kursaal de la Maloja the edge of Lake Maloja (Lake Sils). Impressed with t building, Leland Stanford will use it as a model for the fi men's dormitory. (Jane Stanford's secretary, Bertha Bern later misdirects historians by incorrectly recording in h memoirs the nearby site of Silvaplana.)

Fall **PRESIDENTIAL POLITICS:** Leland Stanford denies a tive interest in seeking his party's nomination for the U presidency, instead endorsing Benjamin Harrison. Sin his senatorial election, Stanford had been presented by t political press as a possible Republican nominee. Aft Harrison's election, the Stanfords develop a long-standi friendship with President and Mrs. Harrison (who visit t Palo Alto Farm in 1891).

# 1890

**STATISTICS:**

Undergraduate enrollment: Approx. 440 as of Oct. 1, 1891; increases to 555 in spring 1892

Graduate enrollment: 37 as of spring 1892

Faculty: 15 in fall 1891; 29 in spring 1892; 58 in fall 1892

Tuition: Free (incidental fees begin fall 1893)

Spring **STANFORD-HUNTINGTON IMBROGLIO:** Suffering ill health, and preoccupied with university planning and senate affairs, Leland Stanford relinquishes his position as Southern Pacific Company president to Collis P. Huntington after a bitter confrontation. Stanford retains presidency of the Central Pacific Railroad and of the Occidental and Oriental Steamship Line, and his positions on the boards of directors of the Southern Pacific and Pacific Improvement companies. When Huntington complains in a statement to the press that the railroad has suffered from Stanford's absences and his obsession with the new university (which Huntington dubs "Stanford's circus"), the feud is front-page news.

October 26 **LELAND STANFORD JUNIOR MUSEUM:** While her husband applies himself to the university project, Jane Stanford turns with enthusiasm to specific plans for the design and construction of a memorial museum on campus. Leland Jr. had not only been a collector, but had aspired to create a public museum broadly dedicated to teaching and scholarship. Mrs. Stanford commissions a building, neoclassical in design and patterned after the Museum of Athens (where her son had visited with Schliemann in 1884). It is one of the largest structures, and the first in California, to use Ernest Ransome's innovative construction method of steel-reinforced concrete. When it opens to the public in 1894, the museum features Leland Jr.'s collections of antiquities and ethnological artifacts complimented by more than 1,500 additions made by Mrs. Stanford, as well as by his parents' notable collections of contemporary Western American landscapes and contemporary and 16th-18th century European Art. During the next 15 years, Mrs. Stanford adds extensively to the collections, especially Egyptian antiquities and Asian and native American art. Patterned after the great museums of Europe, the Stanford Museum is only the fifth American university museum of any size when it opens. By 1903, three additional wings make it the largest privately owned museum in the country.

## 1891

January 14 **SENATORIAL REELECTION:** Stanford is reelected to the U.S. Senate. The Stanfords had returned in October 1890 from a European trip to campaign on behalf of Republican candidates for state legislative office and, consequently, for his reelection to the Senate. Despite poor health, Sen. Stanford travels throughout the state for daily speeches and receptions. Stanford is overwhelmingly reelected to his seat by the new legislature.

March 22 **DAVID STARR JORDAN, FIRST PRESIDENT:** Hoping to open the university in the fall, Leland Stanford recruits as first president David Starr Jordan, the 40-year-old president of Indiana University. A Cornell-educated botanist and natural scientist (M.S., 1872), Jordan taught at midwestern institutes and colleges while turning his attention to the study of fishes. He claimed two other degrees, an M.D. from Indiana Medical College in 1875, which he downplayed as "scarcely earned," and a Ph.D. from Butler University in 1878. He finally settled at Indiana University in 1879 as professor of zoology. (He was named Indiana's president in 1885.) The charismatic and idealistic Jordan is recommended by his mentor, Cornell President Andrew Dickson White and by Daniel Coit Gilman, president of Johns Hopkins. Stanford is attracted to Jordan's educational vision, adaptability, and energy. Jordan and the Stanfords share firm beliefs in individualism, the importance of career-oriented education, and the opportunity of upward mobility through industriousness and diligence. After a private interview with Leland Stanford in Bloom-

*Leland Stanford Junior Museum, 1891, envisioned by Mrs. Stanford as a direct link between her son and the university.*

*David Starr Jordan, first president of the university.*

*Orrin Leslie Elliott, "quiet, cautious, and courageous" first registrar, and his wife, Ellen Coit Elliott.*

*Geologist John Casper Branner, first to be asked to join Stanford's faculty.*

ington, Jordan accepts the post despite two serious reservations: moving to the West Coast, far from the center of American academic life; and the prospect of presiding over a private university "personally conducted" by one of the West's most powerful businessmen and politicians. Jordan and his wife, Jesse Knight Jordan, also a Cornell graduate, make a quick trip to California in April. "No more beautiful site for a university exists in the world," writes Jordan.

March 23 **JOHN CASPER BRANNER:** The day after he accepts the presidency, Jordan asks friend and former Cornell classmate John Casper Branner to join the Stanford faculty. On leave from the Indiana faculty as state geologist of Arkansas, Branner is a noted field geologist. Although not the first faculty member appointed (his arrival is delayed until the university's second semester), Branner is considered first among the early faculty. He becomes an especially influential senior faculty member and, later, vice-president. After forays to Harvard and other northeastern colleges that summer, Jordan will draw the bulk of his first faculty from Cornell and Indiana universities. Writing to Branner from Cambridge in May, Jordan complains: "I'm off on a hunt for professors, but find my best hunting grounds at Cornell. In the 'Back Bay' where I am now, are men whom nothing would induce to go west of Springfield, and men whose regret of their lives is that they were born outside of Boston."

April 15 **ORRIN LESLIE ELLIOTT NAMED KEY AIDE:** Orrin Leslie Elliott, the first individual on the payroll, begins work as the president's secretary and registrar. Elliott, another Cornell colleague of Jordan's, received his A.B. (1885) and his Ph.D. from Cornell in economics (1890), and is an instructor at Cornell. Elliott begins work immediately. Jordan's "quiet, cautious, and courageous" friend will serve as de facto dean of admissions, secretary to the university, lecturer in economics, and the president's closest advisor. After his retirement in 1925, Elliott researches and writes *Stanford University: The First Twenty-Five Years* (1937), the first comprehensive account of the university's early years. Ellen Coit Elliott, also a Cornell graduate, plays an influential role as a young faculty wife and student mentor. Her memoir, *It Happened this Way* (1940), describes a more personal side to the "pioneer years" on campus.

April 30 **NO TUITION:** According to a dispatch printed in the *New York Commercial Advertiser,* Leland Stanford decides to make Stanford University tuition-free. As late as March 1889, Stanford had expected to charge tuition but he reconsiders, particularly since the University of California remains tuition-free. This decision requires reductions in other areas, including a smaller initial faculty and scaled-back salaries, news that makes Jordan's search for faculty more difficult. Jordan must turn his search to young men and women of promise whose reputations would develop along with the university's.

June 26 **UNIVERSITY UNDER WAY:** Jordan, Elliott, and

First faculty families move into 10 clapboard houses built along Alvarado Row in 1891.

President Jordan addresses the crowd at Opening Day, Oct. 1, 1891, as Leland and Jane Stanford sit beneath portrait of Leland Jr.

chemistry Prof. George Richardson arrive at the Palo Alto Farm with their families. They set up administrative offices in Peter Coutt's brick library building, then move into the Inner Quad in July. While Elliott gives entrance exams and deals with bags of mail, Jordan travels throughout California during the summer to encourage public support of higher education and to recruit high school graduates.

July 1 **WORKING STUDENTS:** Francis (Frank) Batchelder, a sophomore transfer from Cornell, arrives to work as stenographer in the President's Office. He is not only the first student registered, but among the first in a long history of students who must earn enough to support themselves while attending Stanford. No provision is made for "direct assistance" (scholarships or fellowships) and no special arrangement made for student employment through the Stanford Estate Business Office (which prefers equally cheap but more dependable Chinese labor). Instead, the university circular recommends students arrive with funds to support themselves through at least one semester. Living expenses, including books, room, and board (and excluding travel fares, clothing, laundry), are estimated at about $200 per year. Faculty and staff hire students as stenographers, clerks, janitors, library and laboratory assistants; students also find jobs waiting tables and helping around faculty homes. Hourly wages average around 15 to 18 cents.

September **ALVARADO ROW:** Faculty families move into the first campus faculty housing, 10 pattern-book clapboard houses built in less than three months not far from the Quadrangle. Jordan names it "Alvarado Avenue," despite the fact that it had "not a tree or shrub or blade of green, or any sidewalk or road except the wheel broken track in the blistered adobe," Ellen Coit Elliott later recalls. Susan Branner adds, "It only needed the line of clothes flapping in the wind to complete the picture of a poor quarter in the outskirts of some western town." Mrs. Elliott proclaims it a "row," and Jordan agrees. The new occupants nickname it "the Cornell Colony." (Seven of the first 15 faculty members are originally from Cornell.) The last of these houses is torn down in 1972 to make way for a Law School parking lot.

October 1 **OPENING DAY:** The university opens as a coeducational institution charging no tuition, with 15 faculty. Departments offer courses in engineering and the sciences, humanities and social sciences. On Opening Day, hundreds of family, friends, guests, and the curious, join more than 400 students attending the dedication ceremony in the Inner Quad, under a warm, late summer sun. Principal speakers are Leland Stanford and David Starr Jordan, who notes: "Ours is the youngest of the universities, but it is heir to the wisdom of all the ages, and with this inheritance it has the promise of a rapid and sturdy growth." Other speakers include Martin Kellogg, president of the University of California, and Judge James W. Shafter of the Board of Trustees. After the ceremony, the Stanfords enter-

*Women of first Roble Hall pose on their front steps.*

*The Camp, barracks abandoned by Quad construction workers, provides a low-cost housing alternative for early male students.*

*Encina Hall, patterned after a Swiss hotel that caught Leland's eye, includes a dining hall with all the amenities.*

tain faculty and trustees at their residence, while university Registrar Orrin Leslie Elliott and his young assistant continue registering students and advising on course work "without pause or intermission, not eating or sleeping, for the next 24 hours," as his wife later recounts. At the end of the academic year (May 1892), the number of students has grown to 555, made up of 255 freshmen, 116 upperclass transfers, 37 graduate students, and 147 "specials." Female students initially make up about 20 percent of the student body, an unprecedented 25 percent majoring in sciences (compared to 4 percent nationally). The student body is drawn from across the country, although two-thirds are from California and much of the rest from Western and Midwestern states; 12 foreign students, largely from Japan and Canada, also attend. The unexpectedly large number of students causes a stir at local institutions worried about losing students (43 University of the Pacific students enter Stanford's upperclass ranks alone); however, while University of California partisans are "a little sore and jealous," the public university at Berkeley benefits from Jordan's statewide promotion of higher education and registers a record 520 students.

October **EARLY ACADEMIC POLICIES:** The university's fully coeducational admissions and curriculum policies cause much public debate, but equally controversial is the university's first effort at affirmative action: 147 "special" or probationary students — those applicants who did not meet minimum entrance requirements — make up nearly 25 percent of the first year's student body. Many of th students have been personally encouraged by Jordan d ing his summer whirlwind speaking tour. Aimed at old working students who did not have the opportunity to tend qualified high schools or afford tutoring, this categ ry had been successfully, if more modestly, used at t University of California for "mature" students, usua over 21. Critics in the press belittle this effort as loweri standards too far, but supporters praise Stanford's willir ness to recognize that lack of earlier opportunities shou not be a "fatal disqualification." Elliott ardently defen the policy, noting Stanford's commitment to provide ec cational opportunities to the less privileged. (The gradu tion rate of this first group of specials is 17 percent; comparison, that of the class of 1895 is 54 percent.) Facu enthusiastically support the system (selection is initia in their hands, but shifts in 1897 to a faculty admissio committee). The "specials" category lasts until shor after World War II. Herbert Hoover, reputedly a "speci student, was in fact a "conditional" student admitted regular standing after passing all but one entrance ex (that in English), which he was obliged to make up bef graduating.

October **MAJOR-PROFESSOR SYSTEM:** The univers curriculum begins operation using Jordan's "major-prof sor system" (introduced at Indiana in the 1880s), based a personal selection of electives rather than the more t ditional curriculum. Each freshman selects a profess

*The Pioneer Faculty in spring 1892 on the steps of Encina Hall.*

with whom to study a field of specialization. Major-subject courses may take up no more than one-third of the student's program, with the remainder filled by non-field electives. Like Leland Stanford, Jordan believes that students must develop educational and career goals early, and that with faculty advice, students will select appropriate courses. This system expects faculty to take active roles as mentors and character builders outside the classroom, as well as within.

October **First Student Dormitories:** Encina Hall, built to house 300 men, and Roble Hall, housing 72 women, officially open. Roble has been quickly built of reinforced concrete rather than sandstone. (This first Roble Hall, on Serra Street, later is renamed Sequoia Hall.) Like Encina, it is owned and operated by the Stanford Estate Business Office rather than by the university. The dorms provide lodging, board, heat and light for $20-23/month during the first year. Leland Stanford insists that costs be kept down in order not to discourage students with low incomes. Ironically, food quality turns out to be a more discouraging factor than cost. Contrary to legend, Herbert Hoover was almost certainly not the first student to move into Encina.

October **The Camp:** Students unable to afford Encina or unwilling to put up with its "cold soup, tough dry meat and continual prunes," find rooms with families in nearby Mayfield or Menlo Park, or with faculty families. Cheapest of all are the ramshackle barracks located behind the Quad and power house, on the site of today's Old Union. In one of the four buildings, Mock Chong's restaurant provides simple but plentiful food to visitors (Encina didn't allow guests) for about 20 cents. As the workmen move out, the other three buildings are taken over by "rugged individualists" who shift for themselves for around $3-$8 a month. Cooperative eating clubs spring up soon after, including "Brookfarm," a coeducational group of campus literary figures. In its 11 years, the Camp enjoys a success out of proportion to its numbers and stigma of poverty. Six successive editors of the *Sequoia* live there, and by 1899 residents have received nine of 11 campus first prizes for poetry and fiction. Student scholarship among Camp residents ranks higher than that of Encina or the fraternities. Pressured in 1898 to close down the unsightly buildings, Jane Stanford declines, instead praising the young men living there for sacrificing a steady working-man's income in order to complete a college education. Even after the university opens the Stanford Inn, many students prefer the Camp's restaurant and eating clubs, but the Business Office forces the Camp's closure, after a six-month reprieve by Jane Stanford, in June 1902.

October **First Student Publication:** The first student publication, the monthly *Palo Alto,* is circulated at Opening Day. The first number sells 2,500 copies. This private student enterprise of upperclassmen, intended to be a sophisticated journal of literary merit rather than a news-

President Jordan at bat (far left) and with his team at the faculty-senior baseball game, played on the stubble field in front of Encina.

Despite its size, the Stanford Band, organized in 1893, still took second fiddle to popular mandolin and glee clubs.

While the men's mandolin and glee clubs go on tour, the Women's Mandolin Club plays at campus social events.

sheet, folds after one year, allegedly because editor Holbrook Blinn, a sophomore transfer, is reprimanded by President Jordan after local clergy complain about an illustration of a voluptuous nude harem girl being auctioned off. In fact, Blinn cannot recover costs once the associated students organization refuses to adopt the high-brow newspaper, its staff and printing costs. Blinn, elected president of the class of '94, later drops out and goes on to a successful New York stage career.

October 5 **FIRST FRATERNITY:** Zeta Psi, the first Stanford chapter of a national fraternity, is chartered, followed soon after by Phi Delta Theta (Oct. 22). Fraternities are brought to Stanford by upperclass transfers. Six more fraternities quickly follow: Phi Kappa Psi, Sigma Nu, Phi Gamma Delta, Sigma Chi, Alpha Tau Omega, and Sigma Alpha Epsilon. The number of fraternities grows to 17 by 1898. By mid-decade, fraternity men compete with the men of Encina for control of student government, but make a poor showing until well after the turn of the century.

October 20 **ASSOCIATED STUDENTS OF STANFORD UNIVERSITY:** After an Oct. 9 preliminary meeting, the Associated Students of Stanford University (ASSU) is formally and permanently organized. Committees include: Constitution and Bylaws, School Colors, University Yell, Cooperative Association, Bulletin Board, and College Paper. There is little, if any, control of finances; student managers of the football and baseball teams are chosen for good fellowship rather than financial acumen, and rarely bother to report income or expenses, charged off-handedly to the ASSU. "If anyone wanted to form any kind of [sports] club, dub it Stanford and play anybody, the Student Body made no objection and the faculty committees were silent," remarks a member of the class of '94. Each class also organizes, especially the 20-50 upperclassmen accustomed to such arrangements elsewhere. The freshman class of 1895, newest to college ways, is slowest but makes up for it with enthusiasm and number of officers. The ASSU constitution is substantially rewritten, and offices reorganized for greater accountability, in 1893-94.

November **STUDENT CLUBS:** Clubs and student organizations flourish. During the first semester, upperclassmen experienced in college life launch engineering, biology, chemistry, physics, and English clubs, two choral societies, an athletic association, and Mock Congress (debate). By decade's end there also will be six literary societies, three debate clubs, several law societies, a press club, Democratic and Republican clubs, and numerous science and engineering clubs.

November 14 **FACULTY-SENIOR BASEBALL GAME:** Baseball is the first sport organized; it can be set up anywhere and is commonly understood. The faculty soon joins in, challenging the seniors to a match played on a dirt lot in front of Encina. President Jordan plays first base, while history Prof. George Howard proves a tough pitcher. The sen-

:appa Alpha Theta, founded 1892, first rents
ı large old house in Mayfield for several
ears before moving to Alvarado Row.*

*Like most early fraternities and sororities, Sigma Alpha Epsilon was first located off-campus (on Emerson Street, Palo Alto).*

ors, fielding an experienced team, win 15-12, but the fac-ılty moves on to challenge each of the other classes and lefeats the sophomores the following May. The faculty eam composes its own "yell": "Cigars, Cigars, Cigarettes, ˌeer — Faculty, Faculty, We're right here!" In what be-omes an annual event, the seniors taunt the faculty by vearing dresses and changing position each inning. How-ver, the game represents an important congeniality mong pioneer students and faculty.

lovember 17 **FIRST CAMPUS STUDENT ORGANIZATION:** 'he University Christian Association, modeled after a sim-.ar Cornell University group, is organized. Broadly con-eived and non-denominational, it provides modest serv-ces and bible study. This coeducational effort in February 892 merges into a campus YMCA-YWCA, which publish-s a handbook for new students, and establishes the cus-om of receptions and orientations during the first week of he academic year. For decades, their *Student Handbook* is he primary source of information on student organiza-ions, resources, and campus traditions. The YMCA also perates a successful job bureau for working students and a .ousing information center.

)ecember **FIRST MUSICAL ORGANIZATIONS:** A universi-y orchestra of 11 is established, although the Men's Glee 'lub attracts larger audiences. This first glee club is short .ved, earning a notorious reputation on tour when it runs p unauthorized debts in the name of ASSU. Reorganized in 1893, the Men's Glee Club performs in the Stanford chapel, as well as in opera houses and theaters in Napa, Petaluma, and Sacramento. A ladies' glee club and a mandolin club are also formed. A small band takes shape in September 1893.

December **STOCK FARM'S PEAK YEAR:** In competition, Leland Stanford's trotters garner world records in all seven possible categories. At the end of the year, however, superintendent Charles Marvin leaves Palo Alto to accept a similar post in Pennsylvania, a serious loss to the farm later attributed to a disagreement with stock farm manager Ariel Lathrop (Jane's brother). Only one more record is set by stock farm horses after Marvin's departure. With Sen. Stanford's preoccupation with Washington affairs and development of the university, the stock farm begins a decline that is hastened in 1893 by the senator's death.

December 7 **COOPERATIVE BOOKSTORE:** After organizing in November, a cooperative association is incorporated to purchase books and supplies in San Francisco, selling shares for $2.50 to subscribing students and faculty. A small wooden building is used to sell books and stationery, with a room set up as an office for the *Sequoia.* This organization fails, however, and a new bookstore is organized in 1897 as a nonprofit, independent organization.

December 9 ***SEQUOIA:*** The student magazine *Sequoia,* the first student periodical authorized by the ASSU, is found-

*First Big Game is played at Haight Street Field in San Francisco, March 1892.*

*Star player Guy Cochrane, '96. When Cochrane needs new shoes, thrifty student manager Herbert Hoover gives him new shoelaces.*

*First five years of baseball rivalry with Cal goes to Stanford's highly regarded varsity nine.*

ed. During its first year it provides campus news and faculty contributions, but will turn toward student essays, fiction, and poetry after establishment of the student newspaper, the *Daily Palo Alto,* in 1892.

# 1892

January 1 **FIRST SORORITY:** The first Stanford sorority, Kappa Alpha Theta, is established when the University of the Pacific chapter relocates from San Jose to Stanford. Members move into a large, "old-fashioned" house off campus and in 1894 move to campus. It is followed by Kappa Kappa Gamma (chartered June 10, 1892) and Pi Beta Phi (October 1893). The number of sorority chapters grows more slowly than fraternities (only five by 1898), due in part to the smaller number of women but also to their greater cohesiveness and to the large number of sorority-like clubs and other social outlets for women.

February **BRANNER LIBRARY:** John Casper Branner arrives on campus with his extensive private library, so big it requires its own freight car. The modest general library in the Inner Quad has few science and advanced humanities texts, so many professors make their own book collections available to students. Branner's library is installed in the geology building in the Inner Quad. At his retirement in 1915, he sells the university his collection — more than 10,000 volumes, an equal number of pamphlets, and many maps. His library forms the nucleus of today's Branner Earth Sciences Library, one of several branch libraries that got its start from a faculty member.

March 19 **FIRST BIG GAME:** Tension has been building between Stanford partisans and those of the older, more prestigious University of California, only 40 miles away at Berkeley. Challenged by California students to a friendly football game months earlier, the match takes on symbolic proportions for students of both institutions. Stanford has no equipment, coach, playing field, or uniforms, but a self-organized team assembles in fall 1891. Only a few of its members had seen football played before arriving at Stanford. Practicing on the hard adobe field near Encina (and at times in Encina's hallways), they concentrate on strategy and a few intricate plays. A teacher at a local school, who had played on Lehigh's varsity team, helps coach on weekends. The grudge match is played at the Haight Street Field in San Francisco, and attracts a large local crowd along with hundreds of students. In the excitement, neither team manager remembers to bring a football, causing a delay in start of the game. Taunted as Jordan's schoolboys, Stanford upsets heavily favored and over-confident California and its experienced team, 14-10. Sen. and Mrs. Stanford wire team captain J.R. Whittemore from Washington, D.C.: "We congratulate the football team on their splendid victory over the University of California team." (Legend that Herbert Hoover was manager of Stanford's first football team and that he forgot the football is wide-

*Women students are provided with their own gymnasium and encouraged to exercise, but not compete. Gymnastics inside the first Roble Gym (right and lower right), later nicknamed "Woodpecker Hall."*

*A summer of intensive study at Hopkins Seaside Laboratory on Monterey Bay, established in 1892, promotes a special sense of camaraderie among students and faculty.*

spread, but not true. Carl Clemens, '93, the team's star fullback, served as team manager until 1893. Hoover was elected ASSU's first treasurer in 1893-94, and at that time took over team management and responsibility for thousands of dollars in gate receipts.)

March 19 **CARDINAL RED:** "Cardinal O'er Blue and Gold" screams a local headline after Stanford's unexpected football victory at the first game with Berkeley; thus, Stanford's cardinal red color is confirmed. As early as October 1891, students called for selection of a college color. Many American colleges (at least those fielding popular football or baseball teams) were selecting official colors of combat to distinguish sides and instill pride. Holbrook Blinn, editor of the *Palo Alto,* proposes gold, California's emblematic metal, and white, while the *Sequoia's* editors press for cardinal red, the "color of conquest" (and not unlike Cornell's red). Both gold and white fall by the wayside as too similar to California's blue and gold. By the time of the first contest, vibrant cardinal banners, flowers, and ribbons bedeck train cars, carriages, hotels, and hatbands. A student meeting called by student body president and football captain J.R. Whittemore, '92, selects Cardinal as Stanford's color, and formulates a college yell: "Rah, rah, rah; rah, rah, rah; r-a-h, r-a-h; Stanford!" In 1893, an ASSU "color committee" makes official the precise shade of cardinal from among many red swatches.

Spring **PACIFIC SLOPE HISTORY:** History students take to the field when Mary Sheldon Barnes, newly appointed assistant professor of history, joins the faculty spring semester. Barnes sends students out to interview early settlers and document the neighborhood's native American and Hispanic heritage. While Profs. Howard and Show cover traditional fields of American and European political history, Barnes takes up the relatively new area of Western American history. The course is a campus favorite despite its heavy workload. Barnes promotes undergraduate research using primary sources. Her own efforts and those of her students evolve into several large Pacific Slope manuscript collections in the university library.

April 23 **FIRST STANFORD-CAL BASEBALL GAME:** Stanford fields an exceptionally strong baseball team (which has been practicing on the Oval) against the University of California. The game is played at San Francisco's Central Park. Berkeley has difficulty with pitcher John Capron's curve ball, and Stanford wins, 13-6. Stanford continues to dominate this rivalry, wining 10 of 12 games played with California during the first five seasons. UC will not win the championship round until spring 1897.

June 15 **THE STANFORD ALUMNI ASSOCIATION:** Shortly after the first diplomas are handed out, graduating students organize an alumni association. Although alumni will soon spread across California and the West, the organization centers in San Francisco and Los Angeles. In 1899, the organization begins publication of the monthly *Stan-*

Suffering ill health, Sen. Stanford poses for one of his last portraits. He dies at his Palo Alto home in 1893.

After Sen. Stanford's memorial service, the procession leaves the Quad for the Stanford Family Mausoleum.

*ford Alumnus,* less to represent alumni opinion than to keep alumni informed of campus doings.

June 27 **HOPKINS SEASIDE LAB:** The Hopkins Seaside Laboratory is established on Point Aulon (now called Lover's Point) on Monterey Bay. Two young faculty members, Oliver Peebles Jenkins, a physiologist, and Charles Henry Gilbert, a zoologist, scouted the Pacific Coast seeking appropriate land for a marine laboratory. Timothy Hopkins, foster son of Mark Hopkins and a Stanford trustee, not only donates funds but promotes the donation of land by the Pacific Improvement Company. Sixteen students attend the opening session, operating out of a wooden laboratory building that measures 25 by 60 feet. In 1917, because of the encroachment of nearby resorts, the laboratory moves about a mile eastward to Point Cabrillo. The same year, the laboratory takes its present name of Hopkins Marine Station, appoints a resident director, and adopts a year-round schedule of classes.

Summer **GEOLOGY FIELD SURVEYS BEGIN:** John Casper Branner and other geology faculty encourage students to work on summer field work in the West and in Arkansas (where Branner is finishing up an extensive state survey). By 1902, the Geology Department's summer field survey trips become a regular, and highly popular, part of the curriculum. Funding by the U.S. Geological Survey, well established by 1894, limits the opportunity to male students until well into the 20th century. Lou Henry, '98, the first woman to graduate from Stanford with a degree in geology (and later First Lady Lou Henry Hoover) must remain on campus cataloging rock specimens.

September 19 ***DAILY PALO ALTO:*** First issue of the *Daily Palo Alto* appears. (When the monthly *Palo Alto* fails, ASSU appropriates the name.) Stanford is only the eighth American university with its own student newspaper. Printed at the office of the *Redwood City Democrat* for the first two weeks, the paper moves on campus when a modest press is installed in the machine shop. It earns a reputation as comparatively well-managed for a student-run business of the era. It is well-edited, if "staid," and recognized for temperate and accurate reporting (especially when contrasted to the sensational journalism of nearby San Francisco). It is nicknamed the DPA, and soon after, "the Dippy," a name that will persist for years after the journal formally changes its name in 1926 to the *Stanford Daily*.

# 1893

April 3 **LELAND STANFORD'S LAST LETTER TO JORDAN:** In a valedictory letter written to President Jordan, Leland Stanford underscores his vision of a university. The rich "can get their education anywhere," Stanford writes, "but the object is more particularly to reach the multitude — those people who have to consider the expenditure of every dollar." Predicting the campus would one day en-

*Mrs. Elliott thought the Inner Quad in 1892 appeared "exactly like a factory," but Mrs. Branner saw "a gem in a coarse setting. How much the Inner Quad has meant to us."*

*Jane Lathrop Stanford, at age 65, takes on administration of the Stanford estate after her husband's death.*

*Prof. Mary Sheldon Barnes, an historian, first woman appointed to the faculty.*

*The new town of Palo Alto is incorporated in 1893.*

compass kindergartens through post-graduate studies and original faculty research, he encourages the teaching of music and the arts as well as the sciences and mechanical arts, law, and medicine. "Palo Alto is one of the most delightful locations in California, take it all in all. . .I hope to see thousands of students there."

April 22 **FIRST STANFORD-CAL INTERCOLLEGIATE DEBATE:** With interest high in public debate, the first debate match with the University of California provides an emotional confrontation and prompts yearly contests. Stanford's first debating society, Alpha, had been founded in October 1891 as all-male, but by early 1892 was coeducational. Three more debating societies quickly followed: Congress, the Euphonia Society, and the Law and Debate Society.

June 20-21 **LELAND STANFORD DIES:** Leland Stanford, 69, dies at his Palo Alto home (he is found sometime after midnight). Stanford's doctor attributes his death to a weak heart. For several months, he has been unable to walk without assistance. He and Jane had returned from three months on the East Coast on May 3. The Saturday after his death, funeral services are conducted in the Inner Quad by an Episcopal bishop, Unitarian minister, and the minister of San Francisco's Grace Church. Stanford's casket is borne by members of the Brotherhood of Locomotive Engineers from the Quad to the new mausoleum. (Shortly thereafter, Leland Jr.'s casket is moved from its original tomb site to the mausoleum.)

July **THE UNIVERSITY GOES AHEAD:** Sen. Stanford's death throws the university, which has been managed as though it were part of the Stanford estate, into severe financial crisis. Several million dollars in bequests to family members must be paid before Jane Stanford receives her inheritance. As the estate goes into probate, assets are temporarily frozen and income to the university stops; expenses and faculty salaries cannot be paid. After two weeks of seclusion, Mrs. Stanford informs President Jordan, "The university will go ahead and fulfill its mission." The probate judge grants Mrs. Stanford, as executor of the Stanford estate, $10,000 per month allowance from proceeds of the estate; most of this she turns over to President Jordan. She significantly cuts estate staff and expenses, while Jordan cuts faculty salaries 12 percent (a salary cut that lasts seven years), and holds off on classroom, library, and laboratory expenditures. The university charges a registration fee for the first time ($10 a semester for regular students, $15 for specials). The machinery slowed, Registrar Elliott notes later, but the university continued to operate smoothly. Despite sensational rumors of a massive exodus of students and faculty, a record number of students register that fall (975) and faculty numbers remain stable at around 65.

September 4 **LAW DEPARTMENT:** The first new department since the university's opening, the Department of Law, is organized. Its first students are three graduate students, 35 undergraduates, and eight special students. Serv-

Prof. J.P. Smith, five geology students, and dog "Modoc," return from 30 days in the Northern California wilderness on the 1893 Stanford Geology Survey.

Activity comes to a halt on the morning the Quad yearbook is distributed. The campus yearbook remains a junior class publication until 1927.

The Sequoia, founded in 1891, soon gives up reporting news and sports to concentrate on things literary.

ing as faculty are former U.S. President Benjamin Harrison and University Librarian Edwin Hamlin Woodruff, who holds a Cornell law degree. Nathan Abbot will join the faculty as department head in 1894. In 1908, the department becomes the School of Law. In 1924, it becomes solely a graduate program.

# 1894

March 9 **FIRST FOUNDER'S DAY:** The first "Founder's Day" is celebrated, nine months after the death of Leland Stanford. Former President Benjamin Harrison is among the speakers. A "memorial day" had been celebrated in May 1892 and May 1893 to commemorate Leland Jr.'s birthday. The annual ceremony will be expanded in 1905, following the death of Jane Stanford, to include the laying of a wreath of flowers at the Stanford mausoleum by the graduating class.

April **TOWN OF PALO ALTO:** The nearby town of Palo Alto, located across the Southern Pacific railroad tracks from the campus, is incorporated between the established communities of Menlo Park and Mayfield. In 1887, Sen. Stanford first envisioned a university village taking shape on a portion of the Palo Alto Farm nearest Mayfield, but later preferred a site beyond university boundaries. The town-site of Palo Alto is plotted out by Timothy Hopkins, who had purchased a portion of the old Seale estate. By summer 1891 the university's main avenue, as designed by Olmsted (and later named Palm Drive) connects the village with the mushrooming campus. A rail station and a few buildings sprang up in 1891, but real development begins in 1893. Since the saloons of Menlo Park, and especially Mayfield, were a concern to Leland Stanford and Timothy Hopkins, early deeds prohibit the manufacture and consumption of alcohol in Palo Alto.

Spring ***STANFORD QUAD:*** Juniors of the class of '95 begin the annual tradition of publishing a student yearbook, the *Stanford Quad.* Until 1927, it is produced by the junior class. After that it is produced by an editorial board open to all students. Its name is chosen because the Quadrangle is seen as the nucleus of campus life and sentiment, and because it has "snap and vigor — a marked characteristic of the university."

May **ENCINA PRANK MAKES NATIONAL HEADLINES:** Following three years of student roughhousing and pranks, someone steals the cigars, wine, and whiskey provided by Jane Stanford to former U.S. President Benjamin Harrison, who has been living in an Encina suite while serving as a guest lecturer spring semester. Since liquor is forbidden on campus, Encina residents defend the action and refuse to pay the university's assessment of $33.60. (The claim is later settled for $28.55, all the Encina Club claims it can raise.) Clashes between Encina students and university officials will peak in 1905-06.

Men and women of the Pioneer Class of 1895 pose for their class photograph in front of Encina Hall.

May **FIRST PH.D. DEGREE GRANTED:** Although graduate students have been present from opening day, the first Stanford doctorate is awarded to George Hall Ashley. Ashley had received his undergraduate degree (mechanical engineer in electricity) from Cornell in 1889 and came to Stanford in 1891 to study geology under John Casper Branner. (Just over 90 years later — in 1985 — Ashley's diploma is returned to the university as a gift of historic value by his granddaughter, Helen Ross Staley.)

June 3 **U.S. GOVERNMENT SUES:** Just as the university starts to regain financial stability, the federal government sues the Stanford estate for $15 million, the entire Central Pacific Railroad debt for loans, with interest, made in the 1860s for construction of the railroad. The bonds are not yet due, nor are individual stockholders or directors liable under California law. However, in an escalating nationwide financial crisis, other railroads are defaulting on federal loans and some government officials worry about significant financial losses. Although Stanford advocates are confident of victory, the suit brings probate proceedings to a halt and a potentially long court battle threatens great expense to the estate. The university again is thrown into a precarious financial position.

# 1895

February **STUDENT HEALTH:** With no hospitals closer than San Jose and San Francisco and few local physicians, Dr. Thomas Wood, head of the Physical Education Department, serves as deputy county health officer providing advice and first-aid. But students are expected to seek their own medical or surgical care and nursing. A volunteer student-faculty organization, the Student Guild, assembles portable sickroom equipment for students suffering from sudden illness. Members pay a fee of 50 cents a semester, an early example of a low-rate, prepaid health insurance plan. Less than half the student body join, however, and facilities remain small until 1903.

May 29 **THE PIONEER CLASS:** Mrs. Stanford, just returned from Washington, honors the first four-year graduating class of undergraduates with a reception at her San Francisco residence. The class of '95 views their counterparts of '92, '93 and '94 as stepchildren "whom accident placed under the care of our alma mater." But "Ninety-five will go upon record as the first class — the pioneers — of the university. . . . The quadrangle is ours by preemption." While the class of '95 takes credit for establishing all precedents, it is in fact upperclass transfers who start many student organizations and who assume leadership in clubs, student politics, and news and literary publications. The Pioneer Class will thrive, however, on rivalry with the succeeding class of '96. The class tries to leave a permanent mark in the form of a plaque on an oak, but a new '95 oak must be selected when the first is cut down to make way for Outer Quadrangle buildings.

*Anne Martin, '96, intercollegiate tennis champion and later noted woman's suffrage activist.*

*Flurry of excitement over Stanford women's basketball victory against Cal is short-lived when faculty disapprove of women in competition.*

*University President Ray Lyman Wilbur was among class of '96 partisans who placed the first class plate. Here he is seen with class officers in 1939. Above right, the 1995 plate is placed in the arcade.*

October 12 **FIRST COURT DECISIONS:** Following a U.S. District Court decision favoring the Stanford estate in June, the U.S. Court of Appeals confirms the decision. Noisy celebrating on the quad is followed by speeches by Jordan, Prof. Edward Ross for the faculty, and students of each class. The little rail station in Palo Alto is painted red. The federal government now moves its case to the U.S. Supreme Court.

# 1896

March 2 **FINAL COURT VICTORY:** Capping two years of court battles, the U.S. Supreme Court unanimously rejects the federal government's claims against the Leland Stanford estate, affirming the principle of limited liability of corporations. With the financial threat to the university's existence removed, a gleeful crowd of students, faculty, and staff gathers in the Inner Quad to hear the official news. Respecting President Jordan's earlier request not to paint the professors or tear down buildings, students proceed to celebrate in Palo Alto. The following morning the little wooden U.S. Post Office on campus wears a coat of Cardinal red paint (and a large red '96) — which Jordan says greatly improves its appearance. Leland Stanford's legacy of $2.5 million in bonds to the university is turned over to the Board of Trustees within a month, but it will take two more years to clear all legacies before Mrs. Stanford receives full control of her own inheritance.

April **FUNDAMENTAL STANDARD:** Jordan's philosophy regarding student conduct takes shape when the university publishes what is later known as the Fundamental Standard: "Students are expected to show both within and without the University such respect for order, morality, personal honor, and the rights of others as is demanded of good citizens. Failure to observe this will be sufficient cause for removal from the University." Beyond this he refuses to go, believing that students know perfectly well what is decent and appropriate behavior, and "that we send away those who violate this condition." Students increasingly voice concern about the lack of clarity and the absence of appeal procedures.

April 4 **WOMEN'S BASKETBALL:** In what is believed to be the first women's intercollegiate basketball game, Stanford beats California 2-1 at the San Francisco Armory. (Basketball scores are low until backboards and dribbling are introduced later.) Mrs. Stanford is sent two tickets, but returns her thanks and regrets. Although the university devotes few resources to athletics, women take up sports for health and fitness. Women students decide on their own to enter competition, and women's basketball teams play nearby Castilleja (1894) and other local schools before taking on the University of California. Students form the Women's Athletic Club (later the Women's Athletic Association) in fall 1895 to encourage women as participants, rather than spectators, of "sport." Because the Faculty Athletic Committee objects to public intercollegiate matches

Plug Ugly, thought up by juniors in 1898, is later banned because of injuries.

*The Stanford Inn, built in 1898, is the only place visitors can buy a meal on campus. Faculty children and their dolls celebrate a birthday on the Inn's veranda.*

for women, the basketball team is virtually disbanded, and competitive sports are confined to tennis and, later, field hockey.

May 25 **CLASS PLATES:** With permission from Jane Stanford, graduating seniors of the class of '96 install a bronze plate with its numerals under the arcade directly in front and at the exact center of the planned entrance to the future church. The numerals, the students proudly point out, can be read whether entering or exiting the church. Not to be outdone, chagrined representatives of the class of '95 later quietly sneak in their plate next to it — some say at night — but must accept a position slightly off-center of the entrance. (Plates are later added for the classes of '92, '93, and '94 as well.) Subsequent classes follow the tradition in what becomes an important part of an annual Class Day event. In 1900, graduating seniors add time-capsules underneath. In his Class Day speech of 1980, then-provost (and future president) Donald Kennedy notes that the sequence around the Quad, using the 512 red tiles in the center row, will end with the plate of the class of 2403 (correcting an earlier estimate of President Jordan's).

Summer-Fall **WOMAN'S SUFFRAGE CAMPAIGN:** Jane Stanford arranges for valuable free railroad passes for Susan B. Anthony and other suffrage campaigners, despite objections of railroad business associates.

Fall **AXE YELL:** Will Irwin, destined to become a distinguished journalist, and fellow student Chris Bradley devise the rhythmic "Give 'em the axe" cheer. Although understood to be figurative, the yell satisfies pent-up feelings toward their cross-bay rivals. Ironically, the yell is also adopted by students at the University of California, especially after 1899, and the two sides have roared it out at each other ever since. The first Stanford cheer to be devised by students was the lusty greeting to Sen. and Mrs. Stanford on Opening Day, 1891: "Wah-hoo, Wah-hoo, L-S-J-U.! Stanford!"

# 1897

May 26 **JASPER RIDGE RESEARCH:** The first of many Ph.D.s based on research conducted at Jasper Ridge is awarded. Used by faculty members and students in the natural sciences since their arrival in 1891, Jasper Ridge is a more than 1,000-acre wilderness area on Stanford land in the foothills behind the main campus that encompasses nine distinct biological environments: grassland, chaparral, open oak woodland, broadleaf forest, redwood forest, stream bank, freshwater swamp, marsh, and lake.

# 1898

May **SPANISH-AMERICAN WAR:** As the United States enters war with Spain, Stanford volunteers of the California

*Gov. Stanford locomotive, brought to campus in 1899, going into the museum 17 years later. At right, it is wedged between columns in the north rotunda.*

*Class of 1895 Oak, seen through the arch beyond Building 100, is later taken down to make way for Outer Quad construction.*

militia get a rousing send off. Thirty-eight are sent to the Philippines; two (one faculty member and one student) are killed in action. Mrs. Stanford tells interviewers of her support for American intervention in Cuba and, subsequently, the Philippines. The conflict prompts Jordan's interest in causes and effects of war, however, and leads to his active participation in the world peace movement. His outspoken views later give the university a reputation for pacifism.

September **Stanford Inn:** The Stanford Inn, a large wooden building with wide verandas, opens between Encina and the Quad. It replaces the Encina dining hall, which is shut down because of persistent complaints about the food. After the Business Office succeeds in demolishing its only competition, the Camp, with its inexpensive Chinese restaurant and eating clubs, for two decades the Inn remains the only place visitors can eat on campus. The Inn, however, improves little on the quality of food available on campus; student eating clubs flourish.

October **Plug Ugly:** Juniors of the class of 1900 initiate the satirical "Plug Ugly" outdoor play. (The plug hats were borrowed from a Berkeley tradition.) The play soon becomes central in the rivalry between juniors and seniors, formalized into an upperclass brawl on the Quad. The event begins with juniors posting irreverent ads for the performance, which the seniors subsequently attempt to rip down. The Plug Ugly skit lampoons seniors "with bad jokes in bad taste." Soon after, the seniors predictably confront their detractors in the Quad. The traditional junior head gear, or "plug" (a battered top hat hardened with layers of thick lead paint), comes in handy as a weapon. Due to the growing number of injuries, the university bans the Plug Uglies in October 1915.

November 2 **Stanford Stone Age:** Launching a major construction program that Jordan will dub "Stanford's Stone Age," Jane Stanford lays the cornerstone for the Thomas Welton Stanford Library (now known as Building 160), among the first of the Outer Quadrangle buildings. Intent on carrying out Sen. Stanford's plans, Mrs. Stanford focuses on completing the quadrangle buildings (the Outer Quadrangle, Memorial Church, and a large Memorial Arch), as well as two neoclassical buildings (a new gymnasium and a library), a chemistry building, and extensive new wings for the museum.

December **Stanford estate clears probate:** More than five years after Leland Stanford's death, the last of the Stanford estate legacies and debts are paid, and Sen. Stanford's estate is discharged from probate court. Jane Stanford gains complete control of Stanford stock and bond investments and property. President Jordan asks to restore faculty salaries, fill gaps in departments and faculty, and buy much needed books and equipment. Some adjustments are made, but Mrs. Stanford determines to complete construction, in her lifetime, of the university's physical plant.

Future first lady Lou Henry Hoover, '98, second from left, and friends model junior plugs.

Not all sororities were Greek-letter chapter houses. "The Combine," is a prestigious group of Roble women.

Frustrated by the loss of the Axe in 1899, Stanford students arrive on the Quad after stealing Cal's senior fence. Cal sends a note of thanks for rubbish removal, and the Axe remains in Berkeley until 1930.

# 1899

January 25 **STANFORD GOLF CLUB:** Math Prof. Robert Edgar Allardice starts the Machrihanish Golf Club of California, commonly known as the Stanford Golf Club. In February, a nine-hole golf course is laid out in the hills above Lagunita, roughly between Alta Vista and Cooksey house. By 1908, the club has 85 members paying $6 yearly.

April 8 **GOV. STANFORD LOCOMOTIVE:** The Gov. Stanford locomotive, given to Mrs. Stanford by the Southern Pacific, is transported to campus. Initially it is stored in an open field near the museum and later covered with a wooden shed. In 1916, a hole is cut in the rear wall of the museum and the engine is cabled and jacked into the building, squeezed between structural columns in the north rotunda, where visitors for decades enjoy climbing on it. In 1963, the hole is again cut and the locomotive is removed. After two decades in various storage facilities, the locomotive undergoes a thorough restoration at the behest of the Pacific Coast Chapter of the Railway and Locomotive Historical Society and goes back on public display on May 2, 1981, at the new California State Railroad Museum in Sacramento.

April 14 **THE AXE:** A bit "fat headed" with their previous success, Stanford athletes endure a year of defeat at the hands of the University of California. (Stanford had been trounced the previous fall 22-0 at the Big Game, and defeated in a close debating contest that spring.) Trying to bolster team spirit after losing the first of the Stanford-Cal baseball series, Stanford yell leader Billy Erb uses a lumberman's axe to complement the axe yell. He beheads a straw effigy dressed in blue and gold at the biggest bonfire rally yet held on The Farm. At the deciding game the next day, Erb uses the axe to chop off lengths of prominently displayed blue and gold ribbon. Since the axe has little effect on California's performance (Cal wins the game and series), it "is not worth a dime," and is largely ignored by Stanford students until Cal students and alumni nab it after the game. The axe again takes on symbolic value as a complicated running melee ensues. To better conceal the axe, a Cal partisan cuts off the handle, and it is later hidden under a young woman's skirt and smuggled onto the Berkeley ferry. The 10-pound blade is nearly recaptured from its Berkeley fraternity safe house, and is finally placed in a bank vault for safekeeping. Unable to get at the axe, a group of Stanford students organized by Will Irwin rip out Cal's senior bench in a midnight raid, hoping to hold it hostage. They receive, instead, a telegram of thanks for the removal of rubbish. As retaliations loom, a committee of two law professors from each school rule on final ownership of the axe. After lengthy deliberations, the professors rule unanimously in Cal's favor: The Axe (now capitalized) is a prize by reason of conquest. For the next 30 years, California retains bragging rights, taking the Axe out of its bank vault at an annual Axe Rally and daring Stanford to take it back. *(See also April 3, 1930)*

Drivers of horseless carriages, first introduced to campus in 1899, cope with muddy roads, including Palm Drive (above). Cars soon are banned from most campus roads.

*Chaparral* first appears in 1899 with jester "Chappie" on the cover (seen here again in 1913).

May 31 **THE STANFORD 500:** In an unexpected amendment to the Founding Grant, Jane Stanford limits the number of female students who may enroll at one time to 500. Women are entering American colleges in record numbers during the 1890s. Female enrollment at Stanford has risen from 25 percent of the student body to more than 40 percent in eight years, fueling public debate regarding the comparative purposes of women's and men's education. Stanford's fully coeducational academic setting — that is, women and men share classrooms, curriculum, major professors, graduation requirements — is heavily criticized by those who see distinctive differences between male and female capacities as well as social roles. Against those who believe the presence of women dilutes men's education, Jordan and Elliott strongly argue that both benefit, the men gaining in sense of responsibility and moral character, the women in self-confidence and clearer life goals. It is noted that Stanford women provide serious academic competition for its male students. Although she has expressed pride in the women's accomplishments, Mrs. Stanford believes men's educational needs must predominate, and fears men will be discouraged from attending. She sets the limitation at 500, despite Elliott's recommendation of a percentage limit. The 500 limit is first reached in 1903, when women are denied admission as "specials." *(See also May 11, 1933, and June 8, 1972)*

September **AUTOMOBILES ON CAMPUS:** A "horseless carriage" first appears on campus when its maker picks up President Jordan and Prof. A.W. Smith for a trip up Mount Hamilton. The trip from San Jose 27 miles to Lick Observatory is completed in a record 5 hours, 20 minutes and earns sensational press coverage. Fearing the effect the noisy machines will have on horse-drawn buses and liverymen's carriages, Jane Stanford closes campus roads to automobiles in 1901, although she later allows Dr. Ray Lyman Wilbur, the university's medical officer, to regularly operate one. The prohibition is relaxed in stages after 1905 (first allowing access during Big Game, then to selected service streets). The automobile ban on Palm Drive is eliminated in 1914.

October 5 ***CHAPARRAL:*** Campus humor magazine, *Chaparral,* is started by student Bristow Adams, following a discussion between Adams, editor of the *Sequoia* (and later a Cornell professor) and Everett Smith (later a Stanford journalism professor) during a boring psychology lecture. A journal of wit and persiflage at best, and colorful bad taste in lesser moments, the magazine replaces *Josh,* copublished by Stanford and University of California students. The cover features the striking figure of "Chappie," a jester with cap, bells, and hammer. Beginning in 1906, the magazine is published by the Hammer and Coffin Society, which is founded on April 17 of that year — the day before the great earthquake. For years, members will deny any connection between the two events.

# 1900

**STATISTICS:**

Undergraduate enrollment: 1,119

Graduate enrollment: 117

Faculty: 75

Tuition: free for undergraduates

January 19 **UNIVERSITY LIBRARY:** Classes are canceled as 250 student volunteers move the university's 45,000-volume library to the new Thomas Welton Stanford Library on the Outer Quad (Building 160). The first University Library had opened in October 1891 in a room in Building 1 with a small collection of 3,000 volumes, hastily assembled to meet the needs of the first year. During the next nine years, many notable gifts and purchases were made, expanding the library's collections dramatically. Among the first of the "Stone Age" buildings to be completed, the new library is dedicated to Sen. Stanford's younger brother Thomas Welton Stanford, who had reassigned his $300,000 bequest from Leland Stanford's will to Jane Stanford. She accepted half, and chose to use it for a new library. Although located as planned by the original architects, the space is neither adequate nor fireproof. In 1904, work begins at a new location (the present site of the Graduate School of Business) selected by Mrs. Stanford for a grand library of neoclassical design. This library is finished (but as yet unoccupied) when the 1906 earthquake damages it so seriously that trustees decide not to rebuild it. The library collection will remain in the Thomas Welton Library until the new Main Library is constructed east of the Quad in 1919.

May 28 **COMMITTEE ON GRADUATE STUDY:** President Jordan commissions a faculty Committee on Graduate Study to formulate regulations for graduate work and to protect the interests of graduate students. During the university's first 10 years, only 10 graduate degrees have been awarded. The faculty remains divided regarding the value of the master of arts degree, uniformity of qualifications for doctor of philosophy degrees, and Leland Stanford's policy of providing no fellowships. Registrar Elliott notes that Stanford undergraduates are encouraged to pursue advanced studies in the East or Europe, and that graduate students elsewhere are not drawn to Stanford due to the lack of fellowships.

November **STANFORD FAMILY STATUE:** A bronze depiction of the Stanford family is installed at the center of Inner Quad Courtyard. Jane Stanford commissioned the statue from Larkin Meade in 1890 during a visit to Florence, Italy, but execution was delayed until 1899. In her memoir, Mrs. Stanford's secretary, Bertha Berner, wrote that "the work was acknowledged to have merit, but Mrs. Stanford was never happy about it." Mrs. Stanford apparently dislikes the initial location and after several months it is moved to the middle of Memorial Court. Despite student objections, trustees in 1915 move it to the museum's main rotunda, and it later resides in an alcove off the main lobby. It is moved to the porch of the Art Gallery around 1967. In 1978, vandals saw off one of Leland Jr.'s thumbs, which the Historical Society pays to repair. The bronze group goes into storage at Ryan Lab and later in the yard at Operations and Maintenance. In 1998, just before commencement, it is installed next to the Stanford Family Mausoleum.

November 6 **TAX EXEMPT STATUS:** California voters, by 67 percent, ratify a state constitutional amendment authorizing the legislature to grant tax-exempt status to the university and to correct a number of legal inconsistencies in the Founding Grant. With Mrs. Stanford's permission, a campaign begins in 1898, aimed first at legislative passage of a constitutional amendment, then at a statewide referendum in 1900. Organized by San Francisco lawyer George C. Crothers, '95, the campaign is conducted and funded entirely by alumni (predominantly Crothers, his brother, Thomas G. Crothers, '92, Francis V. Keesling, '98, and John F. Sheehan, '95) with no official or financial support from the university. George and Thomas Crothers discov-

In 1900, grand space for Thomas Welton Stanford Library in Outer Quad, at left, takes the place of the modest first library crammed in Building 1 of Inner Quad (above left).

Bronze Stanford family statue, located in Inner Quad in 1900, is moved at Mrs. Stanford's request to Memorial Court following completion of Memorial Arch in 1902.

ered defects in the legal status of the university in 1898 when reviewing a contract renewal and new campus location for Sigma Nu fraternity. After discussing the matter with Mrs. Stanford, she confides to them her concern regarding tax assessments on her intended gifts to the university of stocks and bonds. Mrs. Stanford, trustees, and many alumni focus on the importance of protecting university income from excessive taxation, but Crothers fears serious defects in the original grant, the Enabling Act, and Mrs. Stanford's later amendments, could threaten the legal status and future of the university itself. *(See also October 1902)*

November 12 **PROF. ROSS FIRED:** After several years of off-and-on negotiation and procrastination, President Jordan asks Prof. Edward A. Ross, chair of the Sociology Department, to resign. Ross, who had been given several term extensions to find a post elsewhere, complies, but the following day releases a statement to the San Francisco press saying that he has been dismissed over Jordan's wishes because Jane Stanford had been unduly influenced by conservative business associates. A popular member of the faculty since 1893 and a charismatic teacher, Ross first gained public attention for his political activism during the presidential campaign of 1896 and more recently for speeches favoring public ownership of utilities (including the railroads), American labor organizing, and exclusion of Asian labor competition. Ross is not the only faculty member to speak out on political issues, but Mrs. Stanford is uncomfortable with Ross's pro-labor and anti-Japanese stands and questions his moral character. (Mrs. Stanford later argues that Sen. Stanford had intended the university to be free from partisan political pressures, but the university's nonpartisan stance is not articulated until her 1903 address to the Board of Trustees.) Public reaction to Ross's claim that his academic freedom has been abridged greatly surprises Jordan and embarrasses Mrs. Stanford. Jordan has full authority to take such an action, and Mrs. Stanford rarely questions his faculty decisions, but their reluctance to explain the idiosyncratic proceedings further confuses the issue. In the eyes of the Stanford community, Ross's greatest transgression is that he did not "play the game" and go quietly. Nevertheless, the controversy surrounding Ross's dismissal contributes to formal organization of the Stanford faculty in 1904 in order to curb the president's arbitrary powers of promotion and firing. Eventually, this action helps promote nationwide adoption of the tenure system.

## 1901

January 12 **GEORGE HOWARD RESIGNS IN PROTEST:** Faculty anger over the November resignation of sociology Prof. Edward A. Ross grows in January when President Jordan forces out history Prof. George E. Howard, further clouding the academic freedom issue at Stanford. The storm over the Ross Affair would have blown over, Registrar O.L. Elliott later writes, had it not been for Howard. During a class lecture the day following Ross's resignation, Howard, a dynamic lecturer, defended academic freedom and reiterated Ross's accusation of outside influence on

Stone masons work on bas relief frieze depicting the "Progress of Civilization" that runs 250 feet around the top of Memorial Arch. One culminating scene depicts Jane and Leland Stanford on horseback charting a railroad course over the Sierra.

Chemistry Building, opened in 1903, with its many chimneys.

Forced resignations of sociologist Edward A. Ross (left) and historian George E. Howard draw attention to faculty governance and presidential authority at Stanford in 1900 and 1901.

Jordan's action. Howard made no other public statement, but the history professor's class comments were reported by student journalists to the San Francisco press. At Jane Stanford's insistence, Jordan asks for an apology or letter of resignation. Howard chooses the latter, and the university loses an influential pioneer faculty member, who is widely acknowledged as one of the best teachers on campus and an especially effective department head. Numerous additional resignations follow, including prominent professors William H. Hudson of English, Charles N. Little, head of mathematics, and Frank Fetter, incoming chair of sociology. However, while criticism arises in academic circles, the majority of Stanford students, alumni, and faculty express the importance of loyalty to Jordan and respect for Mrs. Stanford's wishes.

November **MEMORIAL CHURCH'S FIRST ORGAN:** A Romantic-style organ, built by the Murray M. Harris Co., is installed in the unfinished Memorial Church. Slightly damaged in the 1906 earthquake, it is put in storage, then reinstalled in the choir loft when the church is rebuilt. In 1915, an echo organ is added in a room behind the wall of the west transept balcony. The Murray Harris is rebuilt in 1925, expanded in 1933, and thoroughly restored in 1995. The 57-stop organ now has 3,702 pipes arranged along both sides of the choir loft.

## 1902

January 1 **STANFORD'S FIRST TOURNAMENT OF ROSES:** In the inaugural Tournament of Roses game in Pasadena, Stanford is pitted against Michigan. Heavily out-manned, Stanford loses 49-0. While it is true that Stanford is the only team during the season to keep "point-a-minute" Michigan under 60 points in a game, it only happened because the West Coast team gave up in the third quarter. The contest is considered such a disaster that tournament officials turn to Roman-style chariot races until football is reintroduced in 1916. (The contest is renamed the Rose Bowl with completion of a new stadium in 1923.)

March ***HAIL, STANFORD, HAIL:*** As a finale to its free concert, and without introduction, the Mormon Tabernacle choir sings *Hail, Stanford, Hail* to an enthusiastic audience in Memorial Church. First written and composed in 1892 by mechanical engineering Prof. Albert Smith and his wife, Mary Roberts Smith (who later joins the Sociology Department faculty), it was little used during the 1890s. The choir's performance, however, is greeted by wild applause and inspires a new tradition when students sing all three verses at a baseball game the following April.

April **STUDENT DRAMA:** After four months in rehearsal, students and faculty of the Greek Department, along with the Orchestra and Glee Club, produce *Antigone* in the original Greek, with Mendelssohn's choral music. The elaborate production is such a popular success, it plays in Los Angeles, Santa Barbara, and Berkeley. Since the university's first year, an array of student and faculty groups have tried everything from home-grown farces, reviews, and melodrama of the pioneer years to more ambitious turn-

*Antigone, performed by students and faculty in original Greek, wins rave reviews in 1902 almost as much for its audacity as for the fine quality of the production. Miss E. Cooksey (right) plays the title role.*

of-the-century productions of Gilbert and Sullivan light opera, Elizabethan plays, and Greek tragedy. The first theatrical performance (a satire in light verse by Charles K. Field, '95) is performed in early 1892 without scenery in the small chapel in Inner Quad (Building 100, at the northwest corner). With completion of the men's gym in 1892, drama productions are produced with knock-down scenery and lights, a portable drop curtain, and baseball bleachers. Long on energy but short on funds, performances transfer in 1899 to the new Assembly Hall in Outer Quad. Class plays and farces are supplemented by more serious work of special drama clubs, a faculty drama club, and the English Club. The Ram's Head "Big Game Gaieties" has its origins in the many original satires and musicals, written and acted by students, that poke fun at faculty and university officials.

Summer **MEMORIAL ARCH:** Work is completed on a towering sandstone Memorial Arch spanning the main entry of the Outer Quad. Designed by Charles Coolidge and modified by Charles Hodges, the arch was built in 1899. It has taken stone carvers two years to complete the 12-foot-high frieze carved into the parapet on all four sides. Carved by Rupert Schmidt, a San Francisco sculptor, and his workmen, the frieze depicts the "Progress of Civilization" by Augustus Saint-Gaudens. One panel — taking a liberal dose of poetic license — depicts Leland and Jane Stanford, on horseback, charting a course for the railroad over the Sierra.

October 3 **AMENDMENTS TO FOUNDING GRANT:** Jane Stanford revises the Founding Grant and her amendments of 1897 and 1899, at the suggestion of legal advisor George Crothers. In what Crothers calls a "radical general revision," required by earlier legal deficiencies in the Founding Grant, Enabling Act and earlier amendments, Mrs. Stanford now withdraws or modifies clauses of doubtful legal or practical value and removes a number of restrictions on the powers of the Board of Trustees. She clears the way for the sale of the Vina and Gridley ranches and other properties by stipulating that only the Palo Alto Farm and San Francisco residence must be retained by the university. She also reverses her earlier prohibitions on outside campuses, a campus elementary school, and boarding houses on campus, and confirms the trustees' power to institute tuition. Also included is a provision calling for the organization of the faculty and trustees and for the institution of regulations governing the appointment and removal of members of the faculty. Still smarting from the Ross Affair, Mrs. Stanford adds: "I desire that the University shall forever be kept out of politics, and that no professor shall electioneer among or seek to dominate other professors or students for the success of any political party." In 1903, George and Thomas Crothers continue to orchestrate a series of legislative acts and court decrees to confirm the university's status as a trust. In a final act to confirm the university's legal foundation, the Board of Trustees submits on June 16, 1903, a 511-page petition written by Thomas Crothers to the Superior Court of Santa Clara County to verify the legality of all university trusts and titles to the university endowment. The subsequent 172-page decree, issued July 3, 1903, is, in effect, the charter of the Universi-

*Museum, with extensive new wings, in 1905 (right). Memorial Church with steeple, before 1906 (below).*

*Salviati studios of Venice put other work on hold to complete Stanford commissions to decorate the interior and exterior of Memorial Church and the front of the Stanford Museum.*

ty, and supersedes all prior grants and amendments.

# 1903

January **CHEMISTRY BUILDING OPENS:** At the beginning of the year, elementary chemistry lecture classes move into the new 60,000-square-foot Chemistry Building, which is praised as one of the best designed and equipped chemistry laboratories in the nation. Chemistry is the first science department to have its own building outside the Quad, although some engineering buildings were located behind the Quad. The sandstone-over-brick building features 16-foot ceilings on the main floor and broad staircases, a large lecture hall, two large labs, a library, and many smaller labs and offices. The laboratories are "fireproof," with concrete floors and brick walls. Corridors are lined with Port Orford cedar wainscoting. Mrs. Stanford sites the building prominently at the university's grand entrance, rather than at its originally intended site behind the Quad. Damaged in 1906, it is modified in the 1910s, 1920s, and 1960s. It serves the department for 85 years.

January 25 **MEMORIAL CHURCH DEDICATED:** Memorial Church, built by Jane Stanford in honor of her late husband, is dedicated in a ceremony that includes 14 clergy of various faiths to emphasize the founders' nondenominational stance. The opening of the church signals completion of the Quadrangle, and is celebrated with much pomp. A month later, on Feb. 22, Ethel Rhodes and William Armfield Holt, both members of the class of 1902, are married in the first wedding ceremony to be held there. Decorative work takes another two years to complete, including the carving of quotations and the application of mosaics, by Salviati and Co. of Venice, on interior walls and on the façade, and placement of stained glass windows designed and constructed by Frederick Lamb, of J. & R. Lamb studios of New York. Although situated at the focal point of the memorial campus, attendance at Memorial Church is voluntary, and services are nondenominational.

February **SALVIATI MOSAICS:** Mauricio Camerino brings from Venice the first designs for the interior and exterior mosaic decoration of Memorial Church. The Stanfords had met Camarino in 1883 while in Venice, where they were impressed by the quality of ancient and medieval mosaic work and by the brilliant restoration of the Church of San Marco by Antonio Salviati & Co. Returning to Europe in 1899, Mrs. Stanford began negotiations with the firm to decorate the interior and exterior of Memorial Church and the façade of the Leland Stanford Junior Museum. In 1904, the Salviati mosaic workshop suspends all other projects, and devotes its full resources to several major Stanford commissions. Mauricio Camerino, who took over the company at Antonio Salviati's death in 1890, personally supervises both the first and second (post-1906 earthquake) installations of the church mosaics.

Spring **COOKSEY HOUSE:** In honor of his recently deceased wife, George B. Cooksey offers to the university for

*View of the Leland Stanford Junior University Oval and Quadrangle from the Stanford Museum roof, around 1905.*

use as a student infirmary a house on a hill overlooking campus. The gift is turned down by Mrs. Stanford, who does not want a hospital located on campus, which fosters the popular belief that gifts to the university are unwelcome. Health facilities remain inadequate for all but minor health problems. The university purchases the house at the end of the year for use as a student residence.

April **TYPHOID EPIDEMIC:** A serious epidemic changes the university's approach to medical care. Within two weeks, an outbreak of typhoid spreads from two cases in a fraternity to more than 200 on campus and in Palo Alto (120 are students). There is no campus infirmary and no fully equipped hospital available between San Francisco and San Jose (where Stanford's infected patients are unwelcome). Dr. Ray Lyman Wilbur, a Cooper Medical College professor and Palo Alto physician, and Dr. William Snow, a professor in the Department of Hygiene and Physical Training, and volunteers from the Student Guild, set up emergency ward facilities on the top floor of Encina for male patients, and in a boarding house in Palo Alto for females. No professional nurses are available. Mrs. Stanford contributes $1,000 to defray expenses of the bankrupt Student Guild. The epidemic results in eight deaths at Stanford, but a much larger percentage survive than among those stricken who are tended at home. The epidemic highlights an ongoing problem: self-supporting students lose work income while recuperating, making it all the more difficult for them to pay high medical costs. When the crisis passes, the Student Guild is reorganized, student membership is made compulsory, and an emergency fund is created. By the end of the year, a residence purchased at Lytton Avenue and Cowper Street in Palo Alto is furnished and staffed with nurses and a cook.

June 1 **BOARD OF TRUSTEES TAKES CONTROL:** Jane Stanford transfers her powers as surviving founder to the Board of Trustees, granting them control of the university's endowment and management. She feels her work of laying the physical and spiritual foundation of the university is finished and prefers that the board take the lead in enacting new and perhaps controversial policies to build the academic program, attract graduate students, and promote advanced instruction and research. Since transfer of power is not legally valid until her death, Mrs. Stanford is elected a member and, subsequently, president of the Board of Trustees on July 6. Hoping to encourage the trustees (who have rarely met up to this time) by granting them a level of independence, she plans an extended trip abroad. She travels to Australia, Asia, and the Middle East, visiting alumni and building the collections of the museum.

Fall **DURAND ARRIVES:** Prof. William Frederick Durand is recruited from Cornell, where he designed marine screw propellers. With a background in fluid mechanics, Durand works on water and power problems in the Western states, then in 1915, at the age of 56, he turns to design of airplane propellers, soon becoming the nation's leading authority. During World War I he plays a vital role in development of military aircraft. Following his 1924 retirement, Durand serves on several high government commissions.

Japanese Student Association poses with President Jordan the year after its founding. Future history Prof. Yamato Ichihashi, '07, stands second from right in top row.

*Student fire fighters pose with their equipment in front of their 1904 firehouse.*

*Aeronautics expert William F. Durand joins the faculty in 1903.*

In 1941, at age 82, he is called to Washington to head a project to develop jet propulsion for aircraft. Durand dies in 1958 at age 99. In 1969, the university dedicates in his memory the Durand Building for Aeronautics and Astronautics Engineering.

# 1904

Spring **JAPANESE STUDENTS:** The growing number of Japanese students — five in 1891, 19 in 1900 — results in establishment of a Japanese Student Association, sponsored by President Jordan and other faculty with strong interests in Pan-Pacific relations. When Mrs. Stanford visits Japan in the spring, 11 Stanford alumni are living there. The first foreign student to complete a Stanford degree was Keinosuke Otaki of Tokyo, who graduated with a bachelor's degree in zoology in 1894.

March 15 **QUAD KEYSTONE:** The keystone in the last arch of the Outer Quadrangle is placed.

March 31 **FACULTY ORGANIZED**: In a move to curb the power of the university president, as conferred by the founders, and clarify faculty promotion and retention policies, trustees adopt the Articles of Organization of the Faculty, worked out by trustee and faculty committees, with concurrence of President Jordan. The articles create the Academic Council of assistant, associate, and full professors to give the faculty a stronger voice in university governance. In a subsequent resolution, adopted March 30, 1906, the trustees decree that faculty dismissals by the president must be approved by trustees following consideration and recommendation by the Advisory Board of the Academic Council. Until this time, the university president has had unlimited authority under the Founding Grant to "remove professors and teachers at will."

April 23 **FIRST WORLD RECORD:** Using a carved spruce pole, Norman Dole, '04, clears the bar in the pole vault at 12 feet, $^{8}/_{25}$ inches at a Stanford-Cal track meet, and sets the first world record by a Stanford athlete. His silver trophy is donated to the University Archives in 1977 by his daughter, Janet Dole Tuffli, '38.

November **NEW FIREHOUSE:** A well-equipped, two-story firehouse is located on Salvatierra Street behind the Quad. It is furnished with two engines, a hand hook and ladder wagon, four ladders, hoses, axes, buckets, and other apparatus. The department consists of five student volunteers who are given free accommodations, but must stay near the firehouse when not in class. A code of signals is devised to specify location, with the alarm given by steam whistles from the power house.

November 12 **CARD STUNTS:** At the first Big Game held on a home campus (this year, at Berkeley), the Stanford rooting section blossoms forth with a large block S formed by strategically placed students wearing white hats and shirts. This much-copied innovation leads to the use of cards and the evolution of complex "card stunts" at Stanford and the University of California. Stanford wins 18-0.

*A Big Game rugby football program cover.*

*Rugby replaces American-rules football, viewed as too much a "gladiatorial combat," at Stanford after Big Game in 1905.*

*A 1904 innovation leading to card stunts: strategically placed Stanford rooters in white hats and shirts to spell out "LSJU."*

# 1905

January 14 **SUSPECTED POISONING INCIDENT:** Jane Stanford drinks a glass of Poland water later found to contain suspicious amounts of strychnine. Upset by the chemist's analysis, and suffering from a bad cold, she recuperates in San Jose while private detectives investigate. At the suggestion of friends on the Board of Trustees, she moves up her plans to tour the Orient rather than return to the San Francisco residence.

February 13 **JEWEL FUND:** In a letter to the Board of Trustees written a week before leaving for Honolulu, Jane Stanford authorizes establishment of the "Jewel Fund" for library purchases, using the proceeds from the proposed sale of her personal collection of jewelry. While attending Queen Victoria's Diamond Jubilee in the early summer of 1897, Mrs. Stanford had attempted to sell her famous collection in London. Given the financial depression of the time, and the number of potential buyers who already had pawned jewels to pay for the London celebration,no one was willing to pay her price. On her return, Mrs. Stanford set aside the jewels for the trustees as a means to complete Memorial Church in the event of her death, but the church is constructed without resorting to their sale. In June 1908, the trustees set aside $500,000 for a book fund, the value of the collection suggested by Mrs. Stanford.

February 28 **JANE STANFORD DIES:** Jane Lathrop Stanford, 76, dies while in Honolulu. Some, including the attending physician, theorize that she was poisoned, and she herself thought so because of the earlier incident at her home in San Francisco. Based on the report of a chemical analyst, who said he found minute traces of strychnine in her bottle of bicarbonate and in her stomach, a coroner's jury rules she was poisoned with "felonious intent." (At that time, small amounts of strychnine routinely were used in some medicines, including Mrs. Stanford's prescription.) The press, especially in San Francisco, print sensational accounts, but no arrests are made and no further official actions are taken. David Starr Jordan and Timothy Hopkins travel to Honolulu to escort the body back to California. At Jordan's request, several Cooper Medical College physicians conduct a second autopsy and in a report submitted to the Board of Trustees, declare probable cause of death to have been a rupture of a coronary artery. The trustees turn down Jordan's request to publish the second autopsy report. Important records regarding the San Francisco investigation and later autopsy are destroyed in the 1906 earthquake. The controversy about the cause of her death continues.

March 24 **JANE STANFORD FUNERAL:** Memorial Church is filled to capacity and a crowd of 6,000 overflows to the Inner Quad for Jane Stanford's funeral. Following the service, mourners form a procession down Palm Drive to the mausoleum. Members of the varsity football team serve as pallbearers. Undergraduates lay flower wreaths at the mausoleum, beginning an annual senior class tradition associated with Founders' Day. Mrs. Stanford's will includes bequests of $3 million to charities and relatives, with the balance going to the university. Including cash from the sale

*Jane Stanford sightseeing in Egypt and posing with alumni in Japan in 1904.*

*Mrs. Stanford, wearing her favorite lace and pearls, sits for her last portrait.*

*Following her death in 1905, Jane Stanford is laid to rest with her husband and son in the Stanford Family Mausoleum. The three sarcophagi are carved from solid pieces of Italian marble.*

of stock in the Southern Pacific Railroad and the Pacific Improvement Company, the total initial endowment provided by the Stanfords has been estimated at about $25 million, not including land and buildings. With Mrs. Stanford's death, the direct link between the university community and its founders is broken.

Spring **STUDENT LIVING CONDITIONS:** Barely half of Stanford's students live in campus dorms or fraternity/sorority houses (389 in Encina, 106 in Roble, and 389 in fraternities and sororities.) Prof. William Snow, chair of the Public Health Committee, reports on a survey of 376 rooming houses and 39 boarding houses: "The living conditions among the 1,600 students thus distributed present in the extremes all the features of over-crowding, poor sanitation, heating, ventilation, and improper food, found in the average tenement districts of a city, but the average living arrangements are satisfactory." Snow's committee notes that in addition to the boarding houses, his committee registered and inspected 15 eating clubs, 14 restaurants, and nine transient hotels.

November 11 **FIRST BIG GAME AT STANFORD:** The annual match with California is held in a new stadium with grandstand seating for 4,500, completed the previous summer in a field between Encina Hall and the county road (later, El Camino Real). Stanford wins in a hard-fought battle, 12-5.

December 11 **RUGBY REPLACES FOOTBALL:** At a joint meeting of President Jordan, UC President Benjamin Ide Wheeler, and faculty from both universities, English rugby is proposed as an alternative to American-rules football. The change shows widespread concern about the commercialization of collegiate sports, especially football. Faculty also worry about financial mismanagement by student athletic committees, and increased game violence. Hoping for significant changes in American football rules, the committee acknowledges the recent success of touring Australian and New Zealand rugby exhibition games, which highlight the sport's open play, fast passing, and emphasis on individual skill rather than on coaching and "gladiatorial combat." Rugby is formally adopted on both campuses the following spring, and the 1906 Big Game is the first of nine played by rugby rules. Although initially unpopular (the decision was made without student or alumni input), rugby is favored at Stanford even after the University of California returns to American-rules football in 1912.

# 1906

April 18 **EARTHQUAKE:** The Great San Francisco Earthquake hits the Bay Area at 5:13 a.m., causing more than $2 million damage at Stanford and killing two persons: Junius R. Hanna and Otto Gerdes. Hanna, a student at Encina Hall, is crushed by a chimney that falls four floors to the basement; Gerdes, a young staff member, is buried in the rubble as the power house chimney collapses. Structures built under Mrs. Stanford's direction after her husband's death sustain greater damage than the original uni-

*Just 14 months after Jane Stanford's death, her beloved church and Memorial Arch, along with her homes in San Francisco and on campus, are badly damaged in the 1906 earthquake.*

versity buildings: The brand-new library and gymnasium are destroyed, the great Memorial Arch at the front of the Quad is badly damaged, and an arcade along the back of the Outer Quad falls. Unreinforced wings of the museum collapse. None of these is rebuilt. Memorial Church sustains heavy damage. In San Francisco, the earthquake is followed by fires that destroy much of the city (including the Stanfords' Nob Hill residence). Within days, a relief center is set up in Palo Alto to gather clothing and food to send to San Francisco, where student and faculty volunteers help distribute them. By the end of the week, the Quad is roped off, guards placed at entrances, classes dismissed, and commencement postponed.

June 29 **RECONSTRUCTION BEGINS:** Reconstruction begins with the president's appointment of three engineering professors, Charles Wing, Charles Marx, and William Durand, to a special earthquake commission. After carefully examining the damage, they recommend which buildings to reconstruct, and set standards for the work. Only immediate repairs can be made before classes resume Aug. 23. Although fall semester opens on time, the earthquake causes a serious financial set-back.

September 15 **THE "CALAMITY CLASS" GRADUATES:** The postponed commencement ceremony occurs in the fall. UC President Benjamin Ide Wheeler is the featured speaker, and for the first time caps and gowns are worn. Students graduating in 1906 had entered the university under happy and ambitious conditions, following the difficult financial problems of the 1890s. The class of 1906 is the university's largest class yet, and has enjoyed better facilities and an expanding campus. However, three of their spring semesters have been disrupted by tragedy — a typhoid epidemic in 1903, Mrs. Stanford's death in 1905, and the 1906 earthquake.

# 1907

Spring **TELEPHONES ON CAMPUS:** The Stanford Business Office staff, tired of answering calls from parents, prospective students, and others, allows a telephone to be installed in the Registrar's Office. When the Business Office moved to campus from San Francisco in 1902, it brought its own telephone. As early as 1891, frequent requests from President Jordan (who particularly wants a system linking his office to principal university buildings) and from Encina Hall have been turned down by the Business Office for fear of expensive use by professors and students. The president has to wait until 1908 for his own phone. In 1909, additional phones are installed in other administrative offices, and within a few years an interdepartmental system is in full operation. (Telephones already have been installed in many private homes and fraternities for some time.)

# 1908

February 5 **THE "LIQUOR REBELLION":** A drunken student returns to Palo Alto from a Menlo Park saloon, enters the wrong house and, thought to be a burglar, is shot and

*Earthquake damage is nearly $2 million, including complete destruction of the new (but as yet unoccupied) library, seen at right and in distance down Lasuen Street, beyond debris of the Quad's east arcade.*

*Statue of scientist Louis Agassiz is head deep in the concrete.*

*Encina residents camp out for several nights because of structural damage and rumors of aftershocks.*

killed. This prompts the Academic Council on Feb. 14 to unanimously adopt a resolution to ban liquor from Encina Hall, fraternity houses, and other student residences, and to expel students guilty of drunkenness. In Stanford's first major student demonstration, several hundred students march to the house of the chairman of the Committee on Student Affairs, Arthur B. Clark. Twelve protesting students are suspended and others are required to take extra units to graduate. The previous November, the Campus Civic Club reported "deplorable conditions" to President Jordan and asked trustees to control deliveries of liquor to campus. In January, the month before the fatality, Jordan had failed to get two liquor licenses revoked.

Fall **FEES INCREASED:** Jordan secures from the trustees an increase in undergraduate incidental fees and tuition fees for law students. For several years since 1900, the fees instituted in 1893 have been waived for students who are California residents, but book and lab fees are increasing. In fall 1910, an "incidental fee" of $15 is reintroduced for those not registered in law or medicine courses.

October **THE TOONERVILLE TROLLEY:** A trolley line is completed using some of the old railroad bed of the original "Bonair Siding" employed during Quad construction. It runs from Palo Alto, up Galvez through the arboretum, past Encina Hall to the campus bookstore and along Panama Street. The line not only speeds the trip to town, but also connects commuting students living in the South Bay who travel on the popular Peninsular Railroad line. Electric lines from Palo Alto and Mayfield had been proposed as early as 1891, but franchise applications did not meet with Sen. Stanford's approval, nor was he ready to construct a line himself. Those needing to get quickly to campus from the towns of Palo Alto, Menlo Park, and Mayfield, and particularly from the train stations, had been served by the horse-drawn buses. For 5 cents a ride, the trolley provides passenger as well as freight transportation until the growing use of trucks and automobiles makes it unprofitable and it is abandoned in December 1929.

October 30 **COOPER MEDICAL COLLEGE:** After years of discussion, Stanford acquires the assets of Cooper Medical College of San Francisco, founded in 1859. This is the first major addition to the Stanford academic program. Acquisition of a medical school just as the university is recovering from substantial earthquake damage and an economic slump reducing its endowment makes the decision unpopular on campus. Seven members of the Cooper faculty are appointed by the university to its new Department of Medicine, joined by seven existing Stanford faculty members. The first independent appointment is that of Ray Lyman Wilbur, who becomes head of the department in 1911. The Medical School will remain in San Francisco until 1959. From the beginning, there are financial difficulties.

December 4 **BOARD ADOPTS OFFICIAL SEAL:** At the suggestion of trustee George Crothers, the Board of Trustees adopts a seal for its exclusive use on contracts, and other legal or official documents. It features a young redwood, with the words "Semper Virens" inscribed above; in the

Toonerville Trolley (seen here in late 1920s) is established in 1908, linking the campus with nearby towns.

*Cooper Medical College in San Francisco is acquired by Stanford in 1908.*

*Trustees' seal* | *President's seal* | *Registrar's seal* | *Commonly used seal*

*One official seal and three adopted "by custom": From left, the official seal of the Board of Trustees; the original president's seal, the registrar's seal embossed on diplomas, and the popular "sheep" version.*

outer ring are the words "Seal of the Leland Stanford Junior University," and the date 1885. Crothers later notes that the motto (translated as "ever green") is meant to stand for perpetuity of life, growth, and strength, "a pledge and resolve that the University shall never become stagnant, unprogressive, self-glorifying, or petrified in its imperfections." With the brief exception of an academic seal adopted in September 1915 (which falls into disuse), this is the university's only officially adopted seal. Three other versions are used "by custom," however: a president's seal, first used by David Starr Jordan, shows a shaggy *El Palo Alto,* with the motto *Die Luft der Freiheit weht* inside, and in the outer circle, "Leland Stanford Junior University," and, curiously, for a university founded in 1885, "Organized 1891." A registrar's seal will evolve with the same wording around the seal (but without the motto) for use on transcripts, diplomas, and other documents. A similar seal, with the same image, and a veritable landscape of mountains and orchard trees (often mistaken for sheep) was popularized as early as the 1890s for use on stationery, jewelry, and other merchandise. Minor variations of this popular seal, often using Jordan's motto, are found today. The motto *Die Luft der Freiheit weht,* first used by President Jordan, is never officially adopted. It will fall out of favor during the two world wars, but is revived in post war years, as President Gerhard Casper notes in 1995, as a guiding principle rather than a slogan.

# 1909

March **ANTI-LIQUOR LAW PASSED:** California state law is enacted that forbids the sale of alcohol within a mile and a half of the boundaries of Stanford University and the University of California, after local citizens complain strongly of many students excessive drinking and their disorderly conduct. Saloons in Menlo Park and Mayfield had been popular with Stanford students from the beginning (Palo Alto was dry due to a clause in the deeds of sale of property within the city limits). Little attention is paid to the law by students, saloon keepers, or city supervisors, and drinking in dorms and fraternities continues despite university regulations and citizen concern.

December **THORSTEIN VEBLEN FIRED:** Thorstein Veblen, associate professor of economics and author of *The Theory of the Leisure Class* and other noted works is fired by President Jordan for having a relationship with a woman who is not his wife. Veblen was hired in 1906 to bring prestige to the Economics Department. According to his biographer, Veblen once told a friend the "president doesn't approve of my domestic arrangements. Nor do I." After Stanford, Veblen finds it hard to get a tenured position, and later co-founds the New School of Social Research in New York. In 1926, in ill-health, he returns to California; he dies in Menlo Park in 1929, at 72.

# 1910

**STATISTICS:**

Undergraduate enrollment: 1,442

Graduate enrollment: 157

Faculty: 112

Tuition: free for undergraduates

Endowment: $26 million

Fall **MOSHER STUDIES WOMEN'S SEXUALITY:** Clelia Duel Mosher, '93, joins the faculty as professor of hygiene and physical training. Only months after arriving at Stanford as a senior transfer in 1892, she began collecting data on women's sexual views and practices. Her 28-year research of 45 women remains unpublished until history Prof. Carl Degler features her results in his important 1973 article on Victorian women. A landmark survey that predates Kinsey by 50 years, Mosher's findings debunk the popular view of Victorian and early 20th-century women as passionless and sexually ignorant. After graduating, Mosher spent several years as an instructor in the Department of Hygiene and Physical training, then earned an M.D. at Johns Hopkins University in 1900. She returns to practice medicine in Palo Alto in 1901.

Fall **TERMAN'S STANFORD-BINET TEST:** Lewis M. Terman joins the Education Department, where he will develop the Stanford-Binet IQ ("intelligence quotient") Test. (Alfred Binet was a French psychologist who developed an earlier test to identify "slow children.") In 1916, Terman publishes *The Measurement of Intelligence,* an enormously popular book based on the concept that a person's innate mental capacity is as measurable as height and weight. In 1922, he moves to the Psychology Department, which he later heads for 20 years. Terman's enthusiasm for IQ tests — and their implications about determining a person's place in society — leads him close to becoming an advocate of eugenics. Later in life, he tells friends he regrets some of his statements about "inferior races."

## 1911

January **LETTER GRADES INTRODUCED:** Letter grades are entered for the first time on report cards. In 1891, there were only four grades: excellent, passed, conditioned, and failed. Excellent was dropped in 1892, but later reinstated. By 1903, excellent, good, fair, and poor were in use and while the faculty could interpret these into A, B, C, and D, none of this was reported to the student, whose report card would show only "passed" or "failed."

April **GRADUATE STUDIES:** A special Academic Council committee recommends a separately administered Graduate School. In a minority report, however, mechanical engineering Prof. Guido Marx persuasively argues for a broader perspective of university study, emphasizing the need for even closer interaction between undergraduates and graduate students. The Academic Council subsequently rejects the committee's recommendation and instead enlarges membership on the Graduate Study Committee to be more broadly representative across subject fields.

Spring **THEODORE ROOSEVELT VISITS:** Theodore Roosevelt returns in 1911 (he planted a tree on campus in 1903). He tours the campus with President Jordan and Prof. John Casper Branner. In a campus lecture, he encourages students to acquire more than expert technical training.

June 4 **DUDLEY HERBARIUM:** Faculty member William Russell Dudley dies. Dudley, a Cornell-trained botanist and member of the pioneer faculty, established a large university collection of botanical books and specimens. The collection is renamed the Dudley Herbarium in his memory and is housed in the Natural History Museum with David Starr Jordan's extensive collection of fish specimens. Both collections are enlarged by faculty and student contributions, and eventually housed in part of the Stanford Museum. In 1976, after growing to 650,000 specimens, the herbarium is moved to San Francisco and

*John Casper Branner, appointed Stanford's second president, walks to his 1913 inauguration with Board of Trustees President Timothy Hopkins.*

*Theodore Roosevelt tours campus with Branner, left, and Jordan, in background, in 1911.*

*Herbert Hoover joins the Board of Trustees in 1911.*

*Clelia Duel Mosher, who joins the faculty in 1910, produces a landmark sexuality study.*

merged with that of the California Academy of Sciences.

October 29 **HERBERT HOOVER ELECTED TO BOARD OF TRUSTEES:** In a move engineered by two business associates on the Board of Trustees, Herbert Hoover is elected to the board — the second alumnus to serve (he takes the place of fellow pioneer classmate George Crothers at the end of Crother's 10-year term), and the first selected by board members. He spends the following months studying academic, financial, and administrative conditions at Stanford and in a long memorandum the following January warns that the university is lagging behind. Over the next two years, he fosters dramatic improvement in faculty salaries, both to attract eminent senior faculty and encourage current professors, recommends strengthening existing departments, instigates changes in the university's financial management, and promotes a campus building boom. "The pot was beginning to boil," writes one Hoover biographer, "and Hoover was stirring it."

# 1912

November 3 **LANE MEDICAL LIBRARY:** A major new building is dedicated at the Medical Department in San Francisco for the Lane Library. Available to department faculty and students, as well as practicing physicians and the general public, it houses the largest medical library in the West. Construction is made possible by a $140,000 gift from the estate of Mrs. Levi Cooper Lane, widow of the founder of Cooper Medical College (the department's predecessor). The building is the first Stanford building, although not on the Palo Alto campus, given by and named after a donor other than the Stanford family.

# 1913

May 23 **JORDAN NAMED FIRST CHANCELLOR:** David Starr Jordan steps down from the presidency, and is named chancellor of the university by the Board of Trustees. The reassignment is the brain-child of Herbert Hoover. It allows Jordan, hesitant to retire, to honorably give up administrative responsibilities without diminution of salary. Jordan now devotes much of his time to the World Peace Foundation. His talk, "Confessions of a Peace-maker" is highly popular in 1914, but after the outbreak of war in Europe, he receives threats and jeers. In 1916, the board does not renew his three-year term as chancellor, ending Jordan's formal relationship with the university. Jordan is not deterred, and speaks against American intervention until the United States enters the war in April 1917. He continues to speak throughout the country on reform topics ranging from education and woman's suffrage to conservation. He composes his rambling two-volume autobiography, *Days of a Man* (1922), in his typically colorful fashion, leaving future generations much poetic drama, but a wealth of misremembered historical details.

May 23 **BRANNER TAKES OVER PRESIDENCY:** John Casper Branner, 63, agrees to serve as second president of Stanford for the last two years of his academic career. Tak-

*After the earthquake, most of Memorial Church is taken down and rebuilt with metal framework.*

*Original church clock face and clock works are given their own wooden tower directly behind the church, near Panama Street, when the steeple is not replaced.*

*Memorial Church, reopened in 1913 with arched stained glass window, is finally complete with new Salviati mosaics on façade in 1916.*

ing office immediately, he is inaugurated Oct. 1, 1913, and serves until Jan. 1, 1916. Branner, a close friend of Jordan and popular pioneer faculty member, served as head of the Geology Department, vice-president, and acting president during Jordan's absences. Branner views his role as a transitional one, bridging pioneer Stanford and a new university generation. The appointment of Branner, a friend and former professor of Herbert Hoover, leads some to suspect the new president will be too compliant to Hoover's potentially jarring reforms, or serve merely as a place keeper for Hoover's own succession to the university presidency. Yet, among his first actions, Branner targets the Medical Department, highly favored by Hoover, as a financial albatross around the struggling university's neck.

August **Medical School:** The Department of Medicine becomes the School of Medicine. During the previous two months, President Branner strongly argued that the Medical Department be separately endowed or jettisoned altogether in order to avoid drastic cuts on campus. He is backed overwhelmingly by campus faculty, but the proposal stuns trustee Herbert Hoover. After heated interchanges, the board, prodded by Hoover, rejects the recommendation but explores a joint agreement with the University of California. When these negotiations fall through, the board decides to maintain the department but concedes that "drastic action" (i.e., threatened elimination of selected campus departments) will not be required.

October 5 **Memorial Church reopens:** Memorial Church is the last building renovated following the disastrous earthquake of 1906. As is done with several other Quadrangle buildings, most of it is taken down to the ground and rebuilt with metal framing. The stained glass rose window is replaced with an arched window. The original spire is not replaced, but the clock and clock works are mounted on a wooden tower behind the church in 1915. The mosaics are restored, and in some places images changed, by late 1916. Contrary to popular belief, the mosaic scene on the façade is neither the Sermon on the Mount nor Christ Welcoming the Righteous into the Kingdom of God. The scene is Christ Blessing the People (Luke 24:50), the only reference in the Bible to Christ having his arms extended upward. The original dedication to Leland Stanford in large letters on the façade is recreated in a less conspicuous spot, and a mosaic water scene with lilies substituted. Unhappy with this result, the Board of Trustees commissions the present simple sandstone design.

# 1914

Summer-Fall **Stanford's Belgian relief efforts:** After Germany invades Belgium in April, Herbert Hoover organizes the Commission for Relief in Belgium and calls for volunteers and charitable contributions. Profs. Frank Angell, Vernon L. Kellogg, and Samuel S. Seward Jr., as well as many students and alumni, volunteer to help staff the commission. In October, President Branner launches local efforts to collect food and clothing; within a month, Stanford groups across the country send money and clothing to the commission.

*The Men's Clubhouse (right) and Women's Clubhouse (not visible), built in 1915, are joined by the new (now old) Stanford Union in 1922.*

*Ray Lyman Wilbur, who declines to wear academic robes as too elitist, with David Starr Jordan at his inauguration as Stanford's third president, 1916.*

*Restaurant in the men's clubhouse is renovated as The Cellar, a popular eatery, seen here circa the 1940s.*

# 1915

February **MEN'S AND WOMEN'S CLUBHOUSES AND THE UNION:** The Men's Clubhouse and Women's Clubhouse are dedicated. Hoping to restore the "solidarity that existed between students and faculty in the old days," Herbert Hoover proposed in 1909 an ambitious plan to build a student union, constructed and maintained by students and alumni and completely independent of the university. Fundraising lags until Hoover appeals to members of the Pioneer Class and Lou Henry Hoover raises funds for the Women's Clubhouse. Construction begins in December 1913. The Men's Clubhouse, initially called "the Union," includes a barbershop, a haberdashery, and a restaurant (first operated by a Japanese cook, and later renovated and called "The Cellar"). The Women's Clubhouse provides a large lounge and a room with a stage. The buildings become headquarters for many student body activities. In 1922, work is completed on the third building of the complex envisioned by the Hoovers, the Stanford Union (then called the "New Union," and today's "Old Union"). It includes dining and dormitory facilities. Mr. and Mrs. Hoover together provide nearly half of the approximate cost of $226,000, with the remainder financed by alumni donations and a student assessment of $1 per semester per student.

October 13 **WILBUR APPOINTED THIRD PRESIDENT:** Ray Lyman Wilbur, '96, graduate of Cooper Medical College, and dean of medicine since 1913, is appointed Stanford's third president. He is inaugurated Jan. 1, 1916. During his exceptionally long term (1916-1943), he oversees a major growth spurt in buildings and in size of student body, reorganization of academic programs, major changes in academic policies, the university's first efforts at fundraising, and budget-cutting brought about by the Great Depression.

# 1916

March **UNIVERSITY TAKES OVER MUSEUM:** The Leland Stanford Junior Museum, badly damaged by the 1906 earthquake and with its collections in disarray, is placed under the University president rather than administered separately by the Stanford Business Office. Although the Museum is open to the public, the university provides little money for facilities, preservation of collections, or new purchases until the 1960s.

September **FRATERNITY REFORM:** "A student's principal business is his study," President Wilbur writes parents of current and prospective students in August. "The student who is not content to lead the simple, clean, industrious life expected on the Stanford campus should go elsewhere." A month later, he targets fraternities. Twice as many students live in fraternities and sororities as in campus dormitories and off-campus housing. The nine sororities maintain high scholarship, good behavior, and solid financial standards, but members of Stanford's 24 fraternities are consistently in the bottom third of scholarship lists (along with varsity football and baseball players, who

The new Encina Gym, built by the Board of Athletic Control. The board, which takes over management and finances of athletics for the university in 1917, is so successful that it funds construction of major sports facilities, Branner Hall, and its own BAC headquarters building on Galvez Street.

*The sign on one of five Stanford ambulances sent to France during World War I.*

are often fraternity members). Chapter houses are falling into disrepair, and local merchants regularly complain to the university about bills long overdue. Wilbur threatens to disband fraternity chapters that do not bring up scholarship records and pay off bills in two years. The war in Europe delays his plans, but in 1919 the Interfraternity Council is organized, and rules formulated regarding freshman pledging, freshman "discipline" (hazing), scholarship, and financial accountability. During the 1930s, substantial repairs are made to many chapter houses (several houses are completely rebuilt), but financial troubles and debate over rushing rules continue.

October 1 **TWENTY-FIFTH ANNIVERSARY OF UNIVERSITY'S OPENING:** Celebration of the university's first quarter century is postponed because it is deemed inappropriate during the early years of the war. Rescheduled for March 10, 1917, the anniversary is celebrated with an afternoon program of music and speeches in the Assembly Hall following annual observance of Founders' Day. Charles K. Field, '95, provides a humorous program at dinner in the Women's Clubhouse.

Fall **END OF TUBBING:** A much needed renovation of Encina Hall makes room for 150 additional men (for a total capacity of 450). Equally important is replacement of bathtubs with showers, thus ending virtually overnight the traditional hazing of freshmen by "tubbing" — holding a freshman's head under water until he "bubbled", or gasped for air. Roughhousing and hazing have been a long-term problem. Student discipline in Encina as well as the fraternities is a clear priority of President Wilbur, who speaks out strongly against hazing as "a combination of cowardice and bullying, absolutely un-American. It overpowers and crushes the individual. At best it is contemptible, and at worst criminal."

## 1917

February **BOARD OF ATHLETIC CONTROL:** The independent Board of Athletic Control (BAC) is created to serve as a de facto athletics department. Previously, athletics was under general oversight of a faculty committee, but teams and events were managed by the Associated Students, an unsuccessful arrangement that often left ASSU bankrupt. Until 1943, the BAC maintains athletic buildings, equipment, and fields; appoints coaches and trainers; and controls funding for and from athletic events. The board manages both an efficient and profitable program: receipts from football games finance construction of the stadium, Branner Hall, Roble Gym, Basketball Pavilion, the Golf Course and Clubhouse, Sunken Diamond, and Encina Gym expansion.

February **STANFORD AMBULANCE UNITS:** The first of five student volunteer ambulance units organized for the American Ambulance Service is sent to France. Unrelenting competition with the University of California persists. Each campus assembles an ambulance corps equipped with an American flag to present to the French commander. These units then race across the Atlantic to be the first

*Thomas Welton Stanford's many benefactions include a new Art Gallery, intended as the corner of a new library-museum quadrangle.*

*Stanford Reserve Officers Training Corps in Inner Quad, 1917.*

to the front. Stanford's ambulance unit wins and its flag is decorated with a Croix de Guerre on July 4, 1917 by French General Marchard. The flag, brought back to the university, is displayed in Memorial Church until the late 1960s (it is preserved today in the University Archives). Fundraising is in part inspired by news of the deaths of Prof. Robert Edouard Pellissier and James Grant Ferguson, '08, both killed in France the previous summer.

April 27 **SCHOOL OF EDUCATION:** Department of the History and Art of Education is reorganized as the School of Education. Ellwood P. Cubberley, executive head of the former department, is named first dean.

May **WAR-TIME COMMENCEMENT:** Commencement is marked by the presence of men in uniform and the presentation of an American flag to the third Stanford Ambulance Unit. With declaration of war the previous April, the emotional appeal of pacifism has given way to military preparedness. An estimated 90 faculty serve in the Palo Alto area and overseas in Red Cross work, famine relief, or military service. An initial enrollment of 250 students in the Reserve Officers' Training Corps unit, organized in September 1916, jumps to 850 by this spring semester and is ranked among the top 10 in the country. In 1918, Encina and Sequoia Halls become U.S. Army barracks, and a temporary mess hall for 1,200 is erected near the site of today's Meyer Library. The athletics program is taken over by the Student Army Training Corps, and intercollegiate sports competitions are largely discontinued. Most social events are suspended unless they contribute to the war effort, such as fundraising. Volunteers provide medical, social, and recreational support for nearby Camp Fremont.

October 1 **QUARTER SYSTEM:** A four-quarter system of 11 weeks each replaces two semesters of 16 weeks each. The addition of the summer quarter allows faculty and students flexibility in their personal plans and keeps the university operating 11 months of the year.

November **STANFORD UNIVERSITY PRESS:** Stanford University Press is formally established with acquisition of the small private print shop operated on campus by Julius Andrew Quelle. Quelle started in the business in 1892, when, as a student, he borrowed $25 each from 12 professors, bought a second-hand press and type cases, and in a corner of the powerhouse began printing the *Daily Palo Alto* and fulfilling other printing needs. The press prints university publications, student newspapers and alumni journals, as well as books by faculty. Self-sustaining, even during the Depression, the press expands in 1930.

December 6 **THOMAS WELTON STANFORD ART GALLERY:** An art gallery opens to house the notable collection of Australian art donated by Thomas Welton Stanford. Designed by Bakewell and Brown as the corner building of a proposed library-museum quadrangle, it has a high, elaborately carved arch at its front and an arcade along its Serra Street façade (much of this arcade will later be filled in). In addition to books, art work, and funds used for the main library (1900), he also endows a fellowship for psychological and psychic research.

The President's House on the Knoll, built for Ray Lyman Wilbur (above left), is the official residence provided by the university in 1918.

"New" Roble Hall, built to house all women not living in sororities, replaces the old in 1918.

# 1918

April **FLU EPIDEMIC:** Alert medical staff promptly isolate and hospitalize victims during the international influenza epidemic of spring 1918, resulting in a much lower percentage of deaths (only 6 out of 260 cases) than typical nationally. The flu first fills the Army infirmary at Camp Fremont, then Palo Alto's Peninsula Hospital (built in 1910) and the campus Isolation Hospital (built in 1912 in the hills behind the campus, between Los Trancos Creek and Felt Lake). The university also requisitions a fraternity house and two local residences. The epidemic highlights the inadequacy of student medical services. In 1921, the university takes over the Student Guild's functions, and establishes a "hospital fund" to receive assessment fees and dispense benefits.

June **WORLD WAR I ROLL OF HONOR:** At commencement, roll of honor certificates are given to parents or relatives of 68 Stanford men and women who are known to have died in service during the war. Certificates of honor go to 722 students who left the university to enter the U.S. armed services and 18 who joined the services of the Allies. In 1921, President Wilbur reports that 3,393 Stanford men and women (students, alumni, faculty and staff) served during the war in U.S. and foreign service or war-related civilian posts, and that 77 were killed.

June **THE KNOLL:** On a knoll overlooking the campus and Lagunita, a large official residence (the first provided by the university) is built for President Ray Lyman Wilbur and for official university functions. The reinforced concrete Spanish-revival structure is designed by San Francisco architect Louis C. Mullgardt, and landscaping is designed by John McLaren, noted designer of San Francisco's Golden Gate Park. The Wilbur family lives in the house until President Wilbur's retirement in 1943, but his successor, Donald B. Tresidder, chooses not to live there. In October 1943, a wartime unit of the Women's Army Corps is quartered there, followed during demobilization by the Geography Department. In 1946, the newly formed Music Department moves in, using the space for teaching, library, and practice space.

September 28 **ROBLE HALL:** A new Roble Hall for women opens near the lake to house all women not living in sororities. It replaces the original Roble Hall on Serra Street, which is renamed Sequoia Hall and used to house men, then academic functions until demolished in 1996. Considered one of the most up-to-date dormitories in the country when constructed, the new three-story Spanish eclectic structure has three wings of reinforced concrete. Freshmen women are assigned to Roble in 1934 when Lagunita Court is built.

# 1919

Spring **HOOVER WAR COLLECTION:** The Hoover War Collection is founded when Herbert Hoover presents President Wilbur with a $50,000 check to support collection of materials documenting the recent war, relief efforts, and

History Prof. E.D. Adams, right, and colleague Ralph Lutz stand beside bundles of documents destined for the Hoover War Library.

The Main Library, opened in 1919, intended by architects Bakewell and Brown to be the focal point of the proposed library-museum quad, which is never fully built.

the Peace Conference. Materials will be housed in the University Library as a separate collection. Hoover credits the idea to writings of Cornell President Andrew Dickson White, who collected ephemera from the French Revolution. In March 1915, history Prof. E.D. Adams, a friend of Hoover, had reminded Hoover of the need to preserve records of the Commission for the Relief of Belgium. Hoover organizes and finances more extensive efforts of Adams and his associates to gather leaflets, newspapers, government documents, ephemera, books and periodicals. Hoover, while serving as director of the American Relief Administration, sent documents back to the United States on ships that had taken food to Europe. In 1922, the Hoover War Collection becomes the Hoover War Library, with a reading room on the ground floor of the Main Library.

July 14 **UNIVERSITY LIBRARY:** A new Main Library, designed by Beaux Arts architect Arthur Brown Jr. of San Francisco, is occupied. Although discouraged from adding ornamentation, he includes three bas relief figures on the façade to represent art, philosophy, and science. Brown and his partner, John Bakewell, intend the library to be the focal point of a proposed library-museum quadrangle. At the dedication, pioneer faculty member John Maxon Stillman predicts the library will be adequate for the next 50 years. The Thomas Welton Stanford Library in the Outer Quad is remodeled for administrative offices.

November **RETURN TO AMERICAN-RULES FOOTBALL:** Once again Big Game is played with the University of California after Stanford returns to American-rules football. Both universities had turned to rugby in 1906 as the more wholesome and individualistic game. After Berkeley drops out of the California Rugby Union in 1912, Stanford-Cal football relations are tense due to disagreements over rules infringements, freshmen eligibility, and scholarship requirements. When Cal returns to American rules in 1915, Stanford plays Big Game with the University of Santa Clara, 1915-1917, and with Army in 1918. Even though Stanford students, alumni, and faculty now prefer rugby over football, many wish to return to the spirited competition with Cal. Others voice the need for higher gate receipts. Stanford's return to American-rules football follows major changes nationally in the sport, including improved refereeing and harsher penalties, and campus changes made in coaching, training, and financial management.

December **STEINBECK:** Future Nobel Laureate John Steinbeck of Salinas, who chose Stanford because of its then-free tuition, receives a "C" in freshman English. Steinbeck supports himself and lives in Encina Hall and in various modest rooms in Palo Alto. He drops out in 1921, re-enters as a journalism major in 1923, and drops out again in 1925. Later he says that he considered his college career a waste of time, but found two good English teachers in Profs. Edith Mirrielees and Margery Bailey. In 1975, the University Libraries acquires the manuscript of his novel *Cannery Row* as its four millionth book, and in 1999 adds significantly to its collection of Steinbeck manuscripts, letters, photographs, and books.

# 1920

**STATISTICS:**

Undergraduate enrollment: 2,165

Graduate enrollment: 283

Faculty: 150

Tuition: $120 per year

Endowment: $26 million

January 1 **UNDERGRADUATE TUITION STARTS:** The trustees, facing a financial crisis caused by fixed endowment income and a rising cost of living, institute the university's first undergraduate tuition — $40 per quarter. Herbert Hoover, returning to national acclaim from his European food relief work, leads the board in pushing through this break with the founders' intention of a tuition-free education, at the October 1919 meeting. Although there are complaints about the abrupt change, arguments of students and parents die down when Hoover points out the number of automobiles belonging to students and "the receipts of the ice cream parlors in the neighborhood would go a long way toward the needed increase in income." Students unable to pay are offered an alternative of seven-year interest-bearing notes. Most of the tuition income is immediately passed along in across-the-board pay increases for the faculty. Two years later, tuition goes from $40 to $75 per quarter.

May **CON HOME OPENS:** Stanford Home for Convalescent Children opens in part of the Palo Alto Farm residence of Leland and Jane Stanford that was spared by the 1906 earthquake. Con Home eventually specializes in treatment of long-term diseases in children and becomes the Children's Hospital at Stanford.

Fall **LOWER DIVISION/UPPER DIVISION:** In a significant reorganization of undergraduate education, the major-subject system that dates to 1891 is replaced for freshmen and sophomores with a new Lower Division described as a "frank reincarnation" of liberal education. During their first two years, students must take courses in English, history, science, foreign language, and citizenship. At the beginning of the junior year, students move to the Upper Division and begin work in a major department. The academic committee that makes this proposal notes that it considered calling the new organization "junior college" rather than "Lower Division," but rejected the idea because the word "junior" already appears in the official name of the university.

Fall **"BAWL-OUT":** For the first time, students' grade point averages are published in the university's directory. Because of the practice, the directory becomes known as the "Bawl-Out." Students protest, to no avail, during the 1920s, and in 1933 the *Stanford Daily* begins an anti-Bawl-Out campaign. President Wilbur declares: "You make your record. We merely keep it." Publication of grade points stops briefly in the 1940s and ends for good with the 1957-58 issue.

## 1921

March **HOOVER TO CABINET:** Herbert Hoover, a member of the Pioneer Class of '95, joins the Harding administration as secretary of commerce. This is the first cabinet appointment from Stanford.

May 23 **HONOR CODE:** The Student Honor System — later called the Honor Code — is approved by faculty after 1,750 students sign petitions seeking responsibility for honesty in academic work. The code, which is the application of the "Fundamental Standard" to academics, has students monitor their own conduct as well as that of their fellow students. *(See also April 1896)*

Summer **TERMAN'S GIFTED CHILDREN:** Lewis M. Terman begins his lifelong study of 1,528 gifted children. Terman began investigations of gifted children in 1904 when he encountered the theory that exceptionally bright children might suffer physical or mental illness or social maladjust-

Convalescent Home gets its start in the old Stanford family home in 1920.

The Basketball Pavilion, used for rallies and dances, as well as basketball, opens in 1922. A student assessment helps pay for it.

ment. The children chosen, often referred to as "Termites," have IQs ranging from 135 to 200. When Terman dies in 1956, the work is continued by the husband-wife team of Prof. Robert Sears and Prof. Pauline Sears. The longest psychological study ever conducted, the project produces evidence that exceptionally intelligent children grow up to be more successful, better satisfied, and more productive than average people. However, the gifted eventually seem to have as many emotional difficulties as the rest of the population. The work continues, now in its ninth decade, under the direction of Albert Hastorf, former Stanford provost and professor emeritus of psychology.

July 1 **Food Research Institute launched:** The Food Research Institute is organized to study production, distribution, and consumption of food. The lack of information about world food supplies and requirements prompts Herbert Hoover, who headed American relief efforts in Europe after the war, to secure initial financing for the institute from the Carnegie Corporation of New York.

November 19 **Stanford Stadium opens:** Designed by engineering Prof. C.B. Wing, the stadium, with a seating capacity of 60,000, is built in 4½ months at a cost of $211,000, provided by the Board of Athletic Control, which raises the money through loans and ticket sales. This is one of the university's last big dirt-moving jobs using horse- and mule-hauling equipment. Stanford races Cal in completing their big stadiums. Stanford wins. In the first game held there, Cal defeats Stanford by an embarrassing 42-7. In 1925, the open end is partially closed, adding 11,000 seats. Another 16,000 seats are added in 1927 in 14 rows hidden by an arched superstructure on the top rim, bringing capacity close to 90,000. With seat losses due to later modifications, current capacity is 85,500.

# 1922

January 13 **Basketball Pavilion:** A large pavilion mainly for basketball but also to be used for student dances and rallies is dedicated across from Encina Hall. Students assess themselves to help retire a construction loan from the Board of Trustees. The Board of Athletic Control and the president's budget also contribute; the loan and interest are repaid in 10 years.

February 3 **The "First Million":** Responding to urgent trustee requests for endowment gifts, Stanford students, at an open meeting in the Quad, pledge $105,965 to kick-off a new campaign — called the "First Million" — to raise $1 million in endowment for faculty salaries. The General Education Board, a foundation created by John D. Rockefeller, offers $700,000 if the university raises $300,000. Alumni meetings soon produce pledges for the remaining amount. The campaign's success stimulates a "Second Million," to support building construction, and a "Third Million," for partial endowment of the Medical School. This

*Stanford loses big in the first Big Game at the new stadium in 1921.*

*Stadium construction in 1921 takes just 4½ months. The decorative arcade hides additional seating that is added in 1927.*

overall effort marks the beginning of organized fundraising by the university and the alumni.

March 1 **PRESIDENT BRANNER DIES:** President Emeritus John Casper Branner dies of a heart ailment at 71. He was Stanford's second president, serving from 1913-1915. A distinguished scholar, he was chair of the Department of Geology and Mining from 1891 to 1915.

# 1923

September **ENCINA DINING HALLS OPEN:** The fall term brings welcome news to the men of Encina: their new dining halls, soon called Encina Commons, built directly behind Encina, are at last open. Since Encina's original dining hall was closed in 1898, the residents have mostly eaten at the Stanford Inn or The Camp, when they were open, or eaten at the Stanford Union or joined local eating clubs. The new rooms, which have a capacity of about 500, blend well with Encina's architecture. In addition to two large dining rooms, the commons also provides space in six small rooms for the eating clubs.

Fall **BEGINNINGS OF WESTERN CIV:** "Problems of Citizenship," a course required for freshmen and taught by various faculty members as a team, is inaugurated with History Prof. Edgar Eugene Robinson as director. It is designed to examine the "fundamental political, social, and economic problems of the American people." In 1935 it will evolve into "History of Western Civilization," also developed by Robinson.

# 1924

April **IQ TESTS:** Beginning with fall quarter, all applicants will have to pass a new requirement: achieve a satisfactory score on a supplemental examination ("intelligence test"). The examination will be given in June at numerous locations in California and elsewhere, and also at the university one week prior to matriculation.

Fall **POP WARNER WINS:** In his first year as football coach, Glenn Scobey "Pop" Warner leads Stanford to an undefeated season and a trip to the Rose Bowl using his innovative, complex double-wing attack. Historians credit Warner with invention of the reverse play and the crouching start, and emphasis on the spiral pass. He introduces huddles between plays, assigns numbers to plays, and puts headgear on his team. In 1926 Stanford is awarded the Rissman National Trophy as the top college football team in the country, the only time it is so honored.

# 1925

January 1 **ROSE BOWL LOSS:** Ernie Nevers, playing in

(Right) Officials signal a touchdown. Legendary coach Pop Warner (below, right) with his star player, Ernie Nevers. In his 1924 premiere season, Warner's team is undefeated.

The Varsity Girls promote Stanford spirit.

perhaps his most famous game, leads Stanford against Knute Rockne's "Four Horsemen" of Notre Dame in the Rose Bowl. Despite two previously broken ankles, Nevers plays the full 60 minutes. Stanford loses 27-10, however, when two of Nevers' passes are intercepted and run back for touchdowns. In 1962, *Sports Illustrated* chooses Nevers as the greatest college football player.

January 15 **JORDAN WINS PRIZE FOR PEACE PLAN:** David Starr Jordan, Stanford's first president, wins the $25,000 Rafael Hermen Award for his proposed "world peace education" plan. The contest is sponsored by the World Federation of Education Associations.

January **SCHOOL RANKINGS:** Stanford ranks 14th nationally in overall strength of its graduate programs, according to a survey of academic department heads published in *A Study of the Graduate Schools of America.* Chicago is first.

May 15 **SCHOOL OF ENGINEERING:** The School of Engineering is organized from the departments of Civil Engineering, Mechanical Engineering, Electrical Engineering, and Mining.

Summer **SUNKEN DIAMOND:** During the summer, the open end of the football stadium is filled with material taken from an adjacent field, which in 1931 becomes the Sunken Diamond baseball field. The baseball team celebrates completion of the new diamond by winning the California Intercollegiate Baseball Association championship.

September 30 **GRADUATE SCHOOL OF BUSINESS:** The Graduate School of Business — the first in California — opens with 16 students at the instigation of Herbert Hoover, who says business should be taught on a par with such professions as engineering, law, and medicine. He also wants to halt the flow of graduates who go east seeking business education and careers. Dean Willard E. Hotchkiss is appointed the school's first dean. Hotchkiss has previously successfully organized two other business schools.

Fall **INDEPENDENT STUDY:** The Independent Study Program is launched for exceptional juniors and seniors, guided by a committee first headed by psychology Prof. Lewis Terman and later by history Prof. Edgar E. Robinson. The program is extended to freshman and sophomores in 1931, but dies out entirely during World War II. By the mid-1950s, independent study programs reappear in many departments.

# 1926

August **AERONAUTICS LABORATORY:** The Daniel Guggenheim Fund makes a $190,000 grant to support the development of the Daniel Guggenheim Experimental Laboratory of Aerodynamic and Aeronautic Engineering. This effort will be under the general direction of Prof.

*At his high-voltage laboratory, dedicated in 1926, Harris J. Ryan (right) works on problems of long-distance transmission of electricity.*

Everett Lesley, with emeritus Prof. William Durand as consultant, and will focus on propeller development, Prof. Durand's specialty. Within a short time, a new engineering building and wind tunnel are constructed behind the Quad. Important aerodynamic research is carried out in the 1930s and into the war years. In summer 1939, Charles Lindbergh pays a secret visit to campus to inspect the research work of Durand and others at the Guggenheim Laboratory. He and the aeronautics faculty discuss aviation over lunch at the Stanford Union.

September 17 **HIGH-VOLTAGE LAB:** The Harris J. Ryan High-Voltage Laboratory is dedicated. The laboratory, located in a field that much later is used for faculty housing, is financed by several large corporations concerned with long-distance transmission of power, including General Electric, the Pacific Gas & Electric Co., and the California-Oregon Power Co. Prof. Ryan came to Stanford from Cornell in 1905. Ryan and his associates study power transmission and work on development of insulators to support very-high-voltage power lines. At the opening, 300 guests watch a demonstration of six 2.1-million-volt flashovers through 20 feet of air between electrodes. Ryan later helps solve the problem of transmitting large amounts of power from Hoover Dam to Los Angeles. He continues high-voltage work until his death in 1934.

September 30 ***STANFORD DAILY* IS BORN:** The afternoon student newspaper, the *Daily Palo Alto*, is reborn as a morning newspaper with a new name: the *Stanford Daily*. The time change will allow students who work on the paper to attend morning classes.

Fall **DUTCH MICROBIOLOGIST JOINS HOPKINS:** Cornelis B. van Niel, from Holland, joins the faculty at the Hopkins Marine Station on Monterey Bay. A microbiologist, he devotes his life to research that clarifies the basic mechanisms of photosynthesis. His famous summer quarter microbiology course, a 15-unit battery of lectures and laboratory work, sometimes goes for eight hours at a stretch. Arthur Kornberg, later to become a Nobel laureate for his work in DNA research, takes the course in 1953 and credits it with arousing his interest in microbiology.

# 1927

April 18 **LOWER DIVISION OR JUNIOR COLLEGE?:** At a University Day dinner, President Wilbur causes concern when he announces that the trustees are considering his recommendation that by 1934 all the work of the "junior college" years — i.e., the Lower Division — be turned over to junior college-type institutions, which have been increasing in size and number. Wilbur sees it as a way to focus resources on advanced and hence more important subjects. A similar recommendation was made in 1912 by President Jordan, when he wrote "sooner or later, Stanford must choose whether it will be a college or a university, for

A flying school and Palo Alto Airport operate in the area of Escondido Village from 1928 to 1935.

*Herbert Hoover, '95, is driven around the track at Stanford Stadium, where he accepts the Republican nomination for U.S. president. Community members salute the new president at his campus home on election night in 1928.*

it has not the funds for both." Wilbur's proposal sets off widespread debate about the university's future. In opposition to the proposal are most of the alumni, the athletics board, and the fraternities. With the onset of the Depression and its problems, the idea becomes less promising. On Feb. 11, 1932, the trustees decide that the junior college idea will be dropped and that the Lower Division will continue and possibly even expand.

# 1928

February 28 **FLYING SCHOOL:** The university leases 65 acres on the southeasterly corner of the campus (now the corner of El Camino Real and Stanford Avenue) to Navy Lt. Norman Goddard, a noted airplane ace, for use as a flying school. No university credit will be given for courses taken. A hangar and office building will be erected and a northwest facing 2,400-foot runway will be built. Initially, there will be two Waco planes, plus a monoplane constructed by Goddard. (Lt. Goddard is killed on Jan. 26, 1930, in a glider accident near the Oakland Estuary. The flying school is closed in 1935 as a result of a lawsuit filed by College Terrace residents.)

November 7 **HOOVER ELECTED PRESIDENT:** Herbert Hoover is elected 31st president of the United States. Hoover hears the news at his campus home, now known as the Lou Henry Hoover House. Students and others, led by John Philip Sousa and his band, march to the house and pay tribute to the new president-elect.

# 1929

March 4 **HOOVER AND WILBUR GO TO WASHINGTON:** Hoover asks university President Ray Lyman Wilbur to join him as secretary of the interior; the trustees grant Wilbur a one-year of absence with pay. Chemistry Prof. Robert Eckles Swain is named acting president, but proves indecisive — referring many decisions to Wilbur in Washington. This situation causes increasing problems; leading the *Stanford Daily*, on Oct. 13, 1930, to call for Wilbur to either resign as president or as interior secretary. The Stanford *Chaparral* follows with a satire referring to Wilbur as the university's "president-by-mail." Hoover refuses to release Wilbur, and the uneasy situation continues. Although the trustees reluctantly continue to grant Wilbur year-by-year leaves, the last two are without pay.

August 27 **CARNEGIE INSTITUTION:** The Carnegie Institution's Laboratory of Experimental Taxonomy and Genetics is dedicated on five acres the independent lab leases from the university. Though not directly connected to the university, its group of distinguished scientists helps promote many important research projects.

# 1930

**STATISTICS:**

Undergraduate enrollment: 2,706

Graduate enrollment: 893

Faculty: 271

Tuition: $300 per year

Endowment: $30 million

January 1 **GOLF COURSE OPENS**: With 6,648 yards (now 6,786) of greens and fairways, the Stanford Golf Course opens on rolling former stock farm pastures. Designed by William Bell, who also did the Pebble Beach course, it is one of the finest in the country. Such golfing greats as Lawson Little, Tom Watson, and Tiger Woods will later enjoy the Stanford course.

April 3 **THE "IMMORTAL 21" RECOVER AXE:** Twenty-one Stanford men, mostly from Sequoia Hall, recover the Axe that University of California students grabbed 31 years earlier after a hotly contested baseball game. For three decades, Cal students hide the blade in a Berkeley bank vault, removing it once a year to taunt Stanford at Cal's annual spring Axe Rally. Several recovery efforts fail. Armed with valuable intelligence from those failures, Don Kropp, '26, and his army develop an elaborate plan. After the rally, Stanford's Axe and its Cal custodian, Norman Horner, return to the bank in an armored car. As Horner steps from the vehicle, Howard Avery, '31, dives off the car roof onto Horner and the Axe; at about the same time, Raymond Walsh, '30, sets off a large charge of magnesium flash powder, temporarily blinding Cal students who are posing for a photograph. In the ensuing mayhem, Bob Loofbourow, '29, somehow gets the blade. He calmly tucks it under his sweater and walks to a waiting car that roars off to The Farm at speeds in excess of 60 miles an hour. As the car departs, Art Miller, '31, throws a tear gas bomb, creating more confusion. Stanford men posing as Cal students suggest going to Berkeley's Campanile to organize a pursuit posse. When the Immortal 21 return to campus, celebration begins. Classes are canceled the next morning for a rally. The university presents each of the 21 with a Block S letter (an honor usually reserved for varsity athletes) and a special gold Axe watch charm. For two years the Axe languishes in a bank vault because of fears of a riot if it appears in public. In 1933, the schools agree to make the Stanford Axe the Big Game trophy. It has been stolen at least eight times since, but no prank rivals the drama of the Immortal 21's caper. *(See also April 14, 1899)*

Fall **INDIAN MASCOT ADOPTED:** Following an emotional Big Game rally with an Indian theme, the ASSU Executive Committee officially adopts the Indian as a symbol for Stanford. The Indian symbol first appeared in 1923, the idea of Dr. Tom Williams, class of 1897, varsity football player, an original member of the Board of Athletic Control, and an avid supporter of Stanford sports. Many colleges and high schools had been selecting easily identifiable symbols on the Indian theme. Recent excavation of Indian archeological sites in the campus area, combined with the image of this symbol as the conqueror of bears and other animal mascots, led to its popularity among alumni and the news media; students, however, remained comparatively apathetic until later in the 1920s. By 1937, the symbol of a heroic Indian brave is joined by the shirtless, wide-eyed, boyish "Li'l Injun" created by Tommy Thompson for the *Stanford Daily* and made popular during the 1940s in cartoons by Bob Breer. The school's color, cardinal, continues to symbolize Stanford as well, and "the Cardinal" is used interchangeably with the Stanford Indian both on and off campus. Reacting to objections from American Indians, the Indian mascot is discontinued in 1972. *(See also March 2, 1972)*

October **TUITION GOES UP:** Tuition is raised $25 to $100 per quarter. This is the first increase since 1921.

## 1931

Winter **MILE OF ROSES PLANTED:** After El Camino Real

*In a spectacular feat of daring, the Immortal 21 recapture the Stanford Axe in 1930. The next morning, classes are canceled for a celebration in front of the Main Library. Shades drawn, the Immortals pose with the Axe – held by ringleader Don Kropp – in the lobby of a Palo Alto bank, where they take the Axe for safekeeping. They also proudly display a newspaper headline.*

*One of many cartoons of Indiar mascot, adopted 1930.*

is widened to four lanes, workers plant 500 climbing rose bushes along a fence from San Francisquito Creek to Mayfield. When El Camino is again widened in 1961, the State Highway Department moves the fence and preserves and replants the much-loved "mile of roses."

April **NEW ENTRY GATES:** A quarter century after the university entry gates were destroyed by the 1906 earthquake, a new set soon will be in place. Designed by the firm of Bakewell and Brown, their cost is largely underwritten by the state as compensation for damage it causes widening El Camino Real. The Alumni Association also contributes.

April 17 **WOMEN'S GYMNASIUM DEDICATED:** Roble Gym for women is dedicated, ending nearly 40 years at the "temporary" gym that had come to be called "Woodpecker Hall" for the native bird that pecked on its exterior. Bakewell and Brown designed the Spanish revival gym, which was paid for with gifts solicited by women students and funds from the all-male Board of Athletic Control. In addition to a gymnasium, it includes a large dance studio, an outdoor swimming pool, and a courtyard with fountain. The gym becomes coed in the 1970s.

May 26 **PALO ALTO HOSPITAL:** The 85-bed Palo Alto Hospital opens in the arboretum, not far from El Camino Real. The five-story reinforced-concrete structure is built with funds raised by the city of Palo Alto. It sits on a 10.5-acre site leased to the city for 99 years. Stanford will ope ate the hospital.

September 19 **PRESIDENT JORDAN DIES:** The universit first president and first chancellor, David Starr Jordan, di from heart disease at his campus home at 80. His wido Jessie Knight Jordan, dies Oct. 24, 1952, two weeks shy her 86th birthday.

# 1932

Winter **GREAT DEPRESSION HITS:** The university is fe ing the full brunt of the Depression. Lower returns on i vestments — some even in default — and lower enro ment bring about a $300,000 decline in annual revenu Trustees impose a 10 percent salary reduction in 1933. 1934, they restore half the cut.

March 26 **EASTMAN SMASHES TRACK RECORDS:** Ta blond, and bespectacled Ben Eastman sets a world reco in the 440-yard run, and two weeks later, on April 9, breaks the 880-yard world record. Blazin' Ben took a f second off the 440 record, which had stood for 16 years.

October **SHEEP SOLD:** The Board of Athletic Control se its 300 sheep to Theodore Hoover, dean of engineerin who has a sheep ranch on the coast at Pescadero. Billy M Clintock, the Scotsman who herded the university's she

*The dining hall of Lagunita Court, complete with linen and hashers. The dorm opens in fall 1934, easing a housing shortage brought on by the removal of the enrollment limitation of 500 women.*

*These Palm Drive entry gates, destroyed in the 1906 earthquake, finally are replaced in 1931 with the gates that still stand.*

*Palo Alto Hospital opens in the arboretum in 1931.*

in Highland style for 30 years, is too ill to carry on. The athletic fields now will be clipped using lawn tractors.

November **HOOVER RETURNS TO VOTE:** Trustees, faculty, alumni, and students gather at the entrance to the Quad to greet President and Mrs. Hoover, who have returned to campus to vote at the polling station in the Women's Clubhouse. The soon-to-be-ex-president is "noticeably weary from his hard-fought campaign," according to the *Stanford Daily*. Newspapers and radio networks falsely claim Dr. Wilbur will step aside in favor of Hoover as Stanford president.

# 1933

March 3 **WILBUR RETURNS:** Ray Lyman Wilbur returns to his presidential duties, facing the university's serious financial problems.

May 11 **500 LIMIT REMOVED:** President Wilbur, in his 1933 Annual Report, hits hard on the problems caused by the limitation of 500 women: "For over 30 years the most outstanding handicap in the operation of Stanford University has been the limitation on women to 500, as directed in 1899 by Mrs. Stanford, the surviving founder." By fall 1932, women account for only 14 percent of the total — a situation generating anger and ill will. The problem is made worse by a complicated, hard-to-understand selection process. Each year since 1929, total enrollment — and tuition income — has fallen, even while qualified women are turned away. Finally facing the issue on May 11, the trustees creatively find a way around the 500 limit: They vote to admit additional women "maintaining substantially the same proportion between men and women as existed on May 31, 1899." This action raises the limit to about 40 percent. Three hundred additional women enroll in fall 1933, and the university suddenly has a new problem — a shortage of women's housing, which temporarily limits the total enrollment of women to about 20 percent. The new women are scattered around campus. The completion of Lagunita Court in fall 1934 removes some of the pressure, and women's enrollment rises. By 1937-38, a total of 1,588 women are enrolled — more than three times the old 500 limit. *(See also May 31, 1899, and June 8, 1972)*

May 21 **"ALUMNI UNIVERSITY":** More than 200 attend "Alumni University," the first campus alumni conference, with professors speaking on such topics as "The Leadership that is America," "Rebuilding the Financial Structure," "The Future of American Democracy," and "Can Industry Make Itself Depression-Proof?" This is the beginning of the Alumni Association's extensive continuing education program; earlier Alumni Day and University Day events focused on social activities and entertainment. Following this success, faculty members travel to Los Angeles for a 1934 conference, beginning a long tradition of educational conferences for Southern California alumni.

The campus sheep, long used to cut grass, are sold in 1932.

Hay is harvested on The Farm in 1935. Men from Encina Hall, in the background, sometimes set fire to the stacks using projectiles shot from upper floors.

The Vow Boys promise in 1933 that they will never lose to USC, and they never do.

May 30 **LAMSON MURDER?:** Allene Thorpe Lamson, '26, wife of University Press advertising manager David Lamson, dies in the bathtub of their home at 622 Salvatierra Street, the back of her head gashed and blood splattered everywhere. The couple is well-known on campus — he a regular contributor to the *Stanford Illustrated Review* and she briefly the alumni magazine's managing editor. The death draws national headlines when Lamson is indicted for murder, tried, found guilty on Sept. 16, and sentenced to hang at San Quentin. The case sharply divides the campus community: many are convinced of his guilt but others, led by English Prof. Yvor Winters, launch a campaign challenging the verdict. Meanwhile, Lamson spends his time on death row writing a best-selling book, *We Who Are About to Die*. Eventually he is granted a second trial, which ends in a hung jury. A third trial is cut short by jury irregularities. A fourth trial again ends in a hung jury — nine for conviction, three for acquittal. The case is dropped and Lamson set free on April 3, 1936.

November **VOW BOYS:** After watching their "big brothers" post Stanford's fifth loss in five years to USC, the freshman team in 1932 vowed never to be defeated by the Trojans. During their first varsity year, the "Vow Boys" begin redeeming their much-publicized pledge with a 13-7 defeat of a USC team that was on a 27-game winning streak. Players almost do not make it to the game: their train is delayed five hours near Salinas because of a track washout; they arrive, sleepless, only an hour before kick-off. In their three varsity years, the Vow Boys never lose to USC. They compile a 25-4-2 overall record, allow opponents only 99 points, shut out opponents 20 times, and play in three Rose Bowls. Five of the Vow Boys make All-American.

# 1934

January 8 **STANFORD RADIO PROGRAM:** The University Radio Program Committee produces the first of 34 weekly 15-minute Monday night broadcasts, initially on San Francisco station KPO and later on KGO. Faculty topics range from "The Streamlining of Automobiles" to "The New European Crisis." Campus groups also present cultural programs, including a performance by the *a cappella* choir and readings from *Julius Caesar*. An NBC executive praises the program, calling it "one of the finest educational contributions that is being made on the radio today." The series ends in October 1941.

April 1 **FELIX BLOCH JOINS FACULTY:** One of the first in a wave of European émigrés, physicist Felix Bloch comes to Stanford from Switzerland. In the late 1930s, he begins research on "nuclear induction" — the tendency for the core nucleus of atoms to vibrate when placed in a strong magnetic field and probed with radio waves. After World War II, Bloch and his Stanford colleague William W. Hansen devise ways to detect nuclear magnetic resonance (NMR).

*Hank Luisetti, #7, popularizes the one-hand jump shot in 1936, revolutionizing basketball.*

*Russell Varian, front left, displays the klystron microwave tube invented in 1937 with his brother, Sigurd, standing at left. Others are, clockwise, Prof. David Webster, Prof. William Hansen, who collaborated with the brothers, and John Woodyard.*

Soon after Bloch's discovery, physicists and chemists begin to use techniques learned in NMR as tools for analyzing the structure of large molecules. NMR later emerges as a powerful diagnostic tool in medicine under the new name of magnetic resonance imaging, MRI.

October **STANFORD ASSOCIATES FORMED:** Dr. Harry B. Reynolds, a '96 classmate of President Wilbur, suggests the formation of Stanford Associates to help raise money for the university. At the time of its founding, Stanford was, for a short period, the richest university in the world, and the myth has persisted among alumni and others that the institution does not need any financial help. But because of low return on investments, Stanford's endowment drops to 20th in nation. Serious deterioration of programs and facilities is threatened. Wilbur accepts the Associates' recommendations for dramatic changes in the university's approach to fundraising and public relations. Paul H. Davis, '22, is hired to become head of Stanford Associates, in effect the university's first full-time development director. The Associates' first appeal to alumni in 1935 brings in $35,000. In 1936, the group takes on primary responsibility for encouraging alumni donations through the Stanford Fund and special gifts, bequests, and trusts. In addition to the development function, Stanford Associates later encourages organization of offices responsible for admissions, placement of graduates, news and publications services, Southern California relations, and university relations.

# 1935

April 12 **PEACE DAY:** Students sponsor a Peace Day Assembly of faculty and students to examine ways to avert war and to find permanent paths to peace. Political science Prof. Graham Stuart, recently returned from a trip to Europe, discusses the pros and cons of the League of Nations in the time of crisis.

August **STANFORD — COUNTRY CLUB?:** In her annual report to the president, Dean of Women Mary Yost calls attention to evidence of "a growing tendency of some students to regard the university as a country club rather than as an educational institution." Fueling the "clubby image" of convertibles, golf, tennis, boating, and polo, are two academic surveys that rank Stanford lower than expected and significantly lower than the University of California. The "country club" reputation — which lingers until the start of the war — hampers the university's ability to solicit much-needed alumni support.

Fall **HAYSTACKS:** University officials warn students of the danger posed by their setting fire to the haystacks drying in fields around campus. The university does not own the hay; it is sold to a man who harvests it to earn his living. Students especially like to set fire to stacks near Encina, Toyon, the library, the aviation field, and the stock farm. Encina men have been known to set fires from projectiles shot from upper floors.

Hanna House, designed by Frank Lloyd Wright and built in 1937 for education Prof. Paul Hanna and his wife, Jean. The children's playroom (below) is eventually converted to a dining room.

Dean of Education Ellwood Cubberley and his wife donate a new building for the School of Education, which is constructed in 1938. He refuses to have his name on it.

# 1936

January 1 **Rose Bowl victory:** The Vow Boys wind up their careers defeating Southern Methodist University 7-0 in the Rose Bowl.

February 10 **Endowment problem:** Faced with a static to declining endowment of about $30 million, invested mostly in low-yield rail and public utility bonds, many in default, the trustees — urged on by Herbert Hoover — petition the Santa Clara Superior Court for permission to shift part of the endowment to corporate stocks and real estate. Hoover personally presents the petition. The judge quickly grants the requested authority. By Aug. 31, the trustees report that 10 percent of the endowment is in common and preferred stocks. Four years later, the total has risen to 24 percent, with an announced goal of 40 percent.

December 30 **The running one-hand jump shot:** Coach John Bunn's Stanford team shows the Eastern seaboard a new way to play basketball. The old way was to pass the ball 10 to 15 times and then take a flat-footed shot. Stanford's Angelo "Hank" Luisetti revolutionizes the sport by tossing in running one-handers. The new style gives Stanford a 45-31 win over powerhouse Long Island University, breaking that team's 43-game winning streak. The press goes wild over Luisetti, who says, "I got credit for the one-handed shot. I'm sure someone else did it before me, but I did it in Madison Square Garden. Anytime you do something in New York, everyone hears about it." In one game as a senior, Luisetti scores 50 points as Stanford crushes a good Duquesne team 92-27. Under coach Bunn, Luisetti and his teammates are voted unofficial national champions in 1937 (NCAA playoffs are introduced in 1939). Luisetti is All-American for three years and National Player of the Year for two. On Feb. 22, 1987, a 15-foot bronze statue depicting Luisetti making a one-handed shot is dedicated in Maples Pavilion. The artist is Luisetti's former teammate Phil Zonne.

# 1937

March **Invention of klystron:** Collaboration begins between the brothers Russell and Sigurd Varian and physics Prof. William W. Hansen that leads to the invention of the klystron microwave tube, a device for generating high-power microwaves. The klystron is helped by Hansen's earlier invention of the rhumbatron, a copper tank that causes radio waves to surge back and forth in a rhythmic motion. The university provides space and $100 to finance the work of the Varians and Hansen, in return for assignment of patents. Soon, proceeds from a licensing agreement begin providing substantial income to the university that finances more research and, in time, contributes to Stanford's science and engineering programs. The klystron tube makes airborne radar feasible and proves essential to Britain's defense against threatened German

ɫemorial Hall is completed ı 1937 to honor those from :anford who lost their lives ı the first world war. Their ames are inscribed on the roll of honor" in the foyer.

A class session in Frost Amphitheater, finished for commencement in 1937.

Police chief Gordon Davis, seen here in 1945, asks students not to roller skate on the Quad in 1939.

nvasion during World War II. Later, the klystron tube be-omes a cornerstone for microwave research and an im-ortant device for the construction of a variety of high-en-rgy particle accelerators useful in medicine and nuclear hysics, including the two-mile Stanford Linear Accelera-or. On April 20, 1948, the Varians found their own com-any, Varian Associates.

une 13 **FROST AMPHITHEATER DEDICATED:** Laurence rost Amphitheater is dedicated. Donated by Mr. and Mrs. Ioward Frost of Los Angeles, it honors the memory of heir son, John Laurence Frost, who was a member of the lass of 1935. It is created by shaping dirt excavated from ther nearby construction sites.

)ctober 24 **WAR MEMORIAL:** Memorial Hall is dedicated 8 years after it was first conceived as a memorial to Stan-ord's 77 dead from World War I. It is built with funds from tudents, alumni, trustees, and faculty, and houses Memorial Auditorium, which holds 1,700, a small theater, radio broadcasting studio, and the Drama Department. The names of those killed in World War II (289), the Korean War (14), and the Vietnam War (21) are later added n the lobby.

November **HANNA HOUSE:** Prof. Paul Hanna and his wife, Jean, move into the campus house Frank Lloyd Wright designed for them on a hill alongside Frenchman's Road. Wright patterns the house after the honeycomb, using a hexagon as the basic unit of design. It is designated by the American Institute of Architects as one of Wright's 17 best works, and placed on the National Register of Historic Places in 1978. The Hannas in 1975 move out and donate the house to the university, which uses it as the provost's residence until the 1989 Loma Prieta earthquake. The quake severely damages the central chimney and fireplace, which are key to the building's structural framework, and the building is closed. In April 1999, the community celebrates the $2 million restoration of Hanna House with a symposium on Wright. The house is used for nonresidential purposes, such as seminars and receptions, and docents from the Stanford Museum lead public tours.

# 1938

May 6 **BOATHOUSE COLLAPSES:** The weather-beaten Lagunita boathouse balcony collapses under the weight of spectators at the Juniors' Water Carnival, dropping 25 into the water and injuring six, but none seriously. The scene is given national prominence in a *Life* magazine photo. This is the second boathouse on the site, built under the supervision of civil engineering Prof. C.B. Wing in 1913 to replace a smaller structure constructed in 1892 for men. The damaged structure is replaced in 1939 with another wooden structure, painted red and white and financed by the students for $8,250. Designed by Bakewell and Brown, it has a low, rambling style of architecture. *(See also May 1989)*

The Lagunita Boathouse during a 1920s water carnival (left), is similarly overcrowded at the 1938 carnival. As the left-side balcony collapses, a well-dressed spectator hangs on for a time (right), but eventually drops into the water (below).

The derelict boathouse is replaced with a low-slung red-and-white wooden structure that lasts a half century.

November 12 **CUBBERLEY'S BUILDING:** The School of Education building, constructed with funds donated by Dean and Mrs. Ellwood Cubberley, is dedicated. Cubberley stipulated that the building not be named for him, but the library and auditorium inside bear his name. Cubberley joined the university as an assistant professor of education in 1898, and was appointed head of the department within two months. President Jordan told him the department was in disrepute and gave him three years to make it respectable, which he did. Beginning with $400 in 1901, Cubberley carefully invested earnings from his writing and editing, and shortly after his retirement in 1933 gave the university stocks and bonds valued at $367,000. His annual salary during his final year of work peaked at $8,000. Later contributions to the university bring the gift total to $772,000. He dies in 1941.

# 1939

January **ROLLER SKATING:** The latest fad is rolling skating. The university's police chief, Gordon Davis, declares there will be no roller skating in the Quad.

April 20 **PEACE DAY:** Faced with growing war threats in Europe, students schedule a Peace Day conference, which includes speeches and discussions of how to keep America out of any European war. Similar events are held at campuses throughout the country. In a later student survey, more than 92 percent at Stanford oppose armed assistance to France and England; however, 54 percent favor economic aid in the event of a war with the Rome-Berlin-Tokyo Axis.

December 8 **HOOVER TOWER FUNDS FOUND:** President Wilbur announces that the 285-foot Hoover Library tower will be built, largely with funds from two foundations controlled by President Hoover — the American Relief Administration and the Belgian American Educational Foundation. The tower is designed by the firm of Bakewell and Brown. The architectural style — based on Spain's cathedral of Salamanca — draws mixed reviews. The *Daily* calls it a "purposeless departure from traditional Quad architecture."

# 1940

**STATISTICS:**

Undergraduate enrollment: 3,218

Graduate enrollment: 1,146

Faculty: 309

Tuition: $345 per year

Endowment: $30 million

April 8 **FIRST LADY ON CAMPUS:** Eleanor Roosevelt speaks to a capacity crowd at Memorial Auditorium on the day when word comes of Germany's invasion of Norway and Denmark. Her speech deals with the role of young people in the future of America.

September **STUDENT JOHN F. KENNEDY:** John F. Kennedy registers as a graduate student for fall quarter, under a special arrangement allowing him to audit classes. He lives in a cottage behind the house at 624 Mayfield Avenue, and takes classes in business, economics, and political science. With fellow students in October, he registers with the selective service; he enlists in the navy shortly thereafter. He leaves campus around the Christmas holidays.

Fall **WOW BOYS:** Wearing colorful new uniforms and emulating the Vow Boys of the 1930s, Stanford's "Wow Boys" (named by a sports writer) are undefeated, to everyone's surprise, in the regular football season and in the Rose Bowl, where they dispatch Nebraska 21-13. Appointment of new coach Clark Shaughnessy has been controversial — his 1939 team at University of Chicago was shut-out 85-0 by Michigan and similar scores by other teams. Confidence in Stanford's varsity team is not any better — the 1939 squad lost eight of nine games and was characterized by a former Vow Boy as "the worst group of players who have ever worn the Stanford red." But in his first year as coach, Shaughnessy revives the long-forgotten T-formation, bewildering opponents, and utilizes the passing skills of quarterback Frankie Albert. Teams everywhere convert to the T-formation.

## 1941

March 8 **PALO ALTO UNDERPASS:** Ending decades of traffic jams, Palo Altans and Stanfordites celebrate the opening of the University Avenue underpass. The desire to free both communities from the tyranny of the railroad crossing produced an unusual level of cooperation among officials from the university, the city, and the state highway department. In conjunction with this celebration and the university's golden jubilee, the *Palo Alto Times* publishes a 106-page commemorative issue about Stanford.

March 9 **GOLDEN ANNIVERSARY:** On Founders' Day, the university officially opens its 50-year celebration with President Wilbur speaking in appreciation of the Stanfords, whom he had known during his student days, followed by the traditional march to the Stanford Family Mausoleum. The Stanford Brass Choir performs from the Hoover Tower belfry, and in the evening the San Francisco symphony premieres Roy Harris's *Ode to Truth,* composed for the occasion, in Memorial Church.

May 10 **SAM MCDONALD:** Sam McDonald Road is named in honor of the much-beloved superintendent of athletic buildings and grounds. Emanuel B. "Sam" McDonald begins working on campus in 1903, becomes caretaker of athletic property in 1907, and later superintendent. From the early 1920s, he heads the crew and runs the barbecue at Con Home Day, an annual clean-up at the Convalescent Home that caps a week of fundraising activities. Through the years, he wisely invests his modest earnings, acquiring land in the mountains above campus, including 450 acres he donates for public use (now known as Sam McDonald Park). A who's who of alumni, faculty, and students, including President Ray Lyman Wilbur, attend large barbecue parties there. When he retires at age 70 in 1954, the Stanford Press publishes his autobiography, *Sam McDonald's Farm.* He dies in 1957, having lived in the Track House more than 45 years.

*On dedication day for new Hoover Tower in 1941, formal speeches are followed by inaugural ringing of the 35-bell carillon in the tower's observation platform.*

*John F. Kennedy, on campus auditing graduate courses in fall 1940, registers for the draft on Oct. 16 as, from left, Prof. Leland Chapin and students Dwight Hutchinson and Bill Turner look on.*

June 16-19 **COMMEMORATIVE SYMPOSIUM:** Continuing the university's anniversary celebration, a commemorative symposium, "The University and the Future of America," and an academic convocation feature major speakers on education, science, civilization, and the war in Europe. The undercurrent in all speeches is the clash between totalitarianism and democracy. The speeches later are published by the Stanford University Press.

June 20 **HOOVER TOWER DEDICATED:** Following a morning academic convocation in Memorial Church and luncheon at Lagunita Court, the new 285-foot-tall Hoover Library Tower is dedicated. A carillon of 35 bells, weighing nine tons, rings out following formal speeches. The bells, first exhibited at the Belgian Pavilion at the New York World's Fair, had been purchased by the Herbert Hoover-controlled Belgian American Educational Foundation.

August 21 **WAR ATTITUDE:** Debate over whether the United States should enter the European war on the side of the Allies splits the faculty, with 176 signing a petition supporting President Franklin Roosevelt's foreign policy and urging a strong defense against "the totalitarian menace." Hoover, who opposed intervention, responds with a poll of a larger group that has 60 percent "disagreeing" with the petition. Hoover's poll is criticized as "misleading" by many faculty.

October 1 **OPENING DAY + 50:** To mark the golden anniversary of the university's opening, five days of events are held starting Oct. 1, including re-enactment of the opening ceremony from 1891, a black-tie dinner for 1,000 at the Palace Hotel in San Francisco, a panel discussion on the world conflict in Memorial Auditorium, a speech by Herbert Hoover, various social functions, and an appeal to alumni for financial support. The Opening Day re-enactment is held the evening of Oct. 3, after which Charles K. Field, '95, who entertained guests at the 25th anniversary, does so again, this time with a dramatization of Stanford's history, accompanied by slides projected on a large screen in the Inner Quad.

December 8 **WAR PREPARATIONS:** After the Pearl Harbor attack, Californians — and Stanfordites — brace themselves for a possible Japanese invasion. A few days later, the university has its first black-out drill — the campus goes black in three minutes. During the coming weeks, students enter the home-front campaign with fervor: They buy war bonds, give blood to the Red Cross, save junk for salvage drives, and entertain soldiers. Fraternities compete to see who can fill the most sandbags per hour. The Women's Council approves bobby sox as an appropriate alternative to stockings on the Quad. President Wilbur asks for tolerance toward Japanese and Japanese-American students.

# 1942

January 1 **WILBUR NAMED CHANCELLOR:** Ray Lyman Wilbur retires and is named chancellor, but at the request of the trustees continues to lead the university until Aug. 31, 1943. Trustees ask board president Donald Tresidder to make recommendations about the next president.

President Wilbur dedicates Sam McDonald Road in honor of the longtime employee in 1941.

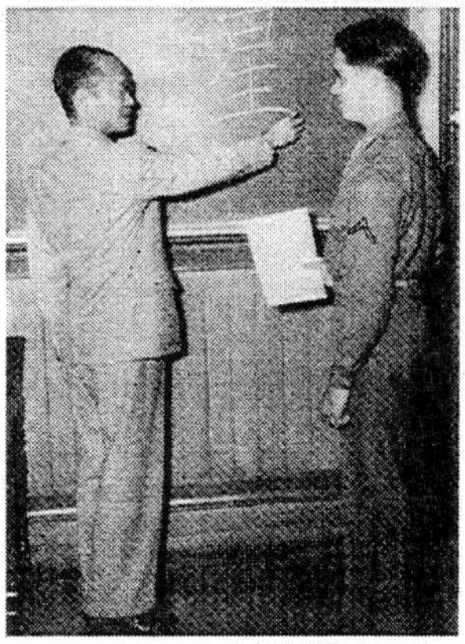

World War II looms heavily on campus as military students eventually outnumber civilians. (Above right) Military students march to class, but leave History Corner more informally (above). (Right) Prof. Shan Wing Chan offers language instruction.

February 19 **EXECUTIVE ORDER 9066:** A U.S. presidential executive order calling for inland internment of all Japanese and Americans of Japanese descent on the West Coast is posted around campus. Until March 27, all persons of Japanese ancestry could voluntarily move to areas east of California, Oregon, and Washington. On May 26, the remaining Japanese students are collected and sent to a temporary processing center at Santa Anita Racetrack in Southern California. Also interned are Japanese history Prof. Yamato Ichihashi, nearing retirement after a long Stanford career, and his wife, Okei. They go initially to Santa Anita and later to Tule Lake in Northern California. Ichihashi is granted a leave of absence and his campus property is watched over by his colleague and friend, historian Payson Treat.

March 28 **BASKETBALL CHAMPS:** The men's basketball team captures the NCAA championship for the first time in university history. Led by coach Everett Dean, they defeat Dartmouth 53-38, despite illness and injuries.

Spring **PROFS GO TO WAR:** Many professors are granted leaves to go into defense plants or government service. Engineering Prof. Frederick E. Terman heads the Radio Research Laboratory at Harvard, which develops countermeasures to radar; physicist William Hansen works long hours at MIT's Radiation Laboratory and at Sperry Gyroscope Co.; Prof. Emeritus William Durand, now 84, works with the National Advisory Committee for Aeronautics in Washington, D.C. The remaining faculty carries a heavy teaching load. The chaplain teaches trigonometry and a music professor teaches engineering drawing.

Spring **MORE PREPARATIONS:** Summer quarter is beefed up so that students can accelerate graduation; freshmen are admitted to summer courses for the first time. At graduation, many are already in uniform. Graduates place a class plate in the Inner Quad made of two-color concrete, to be later replaced with one of traditional bronze.

September **TRAINING ARMY OFFICERS:** The War Department establishes a school (as part of the Graduate School of Business) to train officers for the Army Quartermaster Corps. About 50 future officers are accepted for the fall term.

# 1943

January 21 **DONALD TRESIDDER NAMED PRESIDENT:** Donald Bertrand Tresidder, A.B. '19, M.D. '27, resigns as president of the Board of Trustees to become the university's fourth president. He assumes his post Sept. 1, but, because of the war, has no formal inauguration. Dr. Tresidder, 49, is married to the former Mary Curry, A.B. '15, M.A. '17, and has served as president of her father's Yosemite Park and Curry Company rather than utilize his medical degree. He joined the Board of Trustees in 1939.

May **CAMPUS FILLS WITH SOLDIERS:** Stanford begins receiving its first group of soldier-students for the Army Specialized Training Program (ASTP), a federal program designed to use college and university faculties to train specialists for the military. Within a month, nearly 1,400 soldiers are registered in engineering, language studies, and

*President Tresidder greets Vyacheslav Molotov, the Soviet foreign minister, on a visit to campus in 1945. Molotov was in San Francisco for the United Nations Conference.*

*Members of the Japanese Student Association join President Ray Lyman Wilbur, upper left, on the steps of their clubhouse in 1942. The photograph – an annual tradition – is inscribed to Wilbur May 6, 1942, just before the students leave for wartime internment camps.*

*Donald B. Tresidder (left) is named Stanford's fourth president in 1943. He and his wife, Mary Curry Tresidder, both pilots, often fly to Yosemite, where he had been president of the Yosemite Park and Curry Co.*

pre-medicine, with the number increasing to almost 2,700 by October. Classes operate year-round on a regular and "swing shift" schedule, with lights on until 11:30 p.m. nightly in the Quad. The soldiers completely fill all men's dormitories and start to overflow into fraternity houses, each renamed after a former president of the United States. By fall 1943, total military and civilian enrollment reaches a record 5,324.

# 1944

March **ASTP CUTBACK:** With the war intensifying, the army shifts from long-term training to battlefield action. It announces sharp cutbacks in specialized training programs, including the ASTP, which drops to 430 by spring 1944. By fall 1944, total university enrollment drops to 3,003. President Tresidder quiets fears about the possible negative effect on the university, saying "it is not a question of how it affects the colleges, but how it affects the war effort. It has been a real satisfaction to the administration and faculty to feel that we were making a direct contribution to the war effort. Our real business is not training men for war but training young people for peace. We'll go on with our original business."

April 20 **SORORITIES DISBANDED:** Trustees vote to discontinue sororities and use sorority houses for general women's housing. The ban has been approved by female students following complaints that sorority rush is undemocratic. Trustees say that excessive competition between sorority women and "hall" women has led to "serious disunity." A report from trustees also says "the supervision and counseling in the halls reflects the policies of the university administration more closely than do those of the sororities." In future years, many will believe an often-published story — which is untrue — that sororities were dropped because two women who were rejected committed suicide. *(See also Dec. 13, 1977)*

July 2 **COMMENCEMENT:** Because of the war, less than half those scheduled to receive degrees are on hand for commencement exercises. Of 760 graduates, 412 receive their diplomas in absentia. Not a single graduate of the Medical School appears for the ceremony.

Fall **STUDENT VOTERS:** In a mock election, students vote 2 to 1 in favor of Thomas Dewey for president. Students also supported Dewey four years earlier.

# 1945

January 13 **CAMPUS PLANNING:** President Tresidder appoints San Francisco architect Eldridge Spencer as director of planning, and charges him with developing long-term plans for future use of campus lands and buildings. This is prompted by the prospect of a deluge of returning veterans and resulting need for additional classroom and dormitory space.

February 15 **LOU HENRY HOOVER HOUSE:** Honoring a wish his wife expressed before her death, Herbert Hoover gives the university their campus home as the official resi-

The Row, circa 1947, with Sigma Chi in the foreground. Fraternities, renamed for U.S. presidents, are used by soldier-students during the war. After sororities are abolished 1944, those houses are added to the general pool for women.

Herbert Hoover and his wife, Lou Henry Hoover, at their campus home. In 1945, he donates the home in her memory to the university for use by its president.

dence of the university president. It is named Lou Henry Hoover House. Completed in 1921, the home on San Juan Hill was designed in "early international style" by Mrs. Hoover with help from art Prof. Arthur B. Clark and his son, architect Birge Clark. It is designated a state historic landmark in 1978 and a national historic landmark in 1985.

April 30 **MOLOTOV AT STANFORD:** Taking a break from the United Nations conference in San Francisco, Soviet Foreign Minister Vyacheslav Molotov is received by President Tresidder during a visit to campus. While the conference is in session, President Tresidder campaigns unsuccessfully to have the permanent United Nations headquarters located on Stanford lands.

August 14 **CAMPUS CELEBRATES VJ DAY:** Afternoon classes are interrupted just at 4 p.m. as auto horns join in unison to hail Japan's surrender. A few seconds later, the air raid siren atop Hoover Tower adds to the tumult and at 4:10 the steam whistle at the power plant lets go with a series of short blasts. A victory dance is scheduled at 9 p.m. at the women's gym, with news that all women will be allowed a non-quota 12:30 a.m. lockout.

Fall **STEGNER ARRIVES:** Prominent novelist Wallace Stegner comes to Stanford from Harvard and establishes the Creative Writing Program. Stegner's proposal for a mix of fellowships, prizes, visiting writers, and small publications is funded for five years by oilman Edward H. Jones, brother of English Prof. Richard F. Jones. During the next half century, the program's alumni will include Eugene Burdick, Ken Kesey, Peter S. Beagle, Ernest Gaines, Tillie Olsen, Robert Stone, James D. Houston, Harriet Doerr, Al Young, Larry McMurtry, Alice Adams, and Edward Abbey.

# 1946

January **INFLUX OF VETERANS:** Peacetime registration figures break an all-time record when 4,464 students enroll winter quarter. Of those 1,382 are veterans using the GI Bill of Rights. Spring quarter enrollment rises to 5,028, including 1,950 veterans; enrollment soars fall quarter, when 7,244 students appear, including 4,047 veterans. President Tresidder reports that the vets display "a seriousness of purpose" and maintain higher scholarship records than the general average. University officials scramble for solution to the severe housing shortage, especially for married students.

Spring **NEW HEALTH SERVICE:** A new comprehensive student health service, providing medical, surgical, and hospital care in case of illness or accident, expands the scope of the previously separate men's and women's health service.

September 23 **MARRIED STUDENT HOUSING:** The university opens its first married student housing facility at the Army's war-surplus Dibble General Hospital in Menlo Park. Reconstruction and conversion, rushed in six weeks, yields 320 apartments for married students and other accommodations for approximately 1,500 single students in the area of Middlefield Road and Ravenswood Avenue. After a contest, it is renamed Stanford Village.

*Barracks at the Army's former Dibble General Hospital in Menlo Park in 1946 are transformed into "Stanford Village" for married and single students, to help solve a severe housing shortage brought on by the university's post-war enrollment boom.*

*Students living at Stanford Village wait in line to catch rides to campus.*

November **STANFORD RESEARCH INSTITUTE:** Stanford Research Institute (SRI) is incorporated as a nonprofit organization to provide specialized research services to businesses, foundations, and government agencies. Its board of directors is composed of members of the university Board of Trustees and leaders of several major California corporations. SRI is temporarily housed in the Physics Department, but in May 1947 moves to Stanford Village, which it shares with about 2,500 students, wives, and children. By 1948, it has 150 employees and anticipates at least $1 million in revenue for 1949. One of its first projects is a $150,000 program from the Office of Naval Research to develop a sturdy rubber-yielding plant that would serve as a hedge against possible future war-time rubber shortages. It also takes on a project to investigate the causes and possible cures of smog. It later develops a magnetic check-sorting system. When the village is closed to students in 1965, SRI expands into the remaining available space.

November 1 **PARKING REGULATIONS:** Traffic and parking regulations are put in effect in an attempt to solve problems brought on by 3,000 automobiles that are jamming the campus. Parking on the Oval is made diagonal, and since this limits driving space, traffic is changed to one-way. All cars, motorcycles, and motor scooters must register with the campus Police Department.

## 1947

January **MINERAL SCIENCES:** The School of Mineral Sciences (later the School of Earth Sciences) is formed by joining the Geology and Mining Departments.

January 6 **CAMPUS RADIO:** Campus radio station KSU (later KZSU) has its premiere broadcast, starring Winstead "Doodles" Weaver, '36, a Hollywood comedian. Initially, the student-operated, carrier-current campus station is on the air from 7 p.m. to 11 p.m., Sunday through Thursday, from a studio in Stanford Village. The station's output is carried by direct lines strung through university steam tunnels during the previous Christmas holidays. KSU moves its facilities to Memorial Hall in time for spring quarter.

March **MUMFORD ON STANFORD:** Noted architecture critic and planner Lewis Mumford, who had been hired by President Tresidder, makes his recommendations about future campus growth. The "Mumford Report" strongly urges the university to maintain a greenbelt around its lands to preserve its academic isolation and prevent incursions from nonuniversity entities. "The land that Stanford does not develop for its own purposes should not be developed at all," he writes, reflecting his fear that nearby communities would assume a proprietary point of view. In a prophetic separate letter to Tresidder, Mumford writes: "You are in about the same position that Central Park was in the first 75 years of its existence. The *New York Times* once published a picture showing that if all the proposed buildings and worthy projects that wanted a plot of land [in Central Park] had been built, there would have been no park left. . . . Your successors a century from now will bless you for every acre you hold open."

Fall **POST-WAR ENROLLMENT:** A record 8,223 students

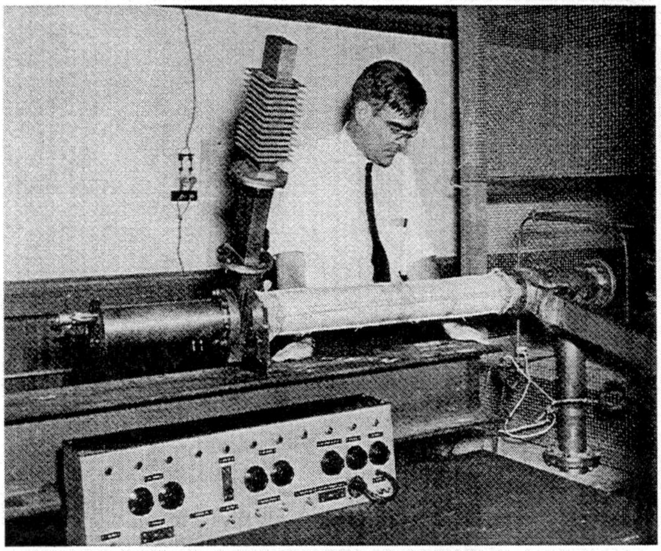

*The early days of linear accelerators: Prof. W.W. Hansen (above) with 3-foot prototype Mark I he builds in the basement of the Physics Department in 1947. (Above right) The first section of the Mark III accelerator in 1949. (Right) By 1952, the Mark III has been lengthened. For safety, cement blocks eventually will completely surround it.*

enroll. Noon and evening classes and a heavier afternoon schedule are instituted.

November **PROTOTYPE ACCELERATOR:** Prof. William W. Hansen, co-inventor of the klystron tube, unveils a three-foot electron linear accelerator prototype, built in the cramped basement of the Physics Department. The linear accelerator offers a means of learning about the performance and structure of the fundamental particles of matter.

# 1948

January 28 **PRESIDENT TRESIDDER DIES:** President Donald B. Tresidder, on a trip to attend a meeting in New York and visit with various alumni, is found dead in his hotel room from a heart attack. He was only 53. On campus, the news causes shock, sadness, and tears. A week later, the student body votes to recommend that the proposed new student union, for which they are raising money, be named for Tresidder. Prof. Alvin C. Eurich, academic vice president, becomes acting president.

May 27 **STANFORD OPERA WORKSHOP:** Benjamin Britten's first and perhaps best opera, *Peter Grimes,* is given its first West Coast-originated production under the direction of Prof. Jan Popper, only three years after its introduction in London. All three performances in Mem Aud are sold out. *Peter Grimes* is such a critical success that the entire production is moved to San Francisco for a single, also acclaimed performance on June 29. The *San Francisco Chronicle* critic calls it Stanford's "greatest musical and dramatic success." Popper came to Stanford from Czechoslovakia in 1940.

Fall **HUMANITIES AND SCIENCES:** Schools of Biological Sciences, Humanities, Physical Sciences, and Social Sciences merge into the School of Humanities and Sciences.

Fall **FIRST FULL-SCALE ACCELERATOR:** Construction is started on a long new laboratory building behind Sequoia Hall to house the new Microwave Laboratory and its planned linear accelerator. The accelerator, based on prototypes developed by Prof. Hansen in 1947, is first operated in November 1950, using three klystron tubes to speed electrons down a 30 foot tube. Called the Mark III, it is expanded, in steps, to 210 feet in 1953 and 310 feet in 1960. In 1963, the Mark III is revamped, and by 1964 its power reaches 1.2 billion electron volts. The Microwave Laboratory is renamed the W.W. Hansen Laboratories of Physics following Hansen's 1949 death, which is from berylliosis (caused by inhaling beryllium used in research). A driven man who worked 16 hours a day for years, Hansen wore a portable oxygen mask of his own design in an effort to complete work under way before he died at 39.

Fall **STATISTICS DEPARTMENT:** The Department of Statistics is launched, reflecting the field's growing importance in such areas as probability theory and statistical decision-making. Many of these developments were stimulated by work of statisticians and mathematicians in World War II. Prof. Albert Bowker is appointed first department head.

November **EURICH LEAVES:** Acting President Eurich an-

*J.E. Wallace Sterling is named Stanford's fifth president in 1948, effective April 1, 1949. A former newsman, he faces Bay Area reporters and photographers at his first press conference (above). Sterling and his wife, Ann, relax at the Lou Henry Hoover House soon after moving in (below). Trustee President Paul C. Edwards inaugurates Sterling in Frost Amphitheater on Oct. 7, 1949 (below left).*

*In 1949, giant footprints climbing upward mysteriously appeared on Hoover Tower. The following year, members of the Stanford Alpine Club repeat their prank, with the feet pointing down.*

nounces he will leave to become chief executive officer of the State University of New York.

November **STERLING NAMED PRESIDENT:** Trustees pick 42-year-old Canadian-born history scholar J.E. Wallace Sterling as Stanford's fifth president. He takes office April 1, 1949. Sterling received his Ph.D. in history from Stanford in 1938. He leaves the position of director of the Huntington Library and Art Gallery in San Marino, Calif. Sterling comments that he is "coming home."

# 1949

April **WOMEN'S RULES CHANGE:** Women vote for a new demerit system to replace lock-ins, fines, and other penalties for lock-out violations. A woman could be put on probation after four demerits and suspended after five.

May 23 **MYSTERIOUS HOOVER TOWER FOOTPRINTS:** Members of the Stanford Alpine Club gain access to Hoover Tower through the steam tunnel and attach giant footprints "climbing" the tower. Rappelling down the side, Bud Gates, '51, tapes two large black feet to the side of the building near the top, then Sherman Lehman, '51, rappels down to add two more footprints farther down, under the direction of ringleader Walt Kane, '49. Julie Boyd, '50, also helps. On May 22, 1950, the crew brings the monster back down, when Lehman and Jim Moore, '51, with help from Gates, repeat the prank with the feet pointing down.

June **ROOF CONTROVERSY:** Following strong reaction of alumni against the flat roof of the new Stern Hall dormitory, the Board of Trustees says "any future building should, so far as possible, blend and harmonize with the original buildings to form a pleasing whole." An alumni survey and letters to the alumni magazine revealed strong opposition to the hall's slate gray color and lack of red-tile roof.

June 26 **PRESIDENT WILBUR DIES:** Chancellor Ray Lyman Wilbur, 74, dies at his campus home of a heart attack. He served as university president from 1916 to 1943.

August 1 **HERBERT HOOVER'S BIRTHDAY:** Frost Amphitheater is jammed with 10,000 for the celebration of Herbert Hoover's 75th birthday.

October 7 **PRESIDENT STERLING INAUGURATED:** With 5,000 alumni, students, and friends of Stanford before him, and 575 academicians beside him in Frost Amphitheater, President J.E. Wallace Sterling calls on education "to produce moral progress to match the material progress of the last half century." Paul C. Edwards, president of the Board of Trustees, notes that the "inauguration of a new president is also the inauguration of a new era in the life of the university.

# 1950

**STATISTICS:**

Undergraduate enrollment: 4,794

Graduate enrollment: 2,841

Faculty: 372

Tuition: $600 per year

Endowment: $44 million

February **LAW SCHOOL HEADQUARTERS:** The Law School moves into newly refurbished quarters in Building 160, the former Administration Building, on the Quad.

August 31 **PLANT COLLECTOR:** Biology Prof. Ira Wiggins is named scientific director of the Navy's Arctic Research Laboratory at Point Barrow, Alaska. He returns to campus after three years to teach and resume his annual plant collecting trips to Baja California. In 1964, he publishes the massive *Vegetation and Flora of the Sonoran Desert* and in 1980 the *Flora of Baja California,* both landmarks of botanical literature.

Fall **DEPARTMENT OF ART AND ARCHITECTURE:** The Art Department, long a stepchild of the academic program, is renamed the Department of Art and Architecture. Faculty size is double that of two years earlier, and major programs are added in art history and architecture. The architecture component, which includes a two-year graduate program, works cooperatively with the School of Engineering, providing a strong technological background for students. In 1970-71, it shifts to the Design Division in Mechanical Engineering, but with funding only for an undergraduate program. The university closes it in June 1977.

Fall **GEOGRAPHY DEPARTMENT:** The geography program is given departmental status. In addition to using maps, charts, books, and occasional field trips in their course of study, students have the option of viewing earth from above in chartered DC-3 airplane trips. The university shuts down geography in 1962.

Fall **LONG-TERM PLANNING:** Reflecting growing pressures to realize income from Stanford's vast vacant lands, trustees agree to start limited commercial development. The first big project will be a 50-acre industrial park adjacent to Barron Park and an 80-acre shopping center facing El Camino. All projects involve long-term land leases. A San Francisco planning-engineering firm is hired to draw up a master plan for 7,000 acres. This work is not satisfactory, and a second firm — Skidmore, Owens and Merrill — is hired to do a plan for 6,000 acres. When submitted in 1953, the Skidmore plan recommends extensive commercial development of the vacant lands, including several self-contained communities in the foothills, housing an estimated 40,000 people. The university's Advisory Committee on Land and Building Development objects to the plan because of the excessive housing and instead recommends increasing the academic land reserve. University trustees decide in 1974 to place the foothills in "academic reserve," foregoing residential and commercial development.

## 1951

April 26 **MODEL UNITED NATIONS:** More than 300 students from 59 western colleges and universities convene at Memorial Auditorium for the first Model United Nations conference. It is sponsored by Stanford's Institute of International Relations, the most active student-run and student-financed program in international relations in the United States. Students take the roles of UN officials and delegates, discussing the same issues as those before the real body. Stanford students serve as the Soviet delegation. The IIR also sponsors conferences, lectures, panels, two radio programs, and a regional information center.

October 1 **BEGINNING OF INDUSTRIAL PARK:** The university leases Varian Associates 10 acres at the vacant edge of university land along El Camino Real, adjacent to Barron Park, for construction of a $1 million research and development lab. Varian is the first tenant in what becomes

The Model United Nations, started at Stanford in 1951, features Tsiang Ting-fu, chief of the Nationalist Chinese delegation, delivering the keynote address in Memorial Auditorium in 1957.

Alf Brandin, university business manager, uses a map of Stanford lands to explain the land development program.

the Stanford Industrial Park (renamed Stanford Research Park in 1974). Later leaseholders include Eastman Kodak (1953), General Electric (1954), Hewlett-Packard (1956), and Beckman Industries (1956).

Fall **EATING CLUBS:** The seven eating clubs move from Encina Commons into their long-awaited new dining facilities next to Toyon Hall. The clubs date to the 1890s, when they were formed as an alternative to fraternities.

# 1952

January 1 **ROSE BOWL LOSS:** After a 9-1 season under rookie football coach Chuck Taylor, Stanford is defeated 40-7 by Illinois in the Rose Bowl. Taylor, nevertheless, is named national coach of the year by his peers. He develops the passing attack.

May **WARREN G. WONKA, STUDENT EXTRAORDINAIRE:** Warren G. Wonka gains national attention when Estes Kefauver, seeking the Democratic nomination for president, writes to thank him for his campaign assistance and express hope of meeting him personally. Wonka first came to Stanford in 1938, when he appeared as a bra salesman in the *Chaparral*. In 1951, he narrowly escaped serious injury in an auto accident near Klamath Falls, Oregon, when a car carrying six band members to the Washington game plunged over an embankment. During his long career, Wonka makes appearances the world over, graduates several times, and advocates a new *Bible* free of "objectionable words and corrupting ideas." Although his attendance is poor, he manages to pull out a "B minus" in Western Civ. Some say Wonka is mythical, but this never has been proved.

Summer **EXECUTIVE PROGRAM:** The Graduate School of Business launches an Executive Development Program. Later called the Stanford Executive Program, it attracts senior-level managers from around the world to an eight-week summer residency program. In 1957, the school starts the Sloan Program, in which middle managers with senior-management potential study for nine months.

July **SUPERMAN:** Two-sport athlete Bob Mathias becomes the first man to compete in both the Rose Bowl and the Olympic Games in the same year. He wins his second gold medal in the decathlon, the first man to win twice. He plays fullback on the Stanford football team.

July 15 **CANCER TREATMENT:** Prof. Edward L. Ginzton, director of Stanford's Microwave Laboratory, and Dr. Henry S. Kaplan, chairman of radiology at the Medical School in San Francisco, team up to fight cancer with one of science's newest weapons — the linear electron accelerator. Under their direction, a compact six-million-volt machine is developed on campus to shoot X-rays at deep-seated cancer tissue. The device is installed at Stanford's Lane Hospital in San Francisco for clinical applications. There, on Jan. 11, 1957, 2-year-old Gordon Isaacs, whose left-eye vision is threatened by retinoblastoma, a form of cancer, is the first patient to be treated successfully with the medical linear accelerator. Varian Associates of Palo Alto produces the first commercial version of the accelerator, named CLINAC, which is a commercial success. In 1971, after 16 years of use on 8,000 patients, Kaplan's first machine is donated to the Smithsonian Institution.

November 6 **BLOCH WINS NOBEL PRIZE:** Physics Prof. Felix Bloch wins a Nobel Prize, the first for Stanford. *(See page 153)*

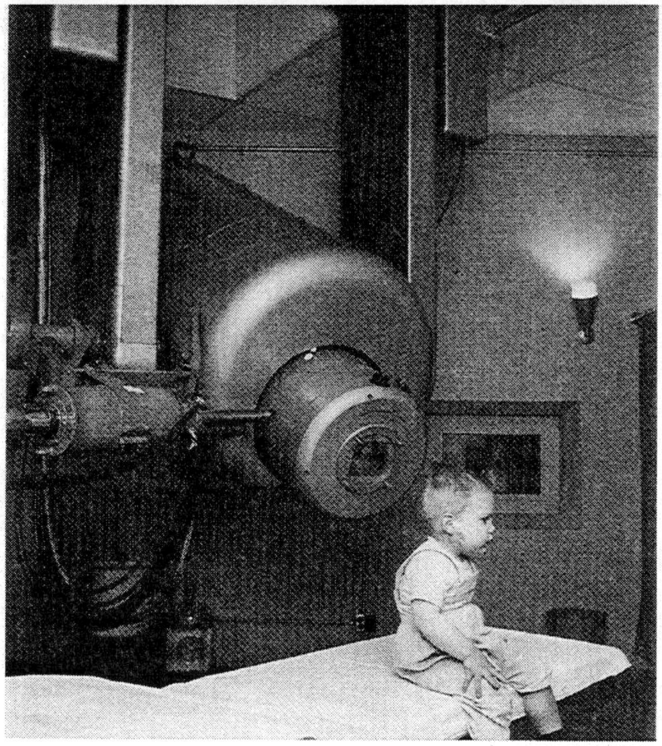

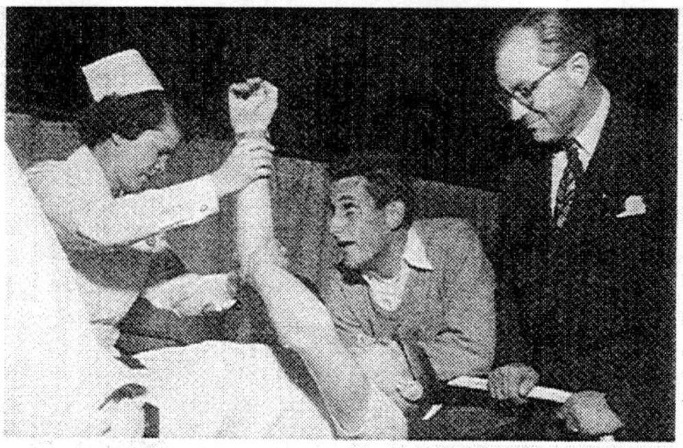

Student Ken Schechter, center, and Dean of Students H. Donald Winbigler watch as the 1953 blood drive concludes with 4,640 pints collected.

Beginning in 1952, Prof. Edward Ginzton, left, and Dr. Henry Kaplan collaborate on the first medical linear accelerator, which successfully treats a child (left) for a form of eye cancer.

# 1953

January 23 **LAST PIONEER DIES:** Douglas H. Campbell, professor emeritus of botany since 1925, dies at his campus home at 93. A leading authority on mosses and ferns, he was the last survivor of those appointed by David Starr Jordan to the original faculty in 1891.

March **COMPUTATION CENTER LAUNCHED:** A high-speed electronic calculator is installed on campus at the instigation of Prof. Albert Bowker, director of the applied mathematics and statistics laboratory, and Prof. Frederick Terman, dean of engineering. The IBM Card Programmed Calculator, with auxiliary equipment for handling punched cards, will perform large computation jobs that take too long using desk calculating machines. It can store 16 words in its electromechanical memory, and will be available for faculty and graduate student research projects. Stanford's first real computer, an IBM 650, is installed in 1956. It holds 2,000 words in its drum memory; in several years it is supplemented with a Burroughs 220. In 1963, the university acquires an IBM 7094 and Burroughs B5000; it also moves the Computation Center to a new building that honors George Polya, emeritus professor and world-famous mathematician. Later, the Administrative Data Services facility is merged into the Computation Center. The center continues to grow rapidly, under various names, in future decades.

April **BIG BLOOD DRIVE:** Near the end of the Korean War, students, in cooperation with the Palo Alto Red Cross, turn the Basketball Pavilion into a huge blood donating center, collecting an amazing 4,640 pints in five days.

April **DORMITORY BUILDING BOOM:** Facing the continuing need for more student housing, the university announces a major dormitory building program. Plans call for a women's dorm (Florence Moore Hall), a replacement for Encina Hall to house male freshmen (Wilbur Hall), a graduate engineering men's dorm (Crothers Memorial Hall), and a large addition to Stern Hall.

November 17 **MED CENTER PLANS:** University trustees approve a recommendation from President Sterling to relocate the School of Medicine and its hospital from San Francisco to the home campus. A 20-member committee will assist in carrying out the plan.

# 1954

January **TISSUE TYPING:** Rose Payne of the Department of Medicine is one of a handful of scientists at the international level whose collaboration leads to discovering the system of histocompatibility antigens in humans. These are the antigens that usually differ between unrelated individuals and provoke reactions that result in the rejection of foreign tissue and transplanted organs. As director of Stanford's Tissue Typing Laboratory for many years, Payne plays a key role in developing techniques to improve the chances of success of organ transplants.

March 15 **TRUSTEES EXPANSION:** The Board of Trustees enlarges its membership from 15 to 23. The expansion, which includes three alumni trustees nominated by the Alumni Association, is sought to increase the geographical diversity of the board, to enable it to take a more active role in fundraising, and to deal with growth of the university.

April **FUTURE LEADERS IN TRAINING:** Peter Bing (future

*Student body Vice President Dianne Goldman (later U.S. Senator Dianne Feinstein) views the gold spike that Leland Stanford used to connect the first transcontinental railroad. After years in a San Francisco Wells Fargo Bank, the "Last Spike" is delivered by armored car in 1954 to the recently reopened museum.*

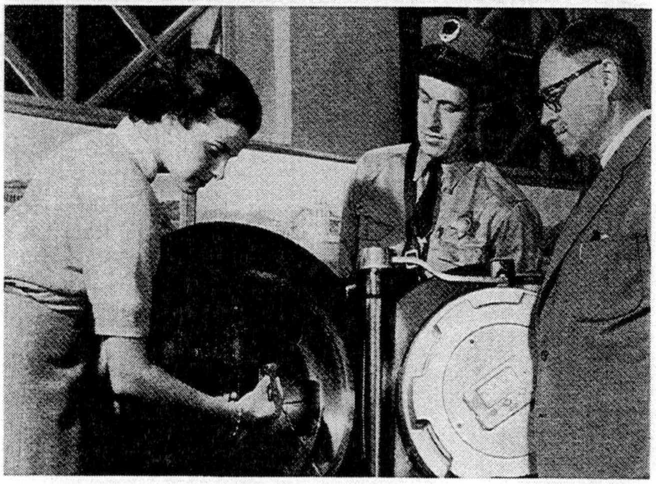

*Stanford Shopping Center opens in 1955.*

president of the Board of Trustees) is elected student body president, and Dianne Goldman (future U.S. Sen. Feinstein from California) is elected vice president.

May 16 **MUSEUM REOPENS:** Stanford Museum, closed since 1945, reopens under the administration of the Art and Architecture Department after extensive refurbishing of the building and reorganization of the collections. Classics Prof. Hazel Hansen and her students have restored many Cesnola-collection Greek ceramics from broken shards thrown together in boxes after the 1906 earthquake. Also on display is the gold spike that Senator Stanford drove to mark completion of the transcontinental railroad. It was transferred from a Wells Fargo vault. Assisting with the reopening is the volunteer support group formed a year earlier, the Committee for Art at Stanford.

September **BEHAVIORAL SCIENCES CENTER OPENS:** With financial backing from the Ford Foundation, the Center for Advanced Study in the Behavioral Sciences opens its headquarters in the foothills behind campus. It is an independent research center that attracts top scholars for a year of study and writing.

# 1955

August 22 **MCCARTHYISM HITS STANFORD:** Fulton Lewis Jr., a conservative syndicated radio commentator, uses his nationwide broadcast to launch an attack on the university. His object is the impending appointment to the law faculty of Herbert Packer, recruited by law Dean Carl Spaeth to conduct a study of the testimony of important witnesses in judicial and legislative inquiries into communist activities in the United States. The study is financed with a $25,000 grant from the Fund for the Republic, an autonomous offshoot of the Ford Foundation run by Robert Maynard Hutchins, former president of the University of Chicago. Facing threats of mass resignation by young law faculty members, President Sterling overrides vocal right-wing objections to Packer's appointment, convincing university trustees of Packer's integrity. Packer is appointed to the faculty Jan. 1, 1956, and spends the next six years assembling and analyzing more than 200,000 pages of testimony from congressional investigations, administrative hearings, and court cases. His book, published by the Stanford University Press in 1962, is described in his Memorial Resolution as "a thoughtful, balanced study of the testimony given by a group of ex-communist witnesses [including Alger Hiss] with particular emphasis on the process of fact finding." As such, "it failed to satisfy extremists of the right or left."

September 1 **TERMAN NAMED PROVOST:** Frederick E. Terman becomes provost, second-ranking officer of the university, and assumes a major role in strengthening the faculty. Son of eminent Stanford psychologist Lewis M. Terman, Frederick was educated at Stanford and MIT. He and his father were both members of the National Academy of Sciences, a rare father and son combination. The younger Terman joined the faculty in 1925 and headed the Electrical Engineering Department from 1937 until he was appointed dean of engineering in 1944. He becomes known as the "father" of Silicon Valley for his role fostering closer ties between Stanford and high technology industries.

September 30 **SHOPPING CENTER OPENS:** Roos Brothers is the first store to open at the Stanford Shopping Center, located on part of Leland Stanford's 19th century vineyard. Fifty stores are planned at a proposed development

Prof. Ronald Bracewell's 32 parabolic antennas are used to study the sun's surface.

Former Russian Premier Alexander Kerensky, right, uses the Hoover Archives to research a book.

Frederick Terman, engineering dean and future provost, right, greets David Packard, left, and William Hewlett in 1952 at the Electronics Research Laboratory. The two entrepreneurs contribute to construction of this and other science and engineering buildings.

cost of $15 million. Income from land leases will help pay higher faculty salaries. Sales tax receipts become a major revenue source for the city of Palo Alto.

November 2 **LAMB WINS NOBEL:** Physicist Willis E. Lamb Jr. wins a Nobel Prize. *(See page 153)*

## 1956

January 3 **ENCINA HALL DORM DAYS OVER:** More than 200 freshmen move out of Encina Hall, home to Stanford men for nearly 65 years. Because of delays completing Florence Moore Hall, Encina is the temporary home for 100 women in fall 1956. It then becomes an administrative office building.

February **KERENSKY AT HOOVER:** Alexander Kerensky, briefly premier of Russia before his government was overthrown by the Bolsheviks in 1917, accepts a position as research associate at the Hoover Institution. During the next five years, he draws on Hoover's wealth of information on Russia to study, write, lecture, and teach seminars. In 1961, he co-authors *The Russian Provisional Government - 1917,* which counters Soviet propaganda about his regime. He dies in 1970 at 89.

February 8 **OVERHAUL OF UNDERGRADUATE EDUCATION:** The most thorough revision of undergraduate curriculum in 35 years is approved by the Academic Council. The Stanford Study of Undergraduate Education replaces the Lower and Upper Divisions with an integrated four-year approach. A new General Studies Program is instituted, which permits students greater freedom to select a variety of courses for a bachelor's degree while increasing the range of general education courses that must be taken. The program also introduces senior colloquia, small seminars that are required of candidates for the bachelor of arts degree before graduation.

April 10 **MONSTER LINEAR ACCELERATOR PROPOSED:** During a meeting at Prof. Wolfgang Panofsky's home, physics Prof. Robert Hofstadter suggests building a linear accelerator 10 to 20 times more powerful than the university's first full-scale accelerator (Mark III). Nicknamed "The Monster" because it would have to be two miles in length, the name later is changed to "Project M" (and ultimately SLAC). Project M is headed by Prof. Edward Ginzton, director of the Microwave Laboratory, who later becomes president of Varian Associates. The university presents a detailed proposal for construction of Project M on Stanford land to the federal government in 1957.

May **FARM OF RADIO TELESCOPES:** Construction is under way on a radio telescope designed by Prof. Ronald Bracewell. It consists of 32 parabolic antennas — 10-foot diameter aluminum dishes — to study the sun's surface and map its temperatures, which it does daily for 11 years after it is completed in 1959. Located on a two-acre meadow Bracewell calls Heliopolis, in the hills behind campus, the telescope is used to monitor solar conditions during the first lunar landing in July 1969. Based in part on information received from Bracewell and colleagues at the Radio Astronomy Institute, NASA officials give the go-ahead for the first American astronauts to land on the moon.

November 1 **SHOCKLEY WINS NOBEL PRIZE:** William Shockley, lecturer in electrical engineering, wins a Nobel Prize. *(See page 153)*

*Physics Lecture Hall ("Physics Tank"), built in 1957.*

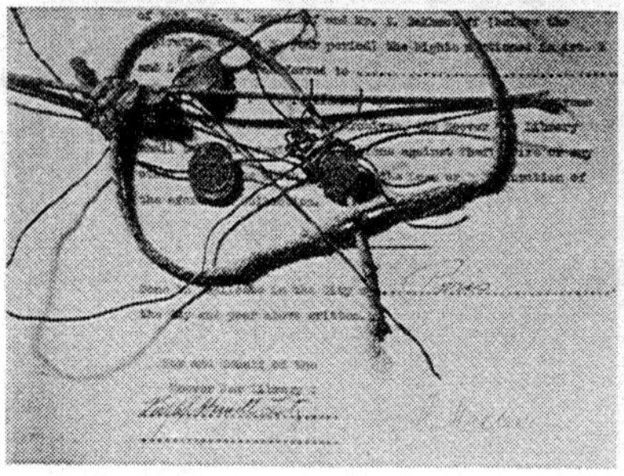

*Russian secret police files are opened in 1957 at the Hoover Institution.*

The Ballad of Baby Doe *gets its West Coas premiere at the 1957 opening of Dinkelspiel Auditorium.*

# 1957

February **SCIENCE QUAD:** A new 30-acre "science quad," designed to stimulate cross-fertilization of ideas among scientists of different fields, begins to take shape across Lomita Drive from the Quad, with construction of the Physics Lecture Hall ("Physics Tank"). The site is one identified as a future science quad in the 1888 Olmsted plan. Construction and existing buildings will provide more than 140,000 square feet of space and additional proposed construction will increase space to about 420,000 square feet in 14 buildings. The region has been developing since 1948, with much of the construction financed through earnings from government contracts and faculty research, especially royalties from the klystron tube. By 1984, growth in the academic program and the increased sophistication of science and engineering render many of the buildings inadequate, and the region often is referred to as Stanford's "industrial slum." The university then begins planning a major redevelopment of the area.

Spring **FRATERNITIES OPPOSE DISCRIMINATION:** The Interfraternity Council unanimously passes a resolution opposing racial and religious discrimination clauses contained in the national charters of 13 of their 24 parent organizations. The resolution officially brings fraternities into line with the university on discrimination issues, and means all fraternities at Stanford will support houses that stand up to their national officers.

May 23 **DINK DEDICATED:** The West Coast premiere of Douglas Moore's Pulitzer Prize-winning opera, *The Ballad of Baby Doe,* marks the opening of the 720-seat Florence Hellman Dinkelspiel Auditorium. The facility, dedicated just before the performance, honors the late wife of Lloyd W. Dinkelspiel, '20, president of the Board of Trustee: Prof. Sandor Salgo is the opera's musical director and Pro Harold Schmidt trained the chorus.

September **COMPUTER SCIENCE:** George Forsythe joi the Mathematics Department as the first faculty memb specializing in computing. The field initially focuses o mathematical and statistical computations and numeric analysis, but Forsythe has a broader vision of potential d velopments in programming languages, artificial intell gence, and machine translation of languages. In 1961, h forms the Computer Science Division of the Mathemati Department. It is spun off in 1965 as the separate Compu er Science Department, one of the first such departmen in the nation. Forsythe's recruitment of outstanding facu ty makes the university a world leader in this new disc pline, and over the years it will be repeatedly ranked fir nationally. In 1972, he dies at 55, a month after he is dia nosed with cancer.

November **PRE-COMMUNIST TREASURE AT HOOVER:** the Hoover Institution, wire and lead seals are broken on wooden boxes stored for 31 years. Inside are the Paris em bassy office files of the Russian czar's imperial secret polic Basil Maklakoff, last pre-communist ambassador to Franc signed a statement that he had burned the files. Instead h hid them and in 1926 shipped them to the Hoover War L brary. Hoover experts describe what Maklakoff sent as mother lode of knowledge on the crucial years leading the overthrow of the Romanovs in March 1917."

December **STANFORD IN ANTARCTICA:** Prof. Robert He liwell leaves for Antarctica, where he will study upper a mosphere physics as part in the 1957-58 Internation Geophysical Year. Helliwell studies "whistlers," signa

*Business School Dean Ernest Arbuckle is voted "Red Hot Prof" in an annual campus fundraiser. The prize: leading a cheer at a football game.*

*In 1958, Landgut Burg, outside Stuttgart, Germany, becomes Stanford's first overseas campus.*

*Judy Muller, KZSU's "Stanford Sadie" before the station is banned in 1958.*

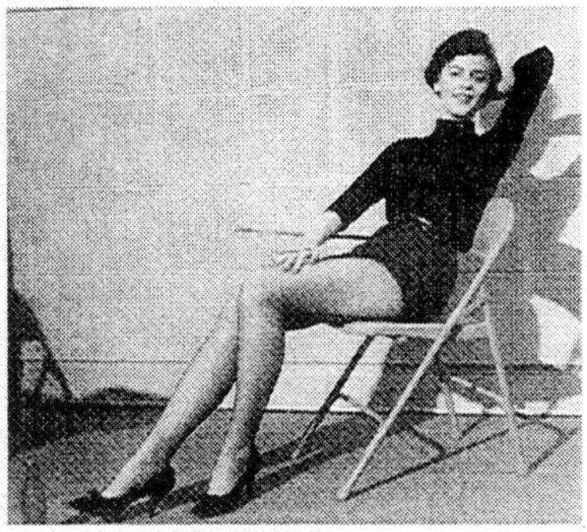

*President Dwight Eisenhower announces support for a two-mile-long linear accelerator at Stanford at a 1959 dinner.*

ıat follow closely the lines of force of the earth's magnet-: field. Stanford scientists visit the Antarctic annually to :udy the phenomenon. In 1969, Prof. John Katsufrakis lo-ates the ideal spot for a research station and in 1973 the :ansmitter is turned on at Stanford's Siple Station. Several ındmarks take on Stanford-related names: "Helliwell ills," "Mount Katsufrakis," and "Stanford Plateau." Siple tation closes in 1988 after its roof caves in.

## 1958

ıne **BUSINESS SCHOOL GROWTH:** Ernest Arbuckle be-omes dean of the Graduate School of Business. In his 10 ears, the Business School faculty more than doubles, :om 29 to 76, while student enrollment increases from oo to 550. The regional character of the student body dis-ppears, and the faculty strengthens the curriculum. A ew $5.5 million headquarters is built flanking the Oval. rbuckle, '33 and MBA '36, has a long association with the niversity: student body officer, assistant to the dean of ıen, manager of his fraternity, Block S winner, professor nd dean, and member of the Board of Trustees.

ıne **ACADEMIC RANKINGS:** Stanford ranks 13th nation-lly in overall quality of graduate programs, according to a 957 survey of academic department heads in a University f Pennsylvania study. Harvard ranks first.

une 24 **FIRST OVERSEAS CAMPUS:** The first campus of he overseas studies program opens in Beutelsbach at andgut Burg, a 30-acre estate 12 miles from Stuttgart, Ger-nany. Enrollment is 33 men and 30 women, sophomores hrough seniors, selected from 197 applicants. Two years ater, two more campuses are opened, France (Tours) and Italy (Florence), with plans under way for a smaller, more specialized program in Tokyo. In 1961, campuses are opened in England (Harlaxton, later Cliveden, then Oxford) and Austria (Semmering, later Vienna).

August **KZSU KICKED OFF:** The university bans student radio station KZSU from the airways for two years due to illegal radio power levels, interference with other stations, and the questionable taste of its broadcasts, including the "Stanford Sadie Show," featuring the seductive voice of a mystery Stanford woman. The Federal Communications Commission had issued numerous warnings to the university, which owns the station.

## 1959

May 14 **STANFORD LINEAR ACCELERATOR (SLAC) APPROVED:** To the surprise and delight of Stanford scientists, President Dwight Eisenhower announces at a gathering of the nation's top scientists and industrialists in New York City that he supports Stanford's proposal to build the world's largest and most powerful atom smasher. The two-mile-long linear accelerator project is approved by Congress in 1961, to be operated by Stanford under the direction of the Atomic Energy Commission (later, the Department of Energy). Construction starts in July 1962.

August 4 **BIG DISH:** Stanford announces that a 150-foot dish antenna — to be the nation's largest radio telescope — will be built on the ridge in the foothills behind campus. It will be a joint venture with the Stanford Research Institute and the Air Force. The huge parabolic reflector "ear," plus the powerful radio transmitter to be built next to it, is designed to detect nuclear bomb blasts in the at-

Plans are announced in 1959 to build a giant radio telescope in the foothills behind campus. It begins operation in 1962.

The Medical Center moves to campus from San Francisco in 1959.

mosphere (at that time a classified project). It is also able to bounce radar signals off the planets and even the sun, leading to more accurate measurements of cosmic distances, planetary surfaces, and other scientific matters. The installation is completed in 1962 and, until the 1970s, plays an important role in the nation's space program, especially in sending and receiving signals to and from Pioneer space probes. After the mid-1970s, scientific advances elsewhere cause NASA to lose interest in the aging dish. Beginning in 1990, SRI and Stanford scientists launch an effort to renovate it and seek new missions. In 1996, the dish helps the Jet Propulsion Laboratory at Pasadena with a Mars project and in February 2000 it joins the unsuccessful search for signals from the lost Mars Polar Lander. With new SRI assignments and continuing Stanford scientific work, the dish is once again well-scheduled.

September 17 **MED CENTER RELOCATES:** Stanford Medical Center, a $27 million complex designed by architect Edward Durell Stone, is dedicated on campus as the new home of the School of Medicine. The school's clinical facilities have been in San Francisco, while the basic sciences, such as anatomy, biochemistry, and physiology, were taught on the Stanford campus. The relocation is expected to help basic scientists and clinicians, who will benefit from proximity to each other and to faculty in other disciplines. In addition to the school and outpatient clinics, the new complex includes the 420-bed Palo Alto-Stanford Hospital Center, owned and operated jointly by Palo Alto and Stanford. The hospital will serve as a clinical base for faculty and local private practice physicians, many of whom serve on the school's voluntary faculty.

October **ESCONDIDO VILLAGE:** Families begin moving into the recently completed first phase of Escondido Village married student housing. The 250 apartments, costing $3 million, are located near the intersection of Escondido Road and Stanford Avenue. Many more units are added later. The housing covers the site of the 1920s-era Palo Alto Airport.

October **LONG-RANGE FINANCIAL PLANNING:** The university initiates long-term financial forecasts with the document "Stanford's Minimum Financial Needs in the Years Ahead." This so-called "Red Book" summarizes academic objectives and their cost. Shortly after its completion, two Ford Foundation executives visit Stanford, inquiring whether the university administration has planned for its next 10 years. They are shown the Red Book. In September 1960, the Ford Foundation announces a large matching grant to Stanford. *(See also April 1961)*

December **COMPUTER DATING PROJECT:** Two electrical engineering undergraduates complete a project, "Marriage Planning Service," for a computer programming course (Math 139). Questionnaires are filled out by 25 men and 25 women drawn from the student body and local residents. The computer initially pairs the two most similar individuals; as further matches are made, the remaining couples are increasingly dissimilar. At a party in Los Trancos Woods where the couples are introduced, the final couple is a freshman male trumpet player in the Band and a nonstudent 35-year-old single mother. This is the first known use of computers for "date matching." No great success is achieved.

# 1960

**STATISTICS:**

Undergraduate enrollment: 5,613

Graduate enrollment: 3,636

Faculty: 619

Tuition: $1,005 per year

Endowment: $134 million

January 7 **NUCLEAR REACTOR UNVEILED:** A 10,000-watt nuclear reactor is unveiled in the old Harris J. Ryan High-Voltage Laboratory. Half of the corrugated steel building is remodeled to house the Mechanical Engineering Department's Nuclear Technology Laboratory. Experts say the reactor is "fool-proof, student-proof, and professor-proof." In 1974, the operation is shut down and fuel rods removed. The building then is used for university storage and studios for Art Department faculty. It is dismantled in 1988 to make way for a 26-unit faculty housing development.

February 11 **POST OFFICE DEDICATED:** Two of the most outdated and crowded facilities on campus finally are replaced by the new post office, dedicated in February, and the adjacent bookstore, occupied in March. Both Lasuen Street buildings are designed by architect John Carl Warnecke, '41. The new post office has 4,176 boxes compared to 1,833 in its predecessor. When that post office, built in 1900, is demolished, the community is surprised to find that the "sandstone" façade is really brick covered with sandstone-colored plaster. The old bookstore will be remodeled as the Western Civilization program library, and later becomes home to the career planning service. Later in the year, this section of Lasuen is closed to auto traffic.

February 12 **PRESIDENTIAL POLITICS:** John F. Kennedy, who is seeking the Democratic nomination for president, speaks to 4,000 inside and outside Memorial Auditorium. Republican presidential hopeful Richard M. Nixon comes to campus on April 11 and speaks at Memorial Auditorium to an overflow crowd (but somewhat smaller than Kennedy's).

April 1 **FRENCH PRESIDENT VISITS:** French President Charles de Gaulle visits the Medical Center and the Stanford Industrial Park.

April 1 **JAPAN STUDY CENTER:** President Sterling presides at the opening of the Stanford Center for Japanese Studies in Tokyo. Unlike Stanford's European campuses, there is no special physical campus. Undergraduates will register at Waseda University and graduate students at Tokyo University. Students also can take courses at other Tokyo institutions, such as Keio University, where the Associated Students already have an exchange agreement.

July 1 **OLYMPIC TRACK AND FIELD TRIALS:** Stanford hosts two-day U.S. Olympic track and field trials in the stadium for the second time. The first was in 1932.

August 23 **FIJI HOUSE BURNS DOWN:** Looking like a scene from *Gone with the Wind,* Phi Gamma Delta's antebellum-style fraternity house burns to the ground. The house was empty, and there are no injuries. The dramatic blaze prompts the university to expand the campus Fire Department.

October 22 **"BEAT CAL" FROM PISA:** Students from the new Stanford campus in Florence travel to Pisa to unfurl an 80-foot "Beat Cal" banner from that city's famous leaning tower.

November 16 **PROFESSOR PRAISES FIDEL CASTRO:** Russian-born professor of economics, Paul A. Baran, an avowed Marxist, causes quite a stir when, after a three-week visit to Cuba, he tells students and press at Cubberley Auditorium that "Castro is one of the great men of this century." Hostile alumni letters soon pour in, threatening to stop donations unless Baran is fired. President Sterling responds with directness: "Professor Baran does not speak for Stanford University. Neither do his opinions represent those of the faculty. . . . A university is, and must be, hospitable to differing points of view, just as a free society has

*A small nuclear reactor is unveiled in 1960 in the old Ryan Lab building.*

*Presidential candidate John F. Kennedy (center of photo, above) draws a huge crowd to his Feb. 12, 1960, talk at Memorial Auditorium. Richard Nixon soon follows. Security is notably lacking.*

*Students vote in 1961 not to integrate the sexes in the the football rooting section, as seen in this 1949 photograph. Also in 1961, card stunts are automated.*

the obligation of respecting a man's right to speak." Sterling also defends Baran's research and teaching ability, and points out that he has tenure and there is no basis for firing him. The "Baran problem" continues, off and on, until 1964, when Baran dies of a heart attack at 54.

December 15 **HOOVER LIBRARY SPLIT:** Exasperated at seemingly constant disagreements with President Sterling and other university officials over control of the Hoover Library, Herbert Hoover surprisingly offers his presidential and related papers — several million items but excluding the "war and peace" papers — to the National Archives, to be placed in a new library being built at Hoover's birthplace, West Branch, Iowa. On Dec. 30, the government accepts the offer. But there is a problem. In 1959, Hoover had formally given Stanford his total archive — part of which he has now offered to the government. After a personal appeal from Hoover, the trustees, in 1961, taking into account Hoover's lifetime of contributions to Stanford, return to him ownership of his presidential and related papers. In time, they are moved to Iowa.

# 1961

January **STANFORD WINERY BECOMES STANFORD BARN:** Leland Stanford's red brick winery, situated on the edge of the Shopping Center, near the Medical Center, is converted to house a bank, a group of international restaurants, and other tenants. Constructed for the Palo Alto Winery around 1886, the building was used after 1915 as a dairy barn and to stable bulls as part of an artificial insemination program. It is now called the Stanford Barn (and often confused with the historic Red Barn, the horse stable near the Golf Course).

March 6 **FRATERNITIES FIGHT RELIGIOUS, RACIAL DISCRIMINATION:** The Stanford chapter of Alpha Tau Omega fraternity has its charter rescinded by the national because it pledges four men of Jewish faith. With university support, ATO continues as a local organization. In 1963, Sigma Nu, frustrated in its two-year effort to end discriminatory racial clauses at the national level, votes unanimously to become a local fraternity, Beta Chi. In April 1965, Sigma Chi fraternity is suspended for one year by its national organization after pledging a black student. In November 1966, the Stanford chapter votes unanimously to sever ties with its national, which refuses to change a policy that allows any of 60 individuals on the national membership committee to veto any chapter pledge. In 1967, Kappa Sigma is suspended by its national, two years after it pledges a black student.

April **PACE CAMPAIGN:** President Sterling announces a three-year, $100 million fundraising drive, Plan of Action for a Challenging Era (PACE), calling it "our boldest venture since the University was founded." Based on a $25 million, three-for-one Ford Foundation challenge grant, it goes over the top by $14 million in 1964. Kenneth Cuthbertson, vice president for finance, later will say of the Ford grant: "More than any single act, it has had an impact which has allowed Stanford to join that handful of institutions which are unique national assets."

April 21 **FOOTBALL SEGREGATION:** By a vote of 2,044 to 951, students veto a proposal to integrate the sexes into

The old post office (above left), with the Stanford Union portal in background. It and the longtime bookstore (above) are replaced in 1960. Before construction of White Plaza, cars line street in the front of the new bookstore (left).

Students from the Florence campus hang a "Beat Cal" banner from the leaning Tower of Pisa in 1960.

one football rooting section.

May 13 ***LAYBOY* SUSPENSION:** Dean of Students H. Donald Winbigler suspends graduate student Brad Efron, editor of *Chaparral,* for publishing a *Playboy* parody called *Layboy* that includes a burlesque of the Virgin Birth. The magazine immediately sells out (or, as some students suspect, the administration seizes the copies). In 1966, Efron joins the statistics faculty. He later wins a MacArthur "genius" fellowship and becomes chairman of his department, head of the Faculty Senate, and chairman of the Advisory Board.

Fall **AUTOMATED CARD STUNTS:** Two math students, as a class project, print instructions for the football rooting section's card stunts using a Burroughs 220 computer. The old method of hand-marking instruction cards took 400 man hours, but the computer prints out 3,465 sets of instructions — one for each rooter — in 13 hours.

November 2 **HOFSTADTER WINS NOBEL:** Physicist Robert Hofstadter wins a Nobel Prize. *(See page 153)*

# 1962

May **STORKE PUBLICATIONS BUILDING:** Thomas M. Storke, '98, editor and publisher of the *Santa Barbara News-Press,* announces he will donate a building for use by student publications, including the *Stanford Daily,* the *Chaparral,* the *Quad, Sequoia* magazine, and others. Two weeks earlier, Storke received a Pulitzer Prize for editorials calling public attention to the conservative John Birch Society.

July 21 **U.S.-U.S.S.R. TRACK MEET:** A U.S.-Soviet track meet opens at Stanford Stadium. Fans — 153,000 in two days — come to watch what turns into an emotional event, with the Cold War rivals joining hands during the closing ceremony and marching in pairs past the stands before a roaring crowd. The winners are the American men and the Soviet women. The event is organized by track coach Payton Jordan, who later says he was inspired by a suggestion from athletic director Al Masters that they put on a track meet that might make some money.

September **ARTIFICIAL INTELLIGENCE:** John McCarthy, who coined the term "artificial intelligence" to describe his efforts to make computers simulate human thought processes, joins the faculty as a professor of computer science. He soon creates the Stanford Artificial Intelligence Laboratory, which supports research in robotics, expert systems, speech understanding, and cognitive science. Stanford becomes a leading international center for both fundamental and applied AI research. McCarthy also develops the concept of timesharing computer systems and is the first to create one, giving rise to a worldwide industry.

September 29 **TRESIDDER MEMORIAL UNION:** A new student union, named in honor of Stanford's fourth president, the late Donald B. Tresidder, is dedicated. It includes a cafeteria, a bowling alley, meeting rooms, and lounges.

# 1963

April 1 **FALLOUT SHELTERS:** Black and yellow civil de-

*After decades as a dairy barn, the Stanford Winery is remodeled and renamed Stanford Barn in 1961.*

*Not Gone with the Wind. Fiji house burns down Aug. 23, 1960.*

*Big Game is delayed a week and the bonfire destroyed during the day in the wake of President John F. Kennedy's assassination.*

*President Sterling in 1963 greets Prince William of Gloucester, who enrolls as a graduate student.*

fense signs are posted on campus identifying basement areas that are newly stocked as nuclear fallout shelters. This act, inspired by the Soviet missile crisis in Cuba, touches off the first major postwar political protest on campus, including a peaceful 24-hour vigil outside President Sterling's home and office. Stanford's shelters, part of a nationwide civil defense program financed by the federal government, are stocked with survival supplies sufficient for a two-week period, theoretically accommodating 6,800 people.

May 6 **WINDS OF FREEDOM FOUNDATION:** University trustees reject gift offers from two individuals who stipulate that their use would be later designated or approved by directors of the Winds of Freedom Foundation, a conservative group that wants to "underwrite the work of distinguished faculty members who are not enamored of socialism." In February 1964, trustees reject $35,000 offered by the foundation for a visiting professor in either economics or political science from a list of candidates it would provide. The sparring continues with several $500 gift offers and rejections. Organized as a nonprofit California corporation in July 1962, the foundation notes in its literature that its "prime purpose. . .is to aggregate funds for gifts to Stanford." Its literature closely resembles the university's in format and carries a Stanford post office box return address. Trustees say they will not surrender authority for solicitation and acceptance of gifts and determination of their use.

Summer **STANFORD IN WASHINGTON STARTS:** A Stanford-in-Washington summer internship program is launched with 14 students. In the next three years, more than 100 students land summer positions in congressional offices and federal agencies. The program soon changes its name to Stanford in Government.

Summer **VOLUNTEERS IN ASIA:** Volunteers in Asia (VIA) begins when 23 students and Dwight Clark, an adviser in Wilbur Hall, travel to Hong Kong at their own expense to teach and help with community projects. In the next 35 years, VIA sends 1,200 volunteers to 14 different countries. It also brings students from Asia to Stanford as part of the Trans-Pacific Exchange program. VIA continues.

July 13 ***TE VEGA* TO INDIAN OCEAN:** *Te Vega,* a 135-foot schooner that has been converted to a research vessel for Hopkins Marine Station, sets sail for a lengthy expedition in the Indian Ocean. Students and faculty serve three-month stints, shuttling to and from ship by air. Initially supported with grants from the National Science Foundation, the *Te Vega* is sold in 1970 because of increasing costs and declining federal support.

September 16 **LIFE ON MARS?:** Profs. Joshua Lederberg, Nobel laureate and chair of genetics, and Elliott Levinthal, mechanical engineering, make headlines when NASA announces that they will design instrumentation for biological experiments to investigate the possibility that life exists on Mars. Their device, known as the Multivator, is a candidate for the first Mars mission lander. A modified payload for biological experiments based on the Stanford model is launched with the Viking Lander on July 4, 1976, but it produces no solid conclusions.

Fall **ROYAL STUDENT:** Prince William of Gloucester, first

In 1963, the 135-foot schooner Te Vega sets sail for research sponsored by Hopkins Marine Station in the Indian Ocean.

Martin Luther King Jr. speaks in Memorial Auditorium in 1964.

Tresidder Memorial Union, honoring the university's fourth president, opens in 1962.

cousin of Queen Elizabeth and seventh in succession to the British throne, enrolls for a year of graduate study in economics and political science. He is the first member of the royal family to attend a coeducational school and the first to study at an American institution. He dies nine years later while competing in an air race.

Fall **MISSISSIPPI BLACK VOTERS:** As part of a growing voter-rights campaign in the South, Allard Lowenstein, former assistant dean of men, and a dozen students travel to Mississippi at their own expense to help local blacks stage a mock election. Among the students are Dennis Sweeney, leader of a new campus political organization called the Student Congress, and David Harris, future student body president. Ten Stanford faculty and 40 student volunteers, the largest group from any university, spend summer 1964 in Mississippi helping blacks register to vote. Sweeney narrowly escapes death when the "freedom house" he occupies in McComb is bombed on June 21. A draft resister, he later becomes a paranoid schizophrenic. On May 14, 1980, he murders Lowenstein in his New York office.

October **NEW INTERNATIONAL CENTER:** Bechtel International Center, a meeting place for Stanford's many foreign students and their families, opens in the old Zeta Psi fraternity house. It is dedicated Jan. 13, 1966. Fire destroyed the I-Center's previous house on Lasuen Street in 1961.

October 26 **CARD STUNTS; NATIONAL ANTHEM PREMIERE:** CBS features the Stanford card section in a special half-time show during the nationally televised Stanford-Notre Dame game. The card section is on the air "live" for seven minutes during which the rooters perform six stunts, including the traditional expanding "S." The stunts are planned by the Axe Committee and put together with the help of a Burroughs 220 electronic computer. Also, the Stanford Band premieres a new rendition of *The Star-Spangled Banner,* arranged by its director, Arthur P. Barnes. It begins with a loud, long drum roll that fades to silence. A lone trumpet plays the first half, the reeds join in softly, and then, as a sports columnist reports in the *San Francisco Examiner,* it builds up "horn by horn, drum by drum and cymbal by cymbal, into a crashing avalanche of sound." The newsman adds: "The last note fell and a stunned silence followed the echoing crescendo. Then from the crowd came a roar." Five weeks later, the Band repeats this version of the anthem at Big Game, which has been delayed a week because of the assassination of U.S. President John F. Kennedy. This time the crowd weeps.

## 1964

April 23 **MARTIN LUTHER KING JR. ON CAMPUS:** In the first of two campus speeches, civil rights leader Martin Luther King Jr. asks an overflow crowd at Memorial Auditorium for help: "In the Mississippi power structure, justice has no meaning. . . . Civil rights issues cannot be resolved from within the state; help must come from the outside." He is interrupted a half-dozen times by prolonged applause. His second campus speech is April 14, 1967, just a year before he is assassinated in Memphis.

May 23 **WHITE PLAZA DEDICATED:** Mr. and Mrs. Ray-

A Shakespearean stage set constructed in Frost Amphitheater for the 1964 Summer Festival of the Arts serves as backdrop for commencement.

*Crews excavating for the Stanford Linear Accelerator Center in 1964 stumble upon a skeleton of* Paleoparadoxia.

*Herbert Hoover with the tower that bears his name. He dies Oct. 20, 1964.*

mond B. White honor their sons, both members of the class of 1949, at the dedication of White Memorial Plaza. William Nicholas White was killed in a training plane accident in 1948 and John Barber White II died in a surfing accident. Designed by landscape architect Thomas Church, the pedestrian and bicycle plaza adjacent to the bookstore and post office replaces part of Lasuen Street. It includes a fountain, soon dubbed "Mem Claw," by artist Aristides Demetrios.

Summer **FESTIVAL OF THE ARTS:** Stanford celebrates Shakespeare's 400th birthday by opening a Summer Festival of the Arts with an Elizabethan theme. Seventy-six events sell 54,000 tickets — more than 94 percent of capacity. The festival includes 21 performances of six Shakespearean plays by three repertory troupes in Frost Amphitheater, concerts, art exhibits, lectures, dances, and dramatic readings. The festival's success spawns annual summer cultural festivals on campus, including a celebration of Mozart in 1965. The festival introduces American Conservatory Theater (ACT) to Bay Area audiences, playing a key role in ACT's decision to take up residence in San Francisco. Budget problems close the festival in 1970.

August **"ELECTRONIC BRAILLE":** Electrical engineering Prof. John Linvill invents a reading machine for the blind that can translate a printed page into a kind of "electronic Braille." An optical scanner converts alphabet letters from visual images to a vibrating array of pins readable by the fingertips. His 12-year-old daughter, Candace, who is blind, tests the device. Linvill later markets an improved version as the Optacon. Its success depends on a very large integrated circuit (VLIC). Stanford becomes the first major university to manufacture its own VLICs. Candace Linvill goes on to graduate from Stanford and become a clinical psychologist.

October 2 ***PALEOPARADOXIA* AT SLAC:** While excavating for the Stanford Linear Accelerator Center, a nearly complete skeleton is found of a *Paleoparadoxia,* a 10-foot amphibian that roamed the area 14 million years ago. Only two other specimens of *Paleoparadoxia* have been found to date — in Japan and Northern California — but neither is as complete or mature as the SLAC specimen. The original fossil is donated to the Museum of Paleontology at Berkeley in exchange for a plaster cast replica, which Adele Panofsky, wife of the SLAC director, painstakingly assembles over a period of nearly 20 years. The replica is completed and dedicated Sept. 4, 1992, and installed in SLAC's new Visitors' Center in November 1995.

October 20 **HERBERT HOOVER DIES:** Longtime university trustee Herbert Hoover, a member of the Pioneer Class of 1895 and former president of the United States, dies at 90.

November 30 **MINORITY OPPORTUNITIES:** President Sterling appoints a faculty-administration committee on educational opportunities for disadvantaged minorities to explore ways the university could be useful in promoting opportunities for African Americans and other minority groups.

# 1965

February **DOG HEART TRANSPLANT:** The dog "Ralphie,"

Associate Prof. Owen K. Garriott is selected for the astronaut corps in 1965. He later flies aboard Skylab.

Engineering Prof. John Linvill in 1964 invents a reading machine for the blind, demonstrated by his daughter, Candace.

Students Will Rogers and Sigourney Weaver perform in Stanford Repertory Theater's *Androcles and The Lion* in the late 1960s. The ambitious repertory company is launched in 1966.

Jazz legend Louis Armstrong performs during a 1965-66 student-organized "Jazz Year."

recipient of a heart transplant from another dog, dies eight months after the experiment. Surgeons have been experimenting for more than five years, but the dogs never survive long. Knowledge gained from this research helps pave the way for human heart transplants.

February 12 **ANTI-VIETNAM PROTEST:** Faculty and students express opposition to American involvement in Vietnam, beginning with a combined faculty-student rally of 400. In March a petition signed by 144 faculty is sent to President Lyndon Johnson urging an end to involvement. Petition drives and rallies continue in April, and a teach-in is held in May.

April **AID FOR HEMOPHILIACS:** Judith Pool of the Medical School develops a new technique for extracting anti-hemophilic globulin, the clotting factor in blood that prevents bleeding in hemophiliacs. The AHG factor, marketed widely by pharmaceutical laboratories, leads to major improvements in the lives of hemophiliacs.

April ***IN LOCO PARENTIS* FADING:** Full confidence in the "maturity and good judgment" of coeds prompts the university to liberalize social regulations for women. Key changes are an extension of freshman dormitory closing hours from 10:30 p.m. to midnight daily (instead of only on weekends) and permission for junior and senior women to extend their unlimited late leaves from 2:30 a.m. to as late as 6 a.m.

May **WORLD RECORD IN TRACK:** The 440-yard track relay team smashes the world record during the West Coast Relays in Fresno, Calif., using a new baton-passing method devised by coach Payton Jordan that then becomes standard practice.

May 11 **HOOVER PAVILION:** Palo Alto Hospital reopens as the Herbert Hoover Pavilion after extensive renovation to bring it up to code and to address a shortage of beds at the Medical Center. Built in 1931 by Palo Alto, the hospital was closed in 1959 when the city and Stanford built its replacement nearby. It continues to serve patients until the late 1980s. Currently it houses administrative offices.

June 17 **UNIVERSITY ARCHIVES ESTABLISHED:** The University Archives and Stanford Collection is established in the University Libraries by the Board of Trustees as the official repository for historical records of the university and the Stanford community. In about 1902, the Library Reference Division began collecting student scrapbooks and letters, faculty papers and correspondence, and other university-related materials. These items are now proving invaluable to Stanford history researchers.

June 29 **PROF. PICKED AS ASTRONAUT:** Owen K. Garriott, associate professor of electrical engineering, is one of six selected for the first NASA team of scientist-astronauts. He has been a senior scientist with the Stanford Center for Radar Astronomy, and in charge of Stanford's satellite monitoring program. He first goes into space on July 28, 1973.

September **FRESHMAN SEMINARS:** A program of small freshman seminars is initiated, to help launch first-year students into the intellectual life of the university. The program starts with 38 seminars enrolling 265 students,

The two-mile-long Stanford Linear Accelerator Center, completed in 1966, is seen here after completion of Interstate 280 in the 1970s.

Staff members use bicycles to check out SLAC's klystron gallery (left), above the accelerator tunnel (below).

and quickly grows in popularity. It continues — with sophomores added in 1980 — until 1991.

September **NEW FACULTY CLUB:** The long-awaited Faculty Club, made possible by a gift from the estate of Lucie Stern, opens for business. Faculty have been without separate dining facilities since the Union, where they had a private dining room since 1922, was superseded by Tresidder Union three years earlier.

October **JAZZ YEAR:** "Stanford Jazz Year '65-'66," a student-organized nine-month series of jazz concerts, lectures, films, and exhibits, is launched with fall quarter concert headliners Louis Armstrong, Ella Fitzgerald, and Duke Ellington. More than 50 other jazz artists, critics, and scholars are scheduled.

November **VIETNAM, PRO & CON:** Some 1,600 signatures are collected in support of U.S. policy in Vietnam; a week later 500 Bay Area faculty and staff sign an open letter asking for an immediate bombing halt.

December **GAY RIGHTS:** The Stanford Sexual Rights Forum registers as a voluntary student organization, the earliest known student group nationally to advocate civil rights for homosexuals. Members also seek change in campus regulations limiting visits between men and women in dormitories, and lobby for access to contraceptives at the Student Health Service. The group is active through spring 1966. In November 1970, the Stanford Gay Students Union organizes. Under a succession of names, it becomes established in the Lesbian, Gay, and Bisexual Community Center in the Old Firehouse.

# 1966

January 31 **STRIKE URGED:** Vietnam protesters at a noon rally call for a university-wide strike, but only a small number of professors cancel classes. In the evening, more than 700 stage a torchlight parade from Cubberley Auditorium to downtown Palo Alto. In April, 135 donors volunteer to donate blood "in physical and moral support" of the Vietnam War effort.

February 17 **SECTARIAN WORSHIP APPROVED:** The Board of Trustees approves sectarian worship services in Memorial Church on a trial basis as part of an overall expansion of the university's religious program. The *Stanford Daily* led a campaign for sectarian services, beginning in January 1964. The university later gets court approval to make the change permanent, overturning a 1902 amendment to the Founding Grant by Jane Stanford that strictly forbade "all denominational alliances." Ministers from a wide variety of denominations have given sermons at the church since it opened in 1903.

February 25 **BING NURSERY SCHOOL:** Succeeding the Stanford Village Nursery School, which had been operated by the Department of Psychology as a laboratory preschool since the late 1940s, Bing Nursery School is dedicated on campus under the direction of Prof. Edith M. Dowley. Funds come from the National Science Foundation and from Mrs. Anna Bing Arnold and her son, Dr. Peter Bing, in memory of his father and her husband. Bing now enrolls more than 400 children in part-time programs. Many of the children are from Stanford families, and others are from families in surrounding communities,

Students protest Selective Service testing and university decision making during a three-day occupation of the President's Office in May 1966.

Annabelle Evans, center, is elected Homecoming Queen in November 1966. Princesses are Eleanor Watkins, left, and Diana Carter. Evans defeated Wendy Wonka - maybe.

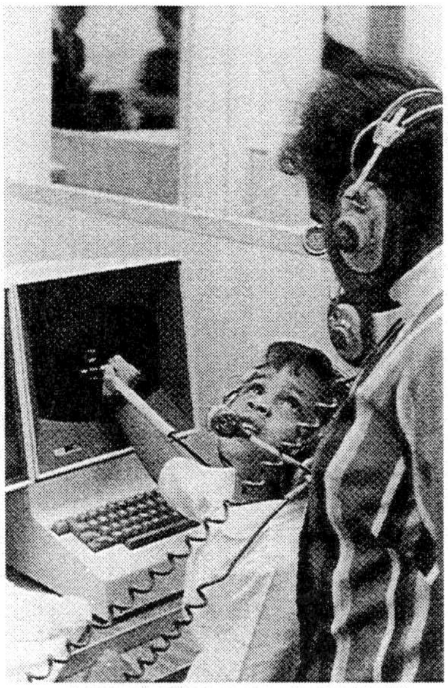

First grader and mother listen to recorded message as part of computer-aided instruction, introduced by professors in 1966.

including some from disadvantaged families that receive financial aid from the school. Faculty members and graduate students from psychology, education, linguistics, and other fields conduct research with the Bing children, ages 2 to 5.

Spring **LINEAR ACCELERATOR COMPLETED:** Construction of Stanford Linear Accelerator Center (SLAC) is completed on schedule and within its $114 million budget under the direction of Prof. Wolfgang K.H. Panofsky, who joined the faculty in 1951. The accelerator provides a new tool for high-energy physics research. During negotiations with the federal government to build SLAC, Panofsky obtained a contractual agreement that the facility would do no classified research, an agreement maintained in subsequent contracts. The facility is dedicated Sept. 9, 1967.

April **STANFORD REPERTORY THEATER:** As part of a university decision to grow dramatically in the arts, the Drama Department begins organizing a professional repertory company — Stanford Repertory Theater — with help from a $300,000 Rockefeller Foundation grant. Nationally known directors, senior and apprentice actors, professional stage and costume designers, and a technical and management staff present at least six major productions each academic year. Highlights of the first season, 1966-67, are *Prometheus Bound* and *That Scoundrel Scapin*. The second season opens with *Antony and Cleopatra*. Budget problems and lack of a good theater contribute to SRT's closure in May 1970.

April **GENETIC SUSCEPTIBILITY TO DISEASE:** Prof. Hugh McDevitt and his group discover that genes responsible for regulating immune responses to infection are clustered together on one chromosome in mice and are linked to those responsible for destroying tissue grafts. Because these genes direct production of protein molecules involved in the body's defense system, McDevitt has found a unique pointer of human vulnerability to disease. By the early 1970s and 1980s, groups at UCLA and elsewhere have established links between such genes and a form of arthritis in humans, as well as other disorders.

May 19-21 **PRESIDENT'S OFFICE SIT-IN:** What starts as a protest against university involvement in Selective Service testing that could affect student draft deferments, broadens into a challenge against faculty and administrative decision-making. Fifteen students begin a three-day occupation of the reception area in the President's Office. Thirty-six students later are charged with violating the Fundamental Standard and are placed on probation for a year.

September **JOURNALISM FELLOWS:** Seventeen journalists arrive as the first group to attend Stanford through the Professional Journalism Fellowship Program. The program provides opportunities for study in any field to mid-career journalists. It later becomes the John S. Knight Journalism Fellowship Program.

September **PASS-FAIL GRADING OPTION:** Pass-fail grading is introduced for undergraduates, but is limited to one course per quarter. It also is restricted to courses outside the student's major and outside general studies requirements. A year later, the pass-fail grading option is expanded to freshman seminars, senior colloquia, undergraduate special seminars, and activity classes.

Meyer Library, completed in 1966.

Student body President David Harris, an outspoken critic of the draft and Vietnam War.

Vice President Hubert Humphrey enjoys a laugh during a campus visit in 1967.

Students at the campus in Florence help during severe floods in 1966.

September **COMPUTERS IN ELEMENTARY SCHOOL:** Profs. Patrick Suppes and Richard Atkinson of Stanford's Institute for Mathematical Studies in the Social Sciences introduce the concept of computer-aided instruction. Students at Brentwood Elementary School in East Palo Alto are among the first in the nation to learn by computer. Working at their own pace, students do interactive math and reading lessons, touching a special pen to the screen to answer questions. They receive immediate feedback.

October **MAJOR EDUCATIONAL STUDY:** President Sterling appoints a nine-member committee to plan a comprehensive review of Stanford's educational program, the first since the 1954-56 Study of Undergraduate Education. It becomes known as the Study of Education at Stanford (SES). The review will be directed by law Prof. Herbert Packer, recently named vice-provost for academic planning and programs, who will chair the study's faculty-student executive committee. It will oversee the work of 10 committees.

November **HOMECOMING QUEEN:** Annabelle Marie Evans of Idaho is elected Stanford's first Homecoming Queen, defeating Wendy Wonka. Rumor has it that Wendy received more votes than Annabelle, but contest officials refuse to reveal the tally. In a campus referendum 20 days later, students vote 791 to 619 to abolish the royal post. Undaunted by her defeat as Homecoming Queen, Wendy enters the Best Foods National College Queen contest in April 1967 and is named a state finalist before contest officials begin questioning her existence.

December **FLOOD AID FOR FLORENCE:** Students raise money and collect nearly a ton of clothing to send to Florence, Italy, site of a major flood. At Stanford's campus in Florence, classes are canceled so students can help salvage Renaissance manuscripts and works of art from world-famous museums.

December 2 **NEW UNDERGRADUATE LIBRARY:** The new undergraduate library is dedicated to the memory of J. Henry Meyer. A San Francisco businessman who moved to Menlo Park in 1900, Meyer donated money for the Lane Medical Library and an endowed fund for the collection of California history manuscripts. The new library is donated by his daughters, Olga Meyer and Alice Meyer Buck. Alice Buck later donates the Buck Estate, between the Golf Course and Menlo Park, to the university. The concept of a separate undergraduate library is later abandoned, and Meyer Library becomes an adjunct to nearby Green Library.

# 1967

January **WOMEN DEMAND OFF-CAMPUS OPTION:** Challenging the university's practice of *in loco parentis,* approximately 350 women students delay payment of room and board bills as a demand for the option of junior and senior women to live off campus. In May, the university announces that up to 100 senior women, chosen at random, will be permitted to live off campus, starting in the fall, but only about 60 of the approximately 400 senior women take advantage of the offer.

January **MEN, WOMEN SHARE HOUSE:** Coeducational

*The university's banners, designed by Prof. Eric Hutchinson, make their premiere at the 1967 commencement.*

housing begins on campus when 31 men and 12 women move into Grove House, the former Phi Delta Theta fraternity house (vacant because the fraternity has been suspended). Along with 17 non-residents, they participate in interdisciplinary seminars at the house. Coed dormitories soon become the most popular option — about 90 percent — in the student housing system both at Stanford and nationally. Experts predict that coed housing will transform the traditional dating-mating game, as men and women begin to regard each other more like brothers and sisters. Stanford's overseas studies centers were coed from the beginning.

January 4 **LYMAN BECOMES PROVOST:** History Prof. Richard W. Lyman, 43, becomes vice president and provost following the 1965 retirement of Frederick E. Terman.

January 12 **DAVID HARRIS PROTESTS DRAFT:** Student body President David Harris, a veteran civil rights worker and outspoken critic of the Vietnam War and the draft, tells a rally of 400 that he will go to jail rather than accept military service. On Feb. 23, he resigns his presidency, saying "I have done all I am capable of doing for the realization of education at Stanford."

February 20 **HUMPHREY DEFENDS VIETNAM WAR:** U.S. Vice President Hubert Humphrey defends American involvement in Vietnam during a campus forum at Memorial Auditorium. Approximately 4,000 fill the auditorium to capacity and cover adjacent plazas. He is greeted with a standing ovation by half the audience. Many students and faculty wear white armbands to show their desire for peace in Vietnam. About 60 audience members quietly walk out in protest after Humphrey finishes his openings remarks, and another 180 leave after he says "the policies which this administration follows [in Vietnam] are the same ones which the late, beloved President [Kennedy] followed. Anti-war demonstrators chant "shame, shame, shame" as he leaves by the back door.

March 16 **STERLING TO RETIRE:** President Sterling tells the Board of Trustees that he intends to retire no later than Sept. 1, 1968. At retirement, the board names him chancellor for life.

March 26 **SWIMMERS WIN CHAMPIONSHIP:** Stanford swimmers win the first of many future NCAA titles, defeating defending champion USC 275 to 260. The men also set six NCAA records at the swim meet in East Lansing, Mich.

April 13 **VIETNAM WAR PROTESTS:** About 400 attend an anti-war rally sponsored by Students for a Democratic Society, after which 150 march to the Stanford Research Institute to protest weapons and chemical warfare research. In May, 169 students sign an ad in the *Stanford Daily* saying they will not fight in Vietnam. Three-quarters also say they will not allow themselves to be drafted.

Spring **STUDENTS STAGE OPERA:** The Student Opera Guild's production of Puccini's one-act *Gianni Schicchi* is a sold-out success.

June 18 **UNIVERSITY BANNERS INTRODUCED:** At the 76th commencement, 10 heraldic banners are carried in the procession — the first public display of the flags newly designed by chemistry Prof. Eric Hutchinson. The British-

*Two thousand community members march from Palo Alto to the Quad to hear a tribute to Martin Luther King Jr.*

*Drs. Norman Shumway, left, and Donald C. Harrison meet the press after they perform the first adult human transplant in the United States in January 1968.*

*The Black Student Union in April 1968 presents demands for increased minority enrollment to Provost Richard Lyman.*

*Spouses of the recipient and donor of America's first heart transplant meet four days after the surgery.*

born Hutchinson, a student of heraldry, made banners for each of the schools, the graduate division, the university, and the president. Their use becomes traditional at commencement. In 1984, Hutchinson adapts the design of the university flag to create a centennial banner.

November 1 **STUDENTS PROTEST CIA, VIETNAM:** Students for a Democratic Society and The Resistance protest campus recruiting by the Central Intelligence Agency, temporarily blocking access to Encina Hall's west wing, where interviews are scheduled. The university starts judicial proceedings against 10 demonstrators. Two weeks later, 2,000 conduct an all-night vigil for peace at Memorial Church in the biggest expression of concern at Stanford since the start of the Vietnam War.

December 15 **GENETICS RESEARCH PROGRESS:** Nobel Laureate Arthur Kornberg and colleagues succeed for the first time in manufacturing synthetic DNA (deoxyribonucleic acid), which displays the full biological activity of the natural molecule of heredity in living organisms. The work demonstrates that scientists can now manipulate enzymes and DNA building blocks to carry out the error-free synthesis of small chromosomes containing several genes, and opens the way for understanding the genetics of more complex organisms and their role in health and disease.

# 1968

January 6 **HEART TRANSPLANT:** The first adult human heart transplant in the United States is performed by Dr. Norman E. Shumway, who has spent the preceding eight years developing the techniques in animal experiments. The recipient, Mike Kasperak, a 54-year-old steelworker, dies 14 days later from kidney and liver failures. Shumway wants to avoid the specter of publicity that characterized similar operations by Dr. Christiaan Barnard in South Africa, but it is not to be. When the decision to perform the transplant is made, calls go out to Stanford nurses. One is at a wedding reception. When the telephone rings, a reporter from the *San Jose Mercury,* also attending the reception, answers. He is asked to find the nurse and convey the message. He does, widely.

April 2 **MINORITY FINANCIAL AID:** Blacks, Mexican-Americans, and other minority students should have priority in obtaining financial aid, an interim committee report for the Study of Education at Stanford (SES) recommends. Headed by Prof. William A. Clebsch, the committee calls for intensified recruiting of minorities, but adds: "No single change in practice could do more to produce an immediate increase in the minority group population at Stanford" than giving students from these groups priority for financial aid. The committee reports that recruitment efforts in recent years have produced an increase in applications from African-Americans: 154 applied for the freshman class entering in 1968, compared to six for the class entering in 1960. The number admitted for 1968 is 71, compared to three in 1960.

April 5 **TRIBUTES TO MARTIN LUTHER KING JR.:** An overflow crowd of 2,400 attends a noon service in Memorial Church for civil rights leader Martin Luther King Jr., assassinated the previous day in Memphis, Tenn. At the same time, about 400 attend a Black Student Union-spon-

*It starts in November 1967, when students (left) block access to campus recruiting by the CIA at Encina Hall. The following May, students stage a three-day sit-in at the Old Union (right) to protest proposed disciplinary action against the CIA protesters. At a courtyard meeting (above), students discuss formation of a student-dominated judicial procedure.*

*On the second try, arsonists in May 1968 destroy the Naval ROTC building, located in the arboretum near Galvez Street.*

sored rally during which an American flag is burned. In the late afternoon, more than 2,000 members of the Palo Alto and East Palo Alto communities stage a silent walk from downtown Palo Alto to the steps of the Quad to hear a tribute to King by B. Davie Napier, dean of the chapel.

April 8 **BLACKS DEMAND INCREASED ENROLLMENT:** Sixty black students quietly walk on stage in Memorial Auditorium to present a series of demands during a morning colloquium convened in response to King's assassination. Many classes have been canceled, and the auditorium is filled to overflowing. The demands include proportional representation of minority groups in the freshman class of 1969-70 and a role for black students in decisions on minority recruiting and admissions. In the evening, Provost Lyman and President Sterling issue a statement committing the university to try to double minority enrollment to about 350 out of 11,500 students by 1970 and also try to double minority employment within a year. The university will start a pilot admission program for at least 10 minority students who do not meet present admission standards. During an April 9 session with 1,000 students, a group of faculty and administrators says the university will hire an admissions officer concerned with minority student recruitment, conduct a fundraising drive for expanded financial aid for minority students, and encourage recruitment of minority faculty and staff members.

April 11 **"DEMANDS MET":** Black Student Union (BSU) leaders emerge from a two-hour meeting with administrators declaring, "They have met our demands." Provost Lyman tells the Academic Council that the administration has rejected the BSU demand for "proportional representation" as "antithetical to the spirit of this university," but will seek faculty support for a goal of more than 100 minority students out of 1,250 in upcoming freshman classes. He says several black students will be employed as admission aides and will consult on selection of a minority admissions specialist. He says the university has not surrendered any of its decision-making powers to any group. "Race relations in America are so serious that every institution must do whatever it can to help," Lyman says. "Ours is the one society on the face of the earth where a reconciliation of the races can take place on a sufficiently large scale to teach its lessons to the world." Faculty and staff establish a Martin Luther King Memorial Fund three days after the assassination. By the end of May, it is at $50,000 in cash and payroll deductions, and growing.

May 6 **PROTEST AGAINST STUDENT SUSPENSIONS:** More than 200 students begin a three-day sit-in at the Old Union, protesting the suspension, proposed by a faculty judicial board, of seven students who demonstrated against the Central Intelligence Agency the previous Nov. 1. In the evening, 1,500 gather in the Old Union courtyard and in a series of votes, they split 3-to-2 against the sit-in tactics, but by a wide margin vote in favor of amnesty for the seven students and formation of a student-dominated judicial review procedure.

May 7 **ARSON DESTROYS ROTC BUILDING:** A fire at 3 a.m. destroys the Naval ROTC building. This is the second fire at the building; it was damaged by arson in March.

May 8 **STUDENTS CLEARED IN CIA PROTEST; SIT-IN ENDS:** After meeting for 13 hours, a committee of five fac-

Fireman clears charred timbers from around President Sterling's desk following a 1968 arson fire that guts his office two months before his retirement.

*President Pitzer meets with members of Students for a Democratic Society outside his office in December 1968.*

*Kenneth S. Pitzer, president of Rice University, is appointed Stanford's sixth president in 1968. He answers questions at his first press conference.*

ulty members, five administrators, and five students announces unanimous agreement on recommendations for a new legislative and judicial structure covering student conduct, consisting of six faculty members and five students. But the committee urges President Sterling to reach an independent decision regarding the seven Nov. 1 anti-CIA protesters. The Academic Council convenes for a special session and, after three-and-a-half hours of debate, votes 284 to 245 to recommend to President Sterling that the proposed suspensions be set aside and no disciplinary action be taken against those sitting in at the Old Union. The Academic Council vote goes against the recommendation of the faculty's own elected executive committee. Sterling reluctantly agrees to the Academic Council recommendations, saying he has "confidence that the great majority of students and faculty on this campus disapprove of coercive tactics and will make that belief known." The faculty asks the students to end the sit-in, which they do. As the 57-hour sit-in is ending, a student referendum favors allowing all employers equal access to campus recruiting facilities by a margin of nearly 6 to 1.

May 16 **STUDENTS OPPOSE SIT-INS:** In a record-breaking turnout, 70 percent of the students voting support the view that forceful occupation of university buildings is "unacceptable behavior." By a 3-to-2 margin they censure student body president Cesare Massarenti for his advocacy and participation in the previous week's sit-in. Activist Denis Hayes defeats topless dancer Vicki Drake 3,458 to 2,136 to be next year's student body president.

June 2 **STUDENTS PAY TRIBUTE TO STERLING:** Led by the Stanford Band, more than 500 students march to the Lou Henry Hoover House to present President Sterling, who will retire on Sept. 1, with a resolution praising his 19 years of service.

July 1 **HOSPITAL UNDER STANFORD CONTROL:** The university becomes sole owner of Palo Alto-Stanford Hospital Center under an agreement approved by the Palo Alto City Council. Stanford pays $1 million cash to the city, assumes $3.5 million worth of hospital construction bond payments over 20 years, and guarantees specified community hospital services until 2008. The hospital center is renamed Stanford University Hospital. Private physicians on the medical staff retain hospital privileges, plus priority to admit patients to 370 of the hospital's 633 beds. The purchase is necessary to permit the School of Medicine freedom and flexibility to develop its academic programs.

July 5 **FIRE DESTROYS STERLING'S OFFICE:** Arson destroys the office of President Sterling. Discovered by Stanford police just before 5 a.m., the fire causes an estimated $300,000 damage, in addition to destroying Sterling's books and personal possessions collected during nearly four decades in higher education.

July 8 **POPULATION BOMB:** Biologist Paul R. Ehrlich's book *The Population Bomb* is published. As it becomes a best-seller, it draws widespread attention to the threat posed by the rapidly expanding global population.

August 19 **KENNETH PITZER APPOINTED PRESIDENT:** Kenneth S. Pitzer, 54, prominent chemist and president of Rice University, is appointed Stanford's sixth president, effective Dec. 1. Student body President Denis Hayes express-

*Students massed in the hallway outside the January 1969 Board of Trustees meeting (right) pour into the Faculty Club meeting room (below) after a student breaks in from the other side to unlock the door.*

*Conservative students disrupt a January 1969 rally of Students for a Democratic Society.*

es "grave reservations" about Pitzer's appointment, but later says it would "in effect destroy this university" to try to stop it. He says he is convinced "a president can be educated by the students." During Pitzer's June 14, 1969, inauguration, trustee John W. Gardner says of the turmoil roiling American campuses, including Stanford: "The extremists, right wing and left wing. . .do not understand that in her hour of agony, America needs physicians, not executioners."

September 1 **GLASER IS ACTING PRESIDENT:** Dr. Robert J. Glaser, vice president for medical affairs and dean of the School of Medicine, serves as acting president until Dec. 1. During his three months, Glaser works with faculty and students to bring war protests under control.

September 12 **FACULTY SENATE BORN:** With the Academic Council membership nearing 1,000, a new faculty representative body, the Faculty Senate holds its first meeting. Physics Prof. Leonard Schiff is elected first chairman. The senate, consisting of 53 (later expanded to 55) representatives elected by the university's seven schools, replaces the nine-member Executive Committee of the Academic Council (the professoriate, plus certain academic and administrative officers). Creation of the senate was first proposed in June 1966 by Prof. Herbert Packer, who sought to promote the role of the faculty as a "coherent, rational, and responsible decision-maker on matters of academic policy." As of 2000, none of its decisions has been overturned on vote of the full faculty.

November **CHICANO ENROLLMENT:** The Mexican-American Student Confederation at Stanford "strongly requests" that the university admit 100 new Mexican-American students during 1969-70. Enrollment of Mexican-American students currently stands at 57. With an intensive five-state recruitment program, the results for fall 1969 pass the goal when 75 freshman, 20 transfer students, and 30 to 40 graduate students bring the campus Chicano total to nearly 200.

November **STUDY OF EDUCATION AT STANFORD:** The first two of 10 reports from the two-year Study of Education at Stanford (SES) are issued. In the coming months, SES recommends a dramatic shift of university teaching resources to the freshman year, a substantial loosening of prescribed courses, major revisions in grading practices, and student opportunities to design their own majors. The committee also advocates continuing educational reform, with a standing committee and an administrative officer. Reforms also are proposed in other areas, including housing, advising, admissions and financial aid, overseas campuses, graduate education, faculty matters, and university governance. Many are adopted, though not all: the suggestion to shift back to the pre-1916 semester system is rejected. An academic planning office is organized to assist students, faculty, and administration in obtaining data on which rational planning can be based. In 1970, the academic advising system for undergraduates is strengthened with a residence-based program, and an advising center is created.

December 3 **PRESIDENT PITZER MEETS SDS:** Two days after taking office, President Pitzer discusses his opposition to the Vietnam War with about 150 representatives of Students for a Democratic Society (SDS).

Conservatives led by Harvey Hukari, right, protest the occupation of the Applied Electronics Lab, urging the administration to stand up to demonstrators.

In April 1969, a group calling itself the April Third Movement wages a campaign against classified and war-related research, and seeks closer control by the university over the semi-autonomous Stanford Research Institute. On April 9, protesters take over the Applied Electronics Laboratory (right), finally voting April 18 (above) to end the occupation.

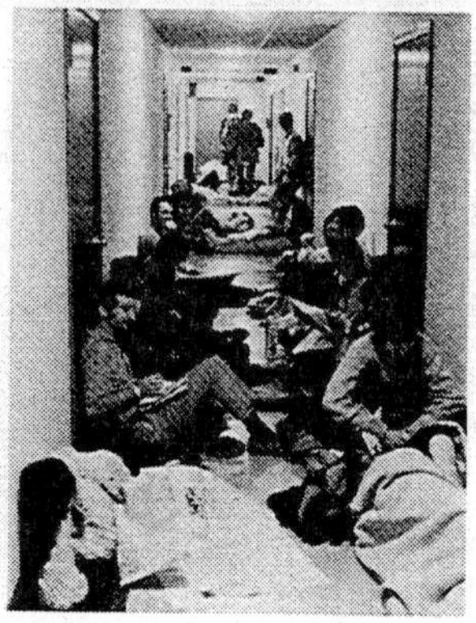

# 1969

January **AFRICAN AND AFRO-AMERICAN STUDIES:** A new interdisciplinary major begins in African and Afro-American studies involving 15 faculty members. It is believed to be the first of its kind at a major private university. Thirteen sophomores and juniors — eight black, five white — sign on as majors.

January 14 **STUDENTS INVADE TRUSTEE MEETING:** About 40 students organized by SDS break into a Board of Trustees' meeting at the Faculty Club, calling on several members to relinquish university or corporate posts and have open trustee meetings, and demanding that Stanford "halt all economic and military operations and projects concerned with Southeast Asia." The meeting is immediately adjourned. Later, 29 students are penalized with probation and fines. More than 1,200 students sign petitions criticizing the disruption.

January 29 **CONSERVATIVES DISRUPT RADICALS:** An SDS rally in the Old Union Courtyard is disrupted by 50 students organized by the Young Republicans and Young Americans for Freedom (YAF), who loudly heckle and wave signs comparing SDS to Hitler. Nevertheless, SDS leader David Pugh allows Harvey Hukari Jr. of YAF to briefly address the crowd. Hukari is editor of the conservative student newspaper *The Arena,* launched in 1968 in reaction to perceived liberal bias in the *Stanford Daily.*

February 11 **ROTC CREDIT DROPPED:** A special student-faculty committee on relations between the university and ROTC department votes 6-3 to deny academic credit for military training and education. The committee says that ROTC departments are, by their nature, incompatible with the university's primary commitment to unrestricted creation and dissemination of knowledge. The recommendation is forwarded to the Faculty Senate, which adopts the proposal two days later, 25-8. Students address the issue in a Feb. 24 referendum, when, by a 3-2 majority, they favor ROTC on campus and credit for parts of the program that are of "genuine academic interest." Trustees in March say that ROTC plays a vital role in the "continued supply of civilian leadership for the military service," and urge President Pitzer to continue negotiations with the Defense Department "leading to appropriate actions which will improve and vitalize this important program." In April, the full faculty votes 403 to 356 to end ROTC academic credit beginning with the 1970 freshman class because appointment of teachers and course content are not subject to usual university controls. President Pitzer begins negotiations with the military to retain ROTC on a noncredit basis, but efforts falter.

March 11 **TRUSTEES MEET STUDENTS:** Five trustees spend two hours in a contentious question-and-answer session with 1,000 students, faculty, and staff in Memorial Auditorium.

April **TELEVISED COURSES:** A program to link engineering firms to campus via a new television network gets its start when the first advanced engineering courses are transmitted to eight Bay Area companies. Frederick Terman encouraged his successor as engineering dean, Joseph Pettit, to start the network after seeing similar systems developed by former student Thomas Martin, dean of engi-

Student body President Denis Hayes addresses 8,000 in a Frost Amphitheater meeting he calls on April 18 to discuss classified and war-related research.

Students elect a "Council of Presidents," headed by Patrick A. Shea, upper right, to run student government. Joining him are John Grube, upper left, Barry Askins, lower left, and Joyce Kobayashi.

Sheriff's riot police, accompanied by faculty observers, enter Encina Hall at 7:15 a.m. May 1, 1969, to clear demonstrators who broke into the administrative nerve center at 1 a.m. Under threat of arrest, the protesters quickly leave.

neering at Southern Methodist University. After 15 years of growth, the Stanford Instructional Television Network (SITN) transmits 170 courses a year in engineering, computer science, math, applied physics, and statistics. It broadcasts 12 hours each weekday on four channels, reaching thousands of students in 100 Bay Area companies and research organizations. The instruction originates in special campus classrooms equipped with cameras, and includes two-way audio feedback to the instructor. At sites beyond the broadcast range, videotapes and local tutors are used in a program of tutored video instruction (TVI) developed in 1974 by Prof. James Gibbons. By the late 1990s, the courses are going to 300 companies using a combination of microwave, videotape, satellite, and two-way digital video technology.

April 3 **APRIL THIRD MOVEMENT BORN:** At a mass meeting in Dinkelspiel Auditorium, students formulate demands to end classified research and war-related research on campus, stopping chemical-biological warfare and counter-insurgency studies at the Stanford Research Institute (SRI), and bringing SRI under closer control of the university. They call themselves the April Third Movement (A3M). Some claim the March 11 session with trustees energized radical and moderate students.

April 9 **PROTESTERS CLOSE ELECTRONICS LAB:** Several hundred A3M protesters occupy the Applied Electronics Laboratory, which does most of the classified research on campus, disrupting its operation for nine days. On April 14, 100 students organized by the Young Americans for Freedom stage a counter-demonstration in which they circle the laboratory with signs reading "End Mob Rule" and "Stop Coercion." The occupation ends on April 18, less than two hours before a deadline imposed by the Stanford Judicial Council. Student body President Denis Hayes calls an unprecedented meeting of the student body that afternoon in Frost Amphitheater. There, 8,000 listen to a discussion of classified and war-related research at Stanford and Stanford Research Institute.

April 25 **COUNCIL OF PRESIDENTS:** Starting a tradition that lasts 27 years, students elect a four-member "Council of Presidents" to run student government. The team consists of Patrick A. Shea, John Grube, Barry Askins, and Joyce Kobayashi. Four-person presidential teams persist until William K. Shen is elected solo ASSU president for 1996-97.

April 30 **PROTESTERS OCCUPY ENCINA HALL:** Members of the A3M testify about their concerns before a trustee committee, then vote to occupy Encina Hall in the evening. Around 1 a.m. they scuffle with 30 conservative students who are blocking the door, but about 200 break into the building through other entrances. Faculty observers say they see numerous incidents of students removing files. University payroll records are ransacked. Provost Lyman summons sheriff's deputies and, under the threat of arrest, the 100 students still there leave the building just before 7:30 a.m. on May 1. Fourteen students subsequently are suspended and 48 more are placed on probation and fined.

May 13 **TRUSTEES SEVER TIES WITH SRI:** Trustees vote unanimously to sever ties with Stanford Research Institute, contrary to the demands of protesters, who want the

Nobel Laureate Linus Pauling receives a standing ovation at his Oct. 15, 1969, Vietnam Moratorium presentation in Memorial Church. More than 8,000 take part in various moratorium events.

*Police use tear gas to disperse students blocking traffic near the Stanford Research Institute building in the Industrial Park. The students are protesting a May 1969 decision by trustees to sever ties with institute.*

*The university in 1969 installs 117 mobile homes – Manzanita trailer park – to cope with a serious housing shortage.*

university to exercise tighter control over the organization. Three days later, about 200 students protesting the action gather at Stanford Research Institute's Hanover Street building in the Industrial Park, blocking traffic on nearby Page Mill Road. After four hours they are dispersed by 130 police using tear gas. Demonstrators smash numerous SRI windows. They return May 19, but are blocked by police. Nearly 100 arrests are made, most of them based on photographs of demonstrators taken by two dozen conservative students from Young Americans for Freedom.

September 24 **MANZANITA TRAILER PARK:** Some 464 students start moving into 117 mobile homes that the university has installed east of Branner Hall to ease a severe housing shortage. Officials say they expect the Manzanita trailer park to remain in operation "not more than five years," but the last of the trailers is not removed until May 1997.

October 15 **VIETNAM MORATORIUM:** In the largest political action gathering in the university's history, more than 8,000 take part in the Vietnam Moratorium, calling for an immediate end to the war. Most classes are canceled or rescheduled as students volunteer their services canvassing in local communities. In the evening, rain forces an outdoor meeting to be moved inside, with Memorial Church and Memorial Auditorium filled to overflowing. Thousands more stand outside in the rain, listening to speeches over loudspeakers.

October 30 **BUDGET PROBLEMS:** A $2.5 million budget cutback in the University's $52 million operating budget over four years is announced. The biggest single factor slowing the university's fiscal growth is the decline in federally sponsored research. Cuts are to be selective, rather than across-the-board, with broad faculty consultation. A year later, the goal is increased to $6 million and the period extended to five years because of new program costs growing out of the Study of Education at Stanford and declining federal support for graduate fellowships. Known on campus as the Budget Adjustment Program (BAP), it gives rise to "bap" as a verb. As the goal is reached in fall 1974, double-digit inflation, a world oil shortage, and a declining stock market create new fiscal problems, and the university announces another program to close a $10 million gap. Stanford is among the first to use long-range forecasting models to predict financial problems. Findings are shared with faculty.

November 11 **BOARD OF TRUSTEES EXPANDS:** Trustees vote to change their body to a minimum of 25 and maximum of 35. In a reorganization recommended by trustee committee headed by John W. Gardner, they add eight alumni trustees to be elected by alumni (four will be 35 or younger and four will be 36 or older). They also reserve two spots for faculty members from other institutions, and include Stanford's president as an *ex officio* member. Students and Stanford faculty are invited to serve, with voting rights, on most trustee committees. The change follows recommendations that the board should be more representative of society — professionally, politically, geographically, and in age distribution. In 1994, direct election of alumni trustees is changed to an application-and-selection process.

# 1970

**STATISTICS:**

Undergraduate enrollment: 6,303

Graduate enrollment: 6,126

Faculty: 1,029

Tuition: $2,400 per year

Endowment: $271 million

January 13 **STANFORD RESEARCH INSTITUTE TO BE INDEPENDENT:** Trustees reach agreement to separate Stanford Research Institute, founded in 1946, from the university. This action is prompted by protests against the institute's war-related and classified research. The organization will change its name to SRI International. The agreement calls for SRI to pay Stanford 1 percent of its gross revenues each year until $25 million has been paid. Thereafter, the payment will drop to 0.5 percent.

February 27 **FRENCH PRESIDENT VISITS:** French President Georges Pompidou visits Stanford Linear Accelerator Center (SLAC).

March 30 **LIMITED CREDIT FOR ROTC:** The faculty approves a one-year trial plan that would allow Army ROTC to offer limited credit. The faculty voted last spring to phase-out credit, but makes this change in an effort to avoid the "punitive clause" in ROTC contracts, which threaten ROTC cadets with immediate enlisted service if they withdraw from the program or the program is stopped.

April 1 **PRESIDENT PITZER DOUSED WITH PAINT:** An unidentified, masked and robed assailant dumps red water-soluble paint on the shoulders and back of President Kenneth Pitzer as he talks with students at Grove House.

April **HUMAN BIOLOGY PROGRAM BORN:** More than 400 register for the first course offered in the new interdisciplinary program in Human Biology, started with a $1.9 million Ford Foundation grant. By 1985 the program will become one of the five most popular majors.

April **ROTC PROTEST:** Crowds of students, including many high schoolers, resort to violence to protest the continued presence of ROTC on campus. A crowd of about 300 roams the campus night after night in early April smashing windows. On April 3, the start of the Academic Council's spring quarter meeting is delayed when 140 demonstrators enter the meeting room. They leave when President Pitzer declares the meeting disrupted, a declaration that could trigger arrests. In a record turnout in mid-April, students vote narrowly in favor of keeping ROTC on campus, but by a nearly-two-to-one margin express the opinion that ROTC should not have academic credit. On April 23, anti-ROTC demonstrators move into the lobby of the Old Union, scuffling with 30 members of the libertarian Free Campus Movement, who lock arms to prevent them from entering. President Pitzer declares the building closed at 5 p.m. and occupants are warned to leave or face arrest. At 1 a.m. the following day, sheriff's deputies arrest 22. Many escape the police, again breaking windows.

April 24 **ARSON DESTROYS LIFE'S WORK:** Several hours after the Old Union sit-in ends, arson at the Center for Advanced Study in the Behavioral Sciences destroys the life work of several prominent scholars, including Prof. M.N. Srinivas, India's leading social scientist, who loses 22 years' worth of research material about caste systems in India.

April 29 **CAMBODIA INVASION PROTESTED**: After reports of an imminent U.S. invasion of Cambodia, a day-long sit-in at the Old Union erupts into a rock-throwing, club-wielding battle between several hundred students and more than 250 police. Tear gas is used to disperse crowds. Sixteen antiwar and anti-ROTC demonstrators are arrested, a dozen injured, and 30 police are hurt by thrown stones and other objects. Afterward, roving rock-throwers break windows in numerous buildings. President Pitzer and Provost Lyman condemn the invasion.

April 30 **ROTC, CAMBODIA PROTEST:** For the second

*Conservative students lock arms in a futile effort to block anti-ROTC demonstrators from entering the Old Union on April 23, 1970.*

*Most of the 4,000 attending a Frost Amphitheater rally on April 30, 1970, (right) favor a nonviolent strike, but demonstrators later break front-door glass at Encina. A group of students who oppose ROTC, but also oppose violence, station themselves (left) between police who are protecting Encina and demonstrators throwing rocks over their heads.*

day, demonstrators demanding immediate elimination of ROTC battle police; they now add withdrawal from Cambodia to their demands. During a Frost Amphitheater rally called to discuss the U.S. action in Cambodia, a radical faction advocates violence, but most of the crowd of 4,000 favors a nonviolent strike. As the rally breaks up, hundreds mass in front of the nearby Athletics Building on Galvez Street, which houses ROTC on its second floor. The crowd moves to the front of Encina Hall, and police arrive shortly after demonstrators break its front-door glass. A group of 300 nonviolent students then forms a line between protesters and police while chanting "Off ROT-C, no rocks." Protesters throw rocks over their heads at police, then move toward White Plaza. Windows are smashed in at least 15 buildings and rocks and red paint are thrown into the homes of Provost Lyman and Provost Emeritus Terman. Police again use tear gas. The violence lasts until about 2 a.m. Earlier in the day, the Faculty Senate, citing changed circumstances, decides to reopen the ROTC issue. Property damage for the month is estimated at $100,000, with 73 injuries in the past two nights.

May 1 **CAMPUS TURMOIL:** About 3,500 meet in Frost Amphitheater to discuss whether to boycott classes or engage in more violence. Most favor the boycott. Hundreds of protesters block entrances to Encina Hall, which houses financial and business offices. President Pitzer warns a special three-hour session of the Academic Council that the university faces an "extreme emergency." Faculty give him a standing ovation when he says he "intend(s) to defend this university." Imposing a curfew is a possibility, he adds. Toward the end of the three-hour session, Pitzer receives a petition signed by 2,000 students, faculty, and staff expressing support for "whatever legal measures must be taken to preserve the integrity, the tranquillity, and the academic viability of our university." Late in the day, three shotgun blasts are fired into the campus home of the Army ROTC commander. No one is hurt.

May 3 **NONVIOLENT STRIKE:** At a White Plaza rally, 1,000 students vote for a nonviolent strike, which begins on Monday, the next day, with most classes canceled. Many strikers continue blocking Encina Hall, the Athletics/ROTC Building, and engineering laboratories. Several departments call mass meetings of students and faculty to discuss responses to the escalation of the Southeast Asia war and campus strife. On May 5, about 30 faculty and student leaders leave for Washington for talks with government officials, as numerous teach-ins about the war are held. The strike continues all week, with Pitzer canceling classes on Friday, May 9.

May 7 **SENATE ENDS ROTC CREDIT:** The Faculty Senate votes to end academic credit for ROTC programs effective Aug. 31. This comes two days after the Air Force, citing low enrollment, announces it will end ROTC at Stanford on June 30, 1971. The senate also condemns America's invasion of Cambodia. The strike continues, with clusters of students blocking entrances to physics, electronics, and the aeronautics and astronautics building, stopping re-

*Plywood panels and masking tape cover windows in many campus buildings following nights of rock throwing in April and May 1970.*

*Richard W. Lyman, appointed Stanford's seventh president on Sept. 24, 1970. He leaves his introductory press conference with his wife, Elizabeth "Jing" (right). Lyman institutes weekly sessions with the student media, carried live on campus radio station KZSU (above).*

search for the Defense Department and shutting down all other work in the laboratories.

May 11 **STRIKE ENDS; JUDICIAL ACTION INITIATED:** After a quiet weekend, the university announces it is filing charges with the Stanford Judicial Council against 55 students in the April 23 and April 29 Old Union sit-ins. Most classes meet, many for the first time in a week. The next day, the university declares the strikers at Electronics Research Laboratory to be in violation of the university disruption policy. Protesters abandon the blockades there and at Encina.

May 18 **ROTC BLOCKADE:** For the 10th day, entrances to the Athletics/ROTC building continue to be blocked 10 hours a day. After a Radical Caucus meeting in Roble Hall, a band of about 75 demonstrators moves swiftly across campus, tossing rocks through windows of the Athletics/ROTC building, aeronautics and astronautics, the Hoover Institution, and smaller buildings. Seven persons involved in earlier incidents are arrested by sheriff's deputies. The blockade ends on May 24, when strikers vow to return if President Pitzer fails to end ROTC.

June **GRADING SYSTEM CHANGE:** Following recommendations from a committee study, the Faculty Senate approves changes in the grading system for undergraduates that will replace "D" and "F" grades with "no credit."

June 4 **FACULTY BARS FUTURE ROTC ENROLLMENT:** In the wake of the Cambodia invasion, the Faculty Senate votes 26-8, with three abstentions, to bar future enrollment of new students in ROTC, a position upheld by the full Academic Council.

June 25 **PRESIDENT PITZER RESIGNS:** Nineteen months after taking over as president, Kenneth Pitzer announces his resignation, effective Sept. 1. In a letter to the Board of Trustees, he says that "deep divisions. . .beset our country" and "as a result, pressures tending to distract or disrupt the educational process have increased significantly. These trends have made it increasingly difficult to obtain the very broad and active support from all those groups who together are responsible for the well-being of the university." At a press conference, he says his resignation was "not forced" by trustees, but that there are "sufficient weaknesses" in support of the university that "needed to be taken into account."

August **OFFICE OF TECHNOLOGY LICENSING:** After a year's pilot program, the Office of Technology Licensing (OTL) is formally established. Income in the pilot year, with part-time help from one person, is $55,000. Thirty years later, OTL staff numbers 26, a new invention is being submitted, on average, each working day, and total income is $36.9 million.

September **INCREASE IN NATIVE AMERICAN ENROLLMENT:** An intensive recruiting effort has led to enrollment of 23 native Americans in the freshman class. The six

Heisman Trophy winner Jim Plunkett leads Stanford to a 27-17 victory over Ohio State in the 1971 Rose Bowl.

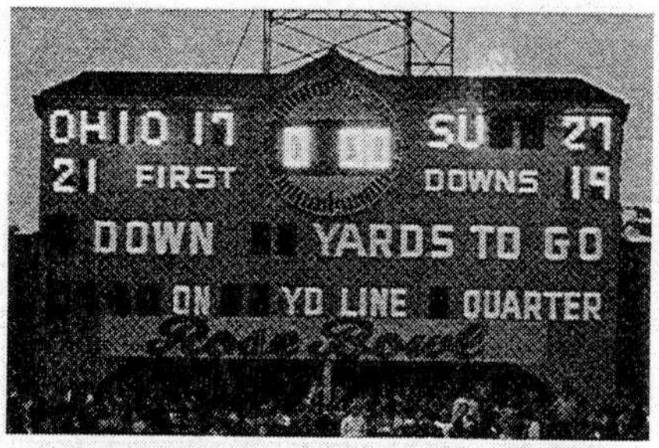

*Noisy anti-war protesters disrupt the Dinkelspiel Auditorium speech of Ambassador Henry Cabot Lodge on Jan. 11, 1971.*

American Indians registered last year suggested the campaign and helped with recruiting. By fall 1973, the number increases to 57 undergraduates and 22 graduate students.

September 24 **RICHARD W. LYMAN NAMED PRESIDENT:** Trustees name Richard W. Lyman, 46, as Stanford's seventh president, effective immediately. An expert in contemporary British history, he joined the History Department in 1958, was named associate dean of Humanities and Sciences in 1964, and was chosen by President Sterling in 1967 to serve as vice president and provost. Lyman has played a key role in dealing with campus unrest. His appointment is widely praised by faculty, alumni, and student leaders. In 1971, Lyman takes his inaugural ceremony "to the people" on a cross-country swing to six major cities. Back home, he begins weekly live press conferences with student journalists on campus radio station KZSU.

# 1971

January 1 **ROSE BOWL VICTORY:** Quarterback and Heisman Trophy winner Jim Plunkett, under the direction of Coach John Ralston, leads Stanford to a 27-17 victory over Ohio State in the Rose Bowl.

January **ARMS CONTROL:** More than 200 students register for a new course on "Problems of Arms Control and Disarmament," a multi-disciplinary undergraduate course organized by the faculty Committee on International Relations. This eventually leads to creation of Stanford's Center for International Security and Arms Control.

January 3 **GRADUATE PROGRAM RANKINGS:** The American Council on Education's rating of graduate programs in 1969 — just published — ranks Stanford faculty among the top five nationally in 16 of 32 fields. Stanford's overall strength is exceeded by only Berkeley, Harvard, and Yale.

January 11 **HENRY CABOT LODGE SPEECH DISRUPTED:** Protesting the war in Vietnam, 50 noisy demonstrators, with hundreds of supporters looking on, interrupt U.N. Ambassador Henry Cabot Lodge while he tries to deliver a speech to a Hoover Institution Conference on the United Nations at Dinkelspiel Auditorium. Lodge finally gives up trying to speak, and Hoover officials find an alternate location where he finishes his presentation before a select audience of 150.

February 10 **STUDENTS SEIZE COMPUTATION CENTER:** Protesting the invasion of Laos by the South Vietnamese, with U.S. air support, students seize the Computation Center during 12 hours of confrontation and violence aimed at shutting down the university. There are 12 arrests and 10 injuries. During a noon White Plaza rally, Associate Prof. H. Bruce Franklin says protesters should "begin to shut down the most obvious machinery of the war, such as the Computer Center." After the rally, 150 demonstrators mill around in the Computation Center, which contains about $5 million in computer equipment. Photogra-

*Protesting the invasion of Laos, students on Feb. 10, 1971, seize the Computation Center. When busloads of deputies arrive, they leave the building, but continue milling around until police "sweep" the area. Graduate student Janet Cooper Weiss exhorts the crowd (left), and H. Bruce Franklin, associate professor of English, argues (right) with a police captain. On Feb. 12, President Lyman suspends Franklin from the faculty.*

phers are banned from the building and a Viet Cong flag is posted overhead. Students vacate the building in the late afternoon when 80 to 100 sheriff's deputies arrive. After repeated warnings that the crowd outside the building should disperse, police conduct a quick sweep that catches protesters, photographers, and reporters off guard. At an 8 p.m. rally in the Old Union courtyard, speakers debate demands and tactics. Franklin calls for a "people's war" in the face of an "occupation army" of police. Small groups "can do their thing, whatever they feel they ought to do...as late at night as possible," he says. Shortly before 11 p.m. the 16-year-old son of a professor is shot in the right thigh while standing near the headquarters of the Free Campus Movement (FCM). Earlier, eight FCM members who watched the Old Union rally were assaulted as they walked across White Plaza.

February 12 **BRUCE FRANKLIN SUSPENDED:** President Lyman suspends Associate Prof. Franklin with pay for allegedly participating in the Jan. 11 disruption of Henry Cabot Lodge's speech and allegedly initiating the shutdown of the Computation Center on Feb. 10. The university obtains a temporary restraining order enjoining Franklin, 16 other named individuals, and up to 1,000 "John Does" from committing destructive or disruptive acts. On March 22, Lyman files formal charges with the Advisory Board. In a petition calling for an inquiry into Franklin's actions at the Computation Center, 24 history, economics, and law professors say "incitement by any faculty member of this university to riot and civil war on campus warrants dismissal."

March **LAND USE PLAN:** Livingston & Blayney, a San Francisco urban planning firm, presents to trustees a detailed report the board commissioned showing alternative uses of thousands of acres of Stanford lands in Santa Clara and San Mateo County and the potential impacts of those uses. The plan explores a range of academic, residential, commercial, and institutional uses of the property. Trustees accept the plan, but take no action on it.

April 9 **HOSPITAL SIT-IN TURNS VIOLENT:** Police end a 30-hour sit-in at the hospital administration offices, arresting 23 of more than 50 demonstrators who cause $100,000 damage protesting the firing of a black employee. Fewer than half those arrested are associated with the university. When police use a battering ram to break through heavy glass doors, demonstrators respond by turning fire hoses on them. Twenty people, mostly police, are injured. In May, the National Labor Relations Board upholds the firing that triggered the protest.

April 12 **POLICE SEARCH *STANFORD DAILY*:** Armed with a search warrant, Palo Alto police search photographic files, desks, wastebaskets, and stacks of old newspapers at the *Stanford Daily* office for photographic evidence of the April 9 hospital demonstration. They leave empty handed after 45 minutes. It is the first known use of a search warrant in an American newspaper office. Past practice calls for use of a court subpoena to obtain such evidence. On May 12 the

Police on April 9, 1971, climb over obstacles to end a 30-hour sit-in protesting the firing of a janitor at Stanford Hospital. Three days later, police armed with a search warrant search the Stanford Daily for photographic evidence.

The annual Native American Pow Wow, seen here in 1974, gets its start in May 1971, when more than 1,000 American Indians gather for their first Stanford encampment.

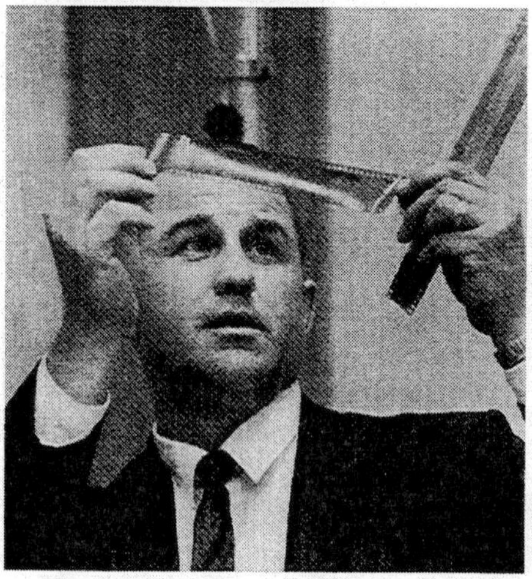

*Daily* files a lawsuit, which is to become known as the *Stanford Daily vs. Zurcher* (Palo Alto's police chief). A U.S. District Court judge declares the search illegal in 1972, as does the U.S. Circuit Court of Appeals in 1977, but in 1978 the U.S. Supreme Court rules 5-3 in Zurcher's favor. During the 12 years following the *Daily* search, based on this precedent, police conduct at least 63 searches nationwide of journalists, lawyers, doctors, and psychotherapists who are not suspects.

April 13 **INVESTMENT RESPONSIBILITY POLICY:** The Board of Trustees becomes the first governing body of a major academic institution to adopt a statement of investment responsibility. It states that in the majority of cases, obtaining maximum financial return is the board's primary fiduciary duty. But "independent consideration and weight" will be given on an individual basis in those cases where "the undesirable social, economic, and political acts of the company involved are direct and substantial." A month later, the board urges General Motors to try to improve conditions for nonwhites in South Africa. In 1978 the board revises its policy: while maximum financial return is still the primary goal, in cases where a company's activities or policies "cause social injury," the board should favor shareholder proposals that would "eliminate or materially reduce" this harm. Divestment will be considered as a last resort, according to the new policy.

April 17 **PLATE TECTONICS:** Prof. Allan V. Cox, a geophysicist, is co-winner of the 1971 Vetlesen Prize — often described as the Nobel Prize of earth sciences — for his paleomagnetic research, which has been fundamental in the development of the plate tectonics theory. That theory holds that the earth's surface is composed of about 16 slowly shifting crustal plates that ride on hotter and less rigid material beneath them.

April 21 **DEMANDS TO END WAR:** A letter signed by nearly 1,600 Stanford women calling for total withdrawal of American forces from Southeast Asia is sent to President Nixon. Also in April, the Academic Council, in a 418-to-249 vote, endorses a Faculty Senate resolution urging Nixon and Congress to bring American involvement in Southeast Asia "to a speedy and complete end."

April 23 **BOMBING AND ARSON DAMAGE:** A bomb planted at the President's Office explodes in the early morning hours, causing $25,000 damage to the roof, attic, and second floor. A campus security guard on duty in the building escapes injury. Three days later, an arson fire guts the Junipero Lounge in Wilbur Hall, causing more than $50,000 damage. The lounge is frequently used for meetings by the Black Student Union. More than 750 faculty and students sign an ad in the *Stanford Daily* deploring the fire.

May 1-2 **NATIVE AMERICAN POW WOW:** More than 1,000 American Indians from Western states gather for the first of what becomes an annual encampment on the intramural fields. The event, featuring religious ceremonies and dancing, is sponsored by the Stanford American

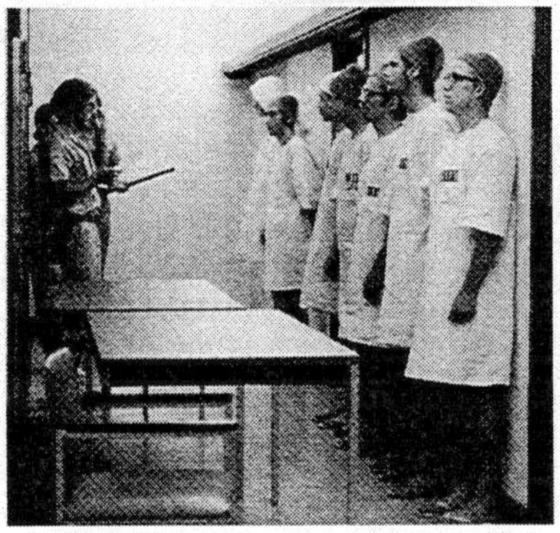

*Students in August 1971 play the roles of prisoners and guards in a psychology class experiment.*

*The faculty Advisory Board in fall 1971 holds hearings on the proposed dismissal of Associate Prof. H. Bruce Franklin. Biology Prof. Donald Kennedy, fourth from left, chairs the board.*

Indian Organization.

August 15 **PRISON EXPERIMENT:** Nine students are "arrested" as part of Prof. Philip Zimbardo's summer quarter course on the "Psychology of the Imprisoned." A dozen other students guard the "prisoners" in a makeshift jail. The planned 14-day experiment becomes a bit too life-like, and Zimbardo suspends it after five days.

September 28 **FRANKLIN HEARINGS:** The faculty Advisory Board, headed by biology Prof. Donald Kennedy, conducts hearings to decide whether Associate Prof. H. Bruce Franklin should be dismissed from the faculty for his role in demonstrations on Jan. 11 and Feb. 10. The hearings, broadcast on campus radio station KZSU, run until Nov. 5, six days a week, five hours a day, with testimony from 110 witnesses.

October **CELL BIOLOGY TOOL:** Genetics Prof. Leonard Herzenberg and colleagues develop a revolutionary new tool for studying basic cell biology. Called the fluorescence-activated cell sorter (FACS), it enables scientists to identify and isolate closely related types of animal cells at rates of up to 5,000 cells per second. FACS machines will aid basic research in laboratories throughout the world.

# 1972

January 1 **ROSE BOWL VICTORY (AGAIN):** With Don Bunce as quarterback, Stanford pulls out a dramatic, last-minute victory over Michigan in the Rose Bowl. With 12 seconds left, Rod Garcia kicks a 31-yard field goal to make the final score 13-12. Four days later, Coach John Ralston announces he's leaving to join professional football. Bunce later earns an M.D. in orthopedics at the university and becomes one of Stanford's team physicians.

January 5 **BRUCE FRANKLIN FIRED:** The faculty Advisory Board votes 5-2 to recommend dismissal of Associate Prof. H. Bruce Franklin on charges of inciting occupation of the Computation Center on Feb. 10, 1971, urging defiance of a police order to disperse, and encouraging a nighttime rally for violent action. He is cleared of charges stemming from the Henry Cabot Lodge incident Jan. 11, 1971. Following the Advisory Board's decision, Franklin holds a press conference, expressing hope there will be more violence on campus. He tells reporters, "Whatever happens is not enough." His wife, Jane, stands at his side holding a carbine she says is unloaded. President Lyman endorses the board's recommendation. On Jan. 22, the Board of Trustees votes 20-2 to uphold the Advisory Board decision, and Franklin is formally dismissed from the faculty on Jan. 24. Scattered incidents follow a rally supporting Franklin attended by 800. A firebomb placed outside the home of Advisory Board member Sanford Dornbusch fails to ignite. Two hundred faculty members sign statements condemning the act and offering a $5,000 reward for information leading to conviction of the person responsible. Franklin and the American Civil Liberties Union file a lawsuit seek-

Timm Williams, a Yurok from Northern California, dances as the band mascot. The university forces him to stop after it discontinues the Indian mascot in 1972.

*Two-for-two: Stanford wins the Rose Bowl for the second year in a row when Rod Garcia kicks a 31-yard field goal with 12 seconds on the clock on Jan. 1, 1972. The final score: Stanford 13, Michigan 12.*

ing his reinstatement. In January 1986 the California State Supreme Court refuses to hear an appeal of a lower court ruling upholding the firing. After leaving Stanford, Franklin is appointed to the Rutgers faculty.

March 2 **INDIAN MASCOT DISCONTINUED:** The ASSU Senate votes 18 to 4 in favor of President Lyman's recommendation that the "Indian" be discontinued as the university mascot. In 1930, the Indian image had joined the color cardinal red to symbolize Stanford athletic spirit, but growing concern for the use of a stereotyped racial image brings increasing criticism from Native American students and staff and other members of the Stanford community. A series of student referenda in 1972, 1975, 1977, and 1981 fails to select an alternative acceptable to all constituencies. The most popular candidates, the Thunderchickens (1972) and the Robber Barons (1975, 1977), are ignored by the Department of Athletics. In 1981, a student referendum, the ASSU Senate, and a university Mascot Advisory Committee favor retaining cardinal alone, which President Kennedy approves. The Stanford Band adopts the Tree as its mascot in 1975 to replace "Prince Lightfoot," Timm Williams, a Yurok from Northern California who had danced with the band as its mascot from 1952 to 1972. Two Band members concoct the Tree as a spoof on mascots.

April **SLAC UPGRADES:** The Stanford Electron Positron Accelerating Ring (SPEAR) is completed as an upgrade of the SLAC facility. This synchrotron storage ring with counter-circulating bunches of electrons and positrons, built under the leadership of Prof. Burton Richter, will provide the data for two Nobel prizes in physics and pioneer the use of synchrotron radiation as a source of intense X-ray and ultraviolet light with many applications.

April 11 **CAMPAIGN FOR STANFORD:** Trustee President Robert Minge Brown announces a five-year drive to raise $300 million, the largest goal yet for any university. In May 1977, the fundraising campaign tops its goal by $4 million, with funds for buildings, endowed chairs, student loan and scholarship funds, and a $132 million boost to the university's endowment. Chancellor J.E. Wallace Sterling serves as co-chair with trustee Richard E. Guggenhime.

April 20 **MORE ANTIWAR PROTESTS:** Protests against the Vietnam War continue. Police break up efforts by 400 to reach Hansen Laboratories during evening torchlit parades. The next day, 1,200 protesters rally at White Plaza against escalation of bombing, after which 600 march around campus. They then vote to "take" El Camino Real. About 100 police repeatedly charge the group at El Camino and Embarcadero, arresting 205 who block traffic.

May 1 **TWO PULITZERS:** Two faculty members are awarded Pulitzer Prizes: Prof. Carl N. Degler for history and Prof. Emeritus Wallace E. Stegner for fiction. Degler wins for *Neither Black Nor White: Slavery and Race Relations in Brazil and the United States*. Degler came to the Stanford faculty from Vassar in 1968. Stegner receives a Pulitzer for his novel *Angle of Repose*. Stegner came to Stanford in 1945 and

A fire of suspicious origin causes $1 million damage to Encina Hall, the main administration building, on June 7, 1972. Lights in the building make it appear the whole structure is ablaze, but the fire is limited to the east wing and the central wing attic.

unched the Creative Writing Program.

lay 9 **WAR PROTESTS (CONTINUED):** Speaking to a oon rally of 900 antiwar protesters at White Plaza, forier Associate Prof. H. Bruce Franklin urges the crowd to take the Old Union and the Placement Center. . .and iove from there to shut down the university." The stuents occupy those buildings; they are moved in the vening, without arrests, by sheriff's deputies. A group of aw School students and professors stages a peaceful iarch to Palo Alto, joined by 700, on May 12. Several days ter, President Lyman meets with government officials in Vashington, D.C., about the impact of foreign actions on ampus. In a KZSU interview from Washington, he reports surprising sympathy" for cutting off federal funds to initutions that have dropped ROTC programs.

ine 7 **ENCINA FIRE:** A nighttime fire, thought by many be arson, causes $1 million damage to Encina Hall, the niversity's main administration building. It starts in the ttic of the central wing, then spreads to the upper floors f the east wing. In the previous four years there had been t least 30 incidents on campus of arson, attempted arson, ombing, or attempted bombing.

ine 8 **MALE-FEMALE RATIO:** The Faculty Senate endorss a committee report suggesting that the university hould make it clear that their are no pre-set targets for the ndergraduate male-female ratio. The committee says the atio should be determined by the nature of the applicant pool. Although gender has not been a criterion for admission in recent years and the enrollment ratios are similar to the application ratios, there is a widespread view that the approximately two-to-one undergraduate ratio is current university policy. The Board of Trustees in September agrees to initiate legal proceedings to remove Jane Stanford's 1899 amendment to the Founding Grant, after which it will rescind its resolution of 1933 limiting women's undergraduate enrollment to about 40 percent. In March 1973, the Santa Clara County Superior Court grants the request, which restores the original provision of the Founding Grant that requires trustees "to afford equal facilities and give equal advantages in the university to both sexes." *(See also May 31, 1899, and May 11, 1933)*

June 29 **DEATH PENALTY DECISION:** Following an oral argument by law Prof. Anthony Amsterdam, the U.S. Supreme Court rules 5-4 in *Furman v. Georgia* that legal executions are "cruel and unusual punishment," in violation of the Eighth Amendment. The ruling spares 640 lives.

July **HOOVER INSTITUTION ON DOMESTIC ISSUES:** The Hoover Institution, long famous as a center for research in international affairs, announces it will focus equal attention on domestic issues, including such problems as immigration, health care, social security, welfare reform, federal regulation of industry, and drug abuse.

September **FEMALE FACULTY:** Associate Prof. Barbara Babcock is the first woman to join the Law School faculty.

*Jasper Ridge, a naturally diverse portion of the Stanford foothills, long a source of study for biology students and faculty, is officially designated a biological preserve in 1973. It includes Searsville Lake.*

The Business School appoints three female assistant professors: Francine Gordon, Linda Sprague, and Myra Strober.

November **LIBRARY TECHNOLOGY:** The automated library system BALLOTS (Bibliographic Automation of Large Library Operations using a Time-sharing System) is installed, a first step in computerizing the University Libraries. Development of BALLOTS started in 1967. It is a computer database that integrates procurement, cataloging, and reference activities.

# 1973

January 3 **OVERSEAS STUDIES:** As student interest in the overseas campuses wanes and the program's academic quality is called into question, a presidential commission issues its review of the program. It recommends continuing and strengthening the overseas campuses by enhancing academic coherence and quality, creating more flexibility in program development, involving the students more directly in the culture and academic programs of host countries, and locating campuses in major cultural centers rather than rural areas. These suggestions are implemented.

January 9 **JASPER RIDGE BIOLOGICAL PRESERVE:** Jasper Ridge, a natural laboratory in the campus foothills, is officially designated as the Jasper Ridge Biological Preserve by the Board of Trustees. It contains all plant communities found in the Coast Range except those of the ocean front, and more than half of those found throughout California. Scientists have been attracted to the ridge since the time of David Starr Jordan. In November 1976, Searsville Lake, leased out for recreational swimming since the 1920s, is closed to the public and incorporated into Jasper Ridge, adding 320 acres to the preserve, which now totals 1,189 acres. The ridge takes its name from jasper, a red form of chert (a rock resembling flint). The preserve is located southwest of Interstate Highway 280, between the Westridge area of Portola Valley and Sand Hill Road. It is fenced and entry is limited.

January 29 ***STANFORD DAILY* SET FREE:** The *Stanford Daily* becomes an independent newspaper, organized as a nonprofit corporation. Although student editors discussed independence as early as 1963, the change is prompted by President Lyman after a *Daily* columnist in 1970 advocated killing prison informants ("take care of snitches," he wrote). A *Daily* editorial says "there will no longer be the threat of potential censorship by the university or the Associated Students," which formerly published the paper and shut it down briefly in 1957 in a dispute over authority to select the editor.

April 14 **BAND SHACK IS HISTORY:** After moving to the old power plant on Galvez Street, the Incomparable Leland Stanford Junior University Marching Band stages a bring-your-own-sledgehammer party to demolish its former

*The Band Shack must go. Everyone gets into the act on April 14, 1973: As a cannon fires, First Lady Jing Lyman starts the action by throwing a bottle of champagne through a window. President Lyman swings his red-ribboned sledgehammer. The Dollies help. The old wooden structure offers more resistance than expected, but eventually collapses.*

headquarters, a wooden structure built 75 years earlier as the campus's public restaurant. The party starts with First Lady Jing Lyman throwing a bottle of champagne into the doomed structure. The band's cannon then sounds and President Lyman delivers the first blow with his red-ribboned sledgehammer. The Band Shack, headquarters since the 1930s, is surprisingly strong, but eventually 200 musicians, alumni, and friends knock it down. Later that night, a "mysterious" fire eliminates the need for a bulldozer. After the next quarter century in the old power plant — now spelled Band "Shak" — the band moves in 1998 to the old Encina Gym, when the power plant is torn down to make way for a new alumni center.

April 24 **WOMEN CAMPAIGN FOR THE SENATE:** Ten women are elected to the 53-member Faculty Senate, the first time since the representative body was formed in 1968 that the senate has more than two women members.

June 7 **LABOR UNION:** United Stanford Employees wins the right to represent 1,500 technical, maintenance, and service workers on campus in a 660-494 vote. In May 1974, the union goes on strike for three weeks during negotiations for its first contract.

June 16 **ROTC ENDS:** Ending 54 years of association between the university and the Reserve Officer Training Corps, 14 undergraduates are the final ROTC officers commissioned at Stanford. The Army ROTC program was established on campus in 1916; Air Force and Navy programs started in 1946. More than 2,000 Army, Navy, Air Force, and Marine officers from Stanford have received commissions. In the future, some students cross-enroll in ROTC at other institutions, including UC-Berkeley, San Jose State, and University of Santa Clara. They receive no academic credit from Stanford for the classes.

October 9 **STUDENT OPTICAL OBSERVATORY:** An optical astronomy observatory with a 16-inch telescope is dedicated on a hilltop near the Golf Course, with university trustees in attendance. It is a monument to student enterprise and determination: Students designed it, raised nearly $50,000 for materials and equipment, and then built the structure themselves. UC-Berkeley donated a salvaged observatory dome, and North American Rockwell gave a $25,000 telescope mount. Student enthusiasm spurs development of a two-quarter course in astronomy for non-science undergraduates, and a one-year course for science majors.

November **RECOMBINANT DNA:** Genetics Prof. Stanley Cohen, research associate Annie Chang, and a team from the University of California at San Francisco led by Prof. Herbert Boyer publish their success in the transfer of selected portions of DNA from one string of DNA to another. This is the genesis of what becomes the biotechnology industry. By the expiration of the patent for the technique, filed in 1974 and managed by Stanford, 478 companies pay license royalties of $255 million, with the net income split between Stanford and UCSF.

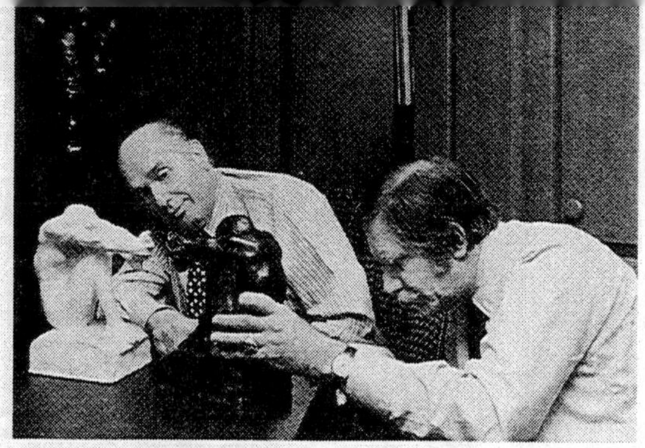

Art Prof. Albert Elsen (right above) and Rodin collector B. Gerald Cantor study two casts of Despair from about 1890. Cantor gives much of his collection to Stanford in 1974. Rodin's Gates of Hell is installed next to the museum in 1985.

Students build an optical observatory in the hills behind campus in 1973.

# 1974

February 11 **RODIN COLLECTION:** B. Gerald Cantor, holder of the largest private collection of Auguste Rodin's sculptures, announces that a significant portion of his collection will be given to the university. In May 1985, a one-acre outdoor Rodin sculpture garden, dominated by Rodin's *Gates of Hell*, opens next to the Museum.

March 8 **STREAKING:** A group of 45 students takes up the latest fad, streaking, running naked across the Golden Gate Bridge at rush hour. They name their run the First Annual Fred Pierce Streak after the retired State Court of Appeals judge who "streaked" Sorority Row in 1918 to win a $5 bet.

March 12 **LAND USE PLAN:** Trustees adopt a new land use policy based on retaining the bulk of the university's open lands for future academic needs. The new policy changes the board's long-standing view of the outlying lands as a financial asset, available for commercial development to earn income for the institution. The lands are to be regarded instead as an academic reserve, held for possible low-intensity educational uses that respect the environment and leave ridge lines and hilltops free of structures.

April 4 **TOP GYMNAST:** Steve Hug wins the NCAA all-around gymnastics title for the third year in a row.

May **SYNCHROTRON RADIATION LABORATORY:** The Stanford Synchrotron Radiation Project (SSRP) becomes a formally constituted entity at SLAC, providing a facility for scientists from many disciplines to use synchrotron-produced X-ray and ultraviolet light beams to study matter at the atomic and molecular scale. This opens the door to a rich variety of studies in condensed-matter physics, materials science, chemistry, and biochemistry, ranging from elucidating the structure of biological enzymes and proteins to detecting impurities on the surface of silicon wafers. The project is renamed the Stanford Synchrotron Radiation Laboratory (SSRL) in 1977.

June **NURSING SCHOOL CLOSES:** The School of Nursing closes after awarding final degrees to 18 women. A 1973 study recommended that a two-year master's program replace the bachelor's program, in which students complete two years of undergraduate work before entering the nursing school for three years. School alumnae press for a new program, but no funds can be found to finance it. Stanford has been the last private, nonsectarian university on the West Coast to offer a bachelor's degree in nursing. The school began in 1897 when six nurses graduated from the Lane Hospital Training School in San Francisco.

October 15 **FLORY WINS NOBEL:** Chemist Paul J. Flory wins a Nobel Prize. *(See page 154)*

# 1975

February **CAMPUS CULTURE:** The Drama Department

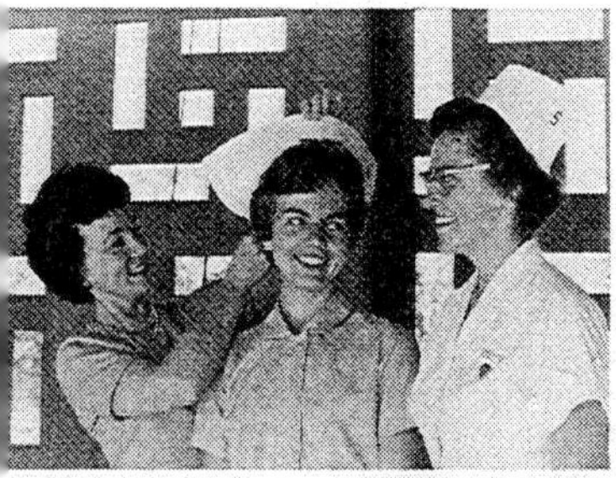

he School of
lursing closes
1 1974.

Prof. David Hamburg and students Steve Smith and Barbara Smuts talk to reporters after the students are released by Zairian guerrillas who kidnapped them, on May 19, 1975, from a primate research center in Africa.

President Lyman plays the role of Sir Rupert Murgatroyd, center, in 1975.

tages *The Beggar's Opera* in the large scene shop behind Memorial Auditorium. The barn-like cavernous room, replete with high windows, huge doors, and aging rafters, is he perfect setting for the bawdy 18th-century musical omedy. In April, President Richard W. Lyman plays Sir Rupert Murgatroyd in the Stanford Savoyard's production of *Ruddigore* at Dinkelspiel Auditorium.

ebruary **UNDERGRADUATE RESEARCH OPPORTUNITIES:** More than 100 undergraduates are taking part in a new program that identifies faculty research projects that have a need for undergraduate assistance. In late 1984, the program begins awarding grant money for undergraduate research. The following spring, the first grants are given for independent research by undergraduates — 54 grants totaling $74,000. By 1999, that number grows to 398 grants totaling $612,000.

March 12 **MEN'S AND WOMEN'S SPORTS PROGRAMS MERGE:** All men's and women's sports programs are merged into a new Department of Athletics, Physical Education and Recreation. The move will better enable the university to comply with Title IX, a federal law requiring colleges to provide equal opportunities for women's sports. Stanford's first scholarships for women athletes are awarded in the fall. The university has 19 intercollegiate teams: 12 for men and seven for women.

April 21 **GRADING SYSTEM:** Concern over "grade inflation" prompts the Faculty Senate to restore the "D" grade, dropped along with the "F" in 1970, effective next fall.

May 19 **STUDENTS KIDNAPPED IN AFRICA:** Three students and a Dutch research assistant are kidnapped from the Gombe Stream Center in Tanzania, Africa, where they have been working with anthropologist Jane Goodall. The kidnappers, insurgents from Zaire led by rebel Laurent Kabila, grab the group during the night and head across Lake Tanganyika to Zaire. They demand ransom of $460,000, arms and ammunition, and the release of political prisoners from Tanzania. After prolonged negotiations and payment of the ransom, all four — students Carrie Hunter, Barbara Smuts, and Steve Smith, and research assistant Emilie Bergman — are released unharmed, the last in late July. Students were first sent to the center three years before to study primate behavior. No more are sent. Kabila later becomes president of the renamed Democratic Republic of Congo, and is assassinated in 2001.

June **ALEXANDER SOLZHENITSYN AT HOOVER:** Soviet dissident Alexander Solzhenitsyn is at the Hoover Institution doing research for his history of Russia in 1917. The Nobel laureate praises the collection, saying, "It is the kind of original source material that the Soviets, in order to rewrite history, either destroyed or refuse to make available to scholars." Solzhenitsyn accepts an appointment as an honorary fellow at the Hoover Institution.

September **CAMPUS PARKING NO LONGER FREE:** The university starts charging students, faculty, and staff for

Soviet dissident Alexander Solzhenitsyn, at Hoover in 1975.

John Chowning launches the computer music program in 1975.

President Gerald Ford dedicates the new Law School building in 1975, before a crowd of 10,000. A woman who tries to assassinate him the next day in San Francisco later says she intended to do it at Stanford.

close-in, convenient parking; remote parking remains free for several years. Revenues are earmarked for parking and transportation needs.

September 21 **PRESIDENT FORD DEDICATES LAW SCHOOL:** U.S. President Gerald Ford speaks to a crowd of 10,000 at the dedication of Crown Quadrangle, new home of the Law School, saying "We must protect every individual from excessive and unnecessary intrusions by a Big Brother bureaucracy." In San Francisco the next day, political activist Sara Jane Moore fires a revolver at the president, but misses when a bystander deflects her arm. Moore later says she had wanted to carry out the assassination at Stanford. However, she had been detained for questioning about her loaded gun, thus missing her trip to campus. Earlier in the month, a woman aimed a loaded gun at the president in Sacramento. Heeding previously published advice by several Stanford faculty experts, Ford sharply curtails public appearances for a month or two.

October 10 **SHARING SHELLS WITH THE EMPEROR:** During a state visit, Japan's Emperor Hirohito meets in San Francisco with Prof. Emerita Myra Keen to talk about seashells, a shared interest. Keen came to Stanford in 1934, first as a curator of fossils, then also as curator of malacology, and later also as professor of paleontology.

Fall **CENTER FOR COMPUTER RESEARCH IN MUSIC AND ACOUSTICS:** Grants from the National Science Foundation and the National Endowment for the Arts help the Music Department open a new Center for Computer Research in Music and Acoustics (CCRMA). It evolved through the efforts of Prof. John Chowning, who, as a graduate student in the 1960s, used Stanford's old Artificial Intelligence Lab in the hills behind campus to develop his dissertation in computer music. There, in the early 1970s, Chowning invented an algorithm to produce realistic music using digital synthesizers. In 1977, Chowning receives a patent for his Frequency Modulation (FM) synthesis process, which the university then licenses to Yamaha. After years of development, Yamaha in 1983 releases the DX-7 synthesizer, which becomes a big-selling favorite with rock bands. The university earns more than $23 million in royalties by the time the patent expires in 1994.

# 1976

January 5 **MARGUERITE SHUTTLE BUS:** A free campus bus service is inaugurated that runs along Serra Street from Escondido Village to the Medical School. Its name, Marguerite, honors the favorite horse of Jasper W. Paulsen, whose horse-drawn "Marguerite" coaches provided much of the university's early transportation. Paulsen got his start as a stable boy for Leland Stanford in the 1880s. After cars forced him out of the campus carriage business, he made a fortune as part-owner of a major oil field in Southern California.

January 13 **ROBERT MCAFEE BROWN:** Nationally promi-

*A huge block "S" mysteriously appears in the Oval after an inch of snow falls on Feb. 5, 1976.*

*A free gasoline-powered "Marguerite" shuttle bus system is inaugurated Jan. 5, 1976. The buses take their name from 1890s horse-drawn carriages.*

nent religious scholar Robert McAfee Brown resigns his faculty position, effective Sept. 1, to return to seminary teaching. The university's earlier denial of tenure to his colleague Jerry Irish, one of the first recipients of the Walter J. Gores award for teaching at Stanford, triggers Brown's decision. Brown has been prominent in social action, particularly against racial injustice and the Vietnam War.

February **STANFORD HISTORICAL SOCIETY LAUNCHED:** A group of campus loyalists starts the Stanford Historical Society. Prof. Emeritus James T. Watkins IV, political science, is first president. One of the first goals of the society, Watkins says, is to produce a chronology of Stanford history.

February 5 **SNOW!:** An inch of snow falls on campus, a day after temperatures are in the 70s. Previously, snow fell on Jan. 21, 1962; Jan. 21, 1932; and Feb. 5, 1887.

June **BEUTELSBACH PROGRAM CLOSES:** In a budget-cutting move, the university closes the overseas study center in Beutelsbach, Germany. It opened in 1958 as the first of Stanford's overseas centers.

September 30 **UNIVERSITY PRESS PRINT SHOP CLOSES:** The university closes the printing division of the Stanford University Press, eliminating composition, printing, binding, and related operations that date back to the university's early days. On July 1, 1993, Cambridge University Press agrees to handle sales and distribution of Stanford Press books outside North America.

October **FACULTY WOMEN ON THE RISE:** New appointments bring the number of women in the Academic Council above the 100 mark, compared to 54 five years earlier. The Academic Council totals more than 1,000 persons of professorial rank.

October 1 **FIRE DEPARTMENT MERGER:** Stanford Fire Department merges with Palo Alto Fire Department in a move that will save the university up to $4 million over the next seven years and will end a long tradition of employing student firefighters.

October 18 **RICHTER WINS NOBEL:** Physicist Burton Richter wins a Nobel Prize. *(See page 154)*

November 9 **STANFORD, BERKELEY LIBRARIES SHARE:** A cooperative venture between Stanford and UC-Berkeley libraries is announced. It will involve a coordinated acquisitions policy to prevent unnecessary duplication of expensive books and allow direct borrowing privileges for faculty and graduate students at both institutions. A bus service — Gutenberg Express — will make daily round trips between the two campuses to facilitate movement of patrons and books.

# 1977

January **FREE COMPUTER TIME:** High-quality interactive computing available for students and faculty 24 hours a

*In a 1977 anti-apartheid sit-in, hundreds occupy the Old Union. The nonviolent action ends with the arrest of 294.*

*LOTS provides free computers 24 hours a day for students and faculty, beginning in 1977.*

*Frederick Emmons Terman Engineering Center, built in 1977, honors the retired provost and former dean of engineering.*

day is launched through LOTS (Low-Overhead Time-Sharing). The name reflects the fact that only four people are needed to staff the system, which is used primarily for student classwork. Initially 48 terminals are connected to a single Digital Equipment Corp. 2040 computer, but by 1985 demand forces LOTS to add its fourth mainframe, with a fifth planned later. LOTS starts with a cluster of terminals in the Center for Educational Research at Stanford (CERAS) and later installs clusters at Tresidder Union and Terman Engineering. The service is free to users, but available only for work not financed by research grants or contracts. Sponsored work is done on the university's more powerful IBM computers.

March **DEEP SEA LIFE:** On a deep-sea expedition along the Galápagos Rift, geology Prof. Tjeerd van Andel and two companions become the first to locate underwater hot springs — at a depth of 10,000 feet — that support a profusion of life on the otherwise barren ocean floor.

May 9-10 **SOUTH AFRICA PROTEST:** The largest display of civil disobedience in Stanford history results in the arrest of 294 persons (of whom 270 are students) in the Old Union. The 16-hour nonviolent sit-in protests apartheid, U.S. corporate investments in South Africa, and the Board of Trustees' refusal to urge Ford Motor Co. to close its operations there. Most of the students are charged with trespassing, failure to disperse, and similar misdemeanors; some also are charged with resisting arrest. No campus judicial charges are filed.

May 12 **COURSE EVALUATION:** After years of off-and-on discussion, the Faculty Senate endorses the principle of universal course evaluation by students and urges its prompt implementation. This evaluation program, originally proposed by the ASSU Task Force on Tenure and Teaching Quality, continues to the present.

October 6 **ENGINEERING BUILDING NAMED FOR TERMAN:** The Frederick Emmons Terman Engineering Center is dedicated, honoring the former dean of engineering and retired provost. The building was constructed with funds donated by William and Flora Hewlett and David and Lucile Packard. Nearly 40 years earlier, Terman encouraged the two men — then recent graduates of Stanford — to start their electronics collaboration in a Palo Alto garage.

December 13 **SORORITIES AGAIN:** Reversing its 1944 ban on sororities, the Board of Trustees approves the concept of "subjectively selected" women's organizations, as long as the groups maintain local control over membership and meet university policies against discrimination. Seven sororities initially are refused recognition because they lack local autonomy, but in January 1981, after satisfying the university's requirements, Delta Gamma becomes the first officially recognized sorority in 37 years. Two years later, the first black sorority, Alpha Kappa Alpha, is granted recognition. In 1997, a university task force bows to demands for equity in Greek housing, and in fall 1998, two sororities — Kappa Alpha Theta and Delta Delta Delta — move into Cowell Cluster.

Graduate student Sally Ride takes her daily run in the hills behind campus. In 1978, she is named to the astronaut corps, and in 1983 she becomes America's first woman in space.

*The Viennese Ball, seen here in 1983, is launched in 1978 by students who attended Stanford in Austria.*

*Governor's Avenue, at the height of its glory in the early 1960s. Many of the century-old eucalyptus are removed in 1978, victims of a three-year drought and old age.*

# 1978

January **WOMEN ASTRONAUTS:** Physics graduate student Sally Ride becomes one of the first six women named to the astronaut corps by NASA. In June 1983 she is America's first woman in space. Ride applied for the astronaut corps after reading a NASA ad in the *Stanford Daily*. She earned bachelor's degrees in English and physics and a master's and Ph.D. in physics, all from Stanford. Future alumnae who join the astronaut corps include the first Hispanic woman, Ellen Ochoa, and the first African American woman, Mae Jamison. In spring 1991, alumna Tamara E. Jernigan carries a Stanford centennial flag and a block "S" volleyball aboard the space shuttle *Columbia*.

January 27 **VIENNESE BALL:** Toyon Hall's lounge is transformed into a palace ballroom as former students from the Vienna campus stage a formal ball for 200 couples. In future years, the ball becomes so popular that students camp out overnight in White Plaza to purchase the highly sought-after tickets. It moves to ever-larger halls, and eventually to a hotel ballroom off campus.

June **TENNIS CHAMPS:** For the first time in intercollegiate tennis history, the men's and women's national championships are won by the same school — Stanford.

June **GOVERNOR'S AVENUE TREES DYING:** Work crews remove at least 100 dead and dying giant eucalyptus trees, victims of a three-year drought. Many are century-old eucalyptus trees planted by Leland Stanford along Governor's Avenue.

July 20 **MAGNA CARTA ON DISPLAY:** Former U.S. President Gerald Ford helps cut the ribbon during dedication of the Herbert Hoover Memorial Building. An original copy of England's Magna Carta is put on display.

October **LELAND STANFORD'S SACRAMENTO HOUSE SAVED:** The state of California acquires Leland and Jane Stanford's Sacramento mansion as part of the state's historic parks system, paying $1.3 million to the Roman Catholic Archdiocese. Jane Stanford had donated the house to the church in 1900. Plans to restore and open it to the public are long delayed.

August 18 **MATH PROFESSOR SLAIN:** Math Prof. Karel deLeeuw is murdered in his office. Graduate student Theodore Streleski turns himself in within 12 hours saying he feels the mathematics faculty has unfairly delayed his graduate study. Following a conviction for second-degree murder based on diminished capacity, Streleski serves seven years in prison.

October **CHINA EXCHANGE:** As part of the thaw in Chinese-American relations, six research scholars arrive on campus from the People's Republic of China for a two-year stay. Several Stanford scholars go to China in 1979.

November 4 **LIBRARY FLOOD:** An eight-inch water main

Math Prof. Karel deLeeuw, who is murdered by a disgruntled graduate student in 1978.

A broken water main causes extensive flooding and library damage in 1978.

Alexander Calder's Le Faucon flies into place in front of the Law School in 1979.

A doughnut-shaped 107-ton superconducting electromagnet for SLAC arrives on 120 wheels in 1979.

breaks near Meyer Library, causing $1 million damage to approximately 45,000 books in the basement of Meyer Library. Local citizens and companies volunteer their help and the books are moved to giant freezers for storage until they can be vacuum dried and then restored. About 7,000 books are damaged at the Law Library when the chilled water system on the roof fails in September 1979. Defective fire sprinkler heads cause library damage in 1981, 1983, and 1989, and a burst pipe in 1981 damages 5,000 doctoral dissertations in the basement of Green Library. Freeze-drying wet books becomes standard salvage procedure.

# 1979

January **WOMEN IN ENGINEERING:** Twenty-five percent of the undergraduates in the School of Engineering are women, up from 5 percent five years earlier.

April 16 **PULITZER FOR FEHRENBACHER:** Don E. Fehrenbacher, professor of history, wins a Pulitzer Prize for his 1979 book, *The Dred Scott Case: Its Significance in American Law and Politics.* The prize follows by two years a Pulitzer awarded for Prof. David M. Potter's *The Impending Crisis: 1848-1861,* published posthumously after Fehrenbacher completed and edited it.

November **ALEXANDER CALDER SCULPTURE:** Alexander Calder's three-ton metal stabile *Le Faucon* (The Falcon) is installed in the Law School courtyard, a gift of Mr. and Mrs. Richard E. Lang of Seattle. It is part of an extensive outdoor art program headed by Prof. Albert Elsen — the largest at any university.

November 23 **HUGE DOUGHNUT:** The heaviest load yet carried over U.S. highways — a 107-ton doughnut-shaped superconducting electromagnet — arrives at SLAC from Chicago. The load, on 120 wheels, travels at 25 mph and takes up two traffic lanes. It will be used in the new Positron Electron Project (PEP).

# 1980

**STATISTICS:**

Undergraduate enrollment: 6,630

Graduate enrollment: 6,236

Faculty: 1,230

Tuition: $6,285 per year

Endowment: $643 million

January 24 **CURRICULUM REFORM:** The biggest curriculum change in a decade is approved without dissent by the Faculty Senate. It includes a new Western culture requirement, with seven additional distribution requirements: 1) literature and the fine arts; 2) philosophical, social and religious thought; 3) human development, behavior and language; 4) social processes and institutions; 5) mathematical sciences; 6) natural sciences; and 7) technology and applied sciences. Entering freshmen will be the first affected.

January 26 **PRESIDENT RICHARD W. LYMAN RESIGNS:** President Lyman resigns effective Aug. 1 to become president of the Rockefeller Foundation in New York.

February 8 **HISTORY CORNER RENOVATED:** A restored History Corner, built in 1903 and renovated in the original style for $8 million, is dedicated.

April 11 **GREEN LIBRARY DEDICATED:** The $14.7 million Cecil H. Green Library is dedicated, two months after opening to students. It is attached to the back of the old Main Library, and connected at each floor. With the addition, library floor space and book capacity double, and seating and study provisions triple. Cecil H. Green and his wife, Ida, made a substantial gift toward construction. The old Main Library will be known as Green West.

April 21 **PEP BEGINS OPERATIONS:** Positron Electron Project (PEP) operations begin at SLAC with first storage of an electron beam in the PEP storage ring at 3:30 a.m. PEP, a joint project of SLAC and the University of California's Lawrence Berkeley Laboratory, is sponsored by the U.S. Department of Energy, and is officially dedicated on Sept. 5. PEP provides SLAC with 10 times higher energy than SPEAR and extends SLAC research into a new regime, where evidence of gluons, the particles responsible for strong forces, is found.

June 13 **DONALD KENNEDY APPOINTED PRESIDENT:** Biologist Donald Kennedy, 48, is appointed Stanford's eighth president, effective Aug. 1. He joined the faculty in 1960, serving as chairman of Biological Sciences from 1965 to 1972 and as chairman of Human Biology from 1974 to 1977. He was recruited to join the Carter administration as head of the Food and Drug Administration in 1977, but returned to campus in July 1979 to become provost. At his Oct. 12, 1980, inauguration as university president, Kennedy urges faculty to overcome the alienation of the late 1960s and once again become involved in the lives of students outside the classroom. He also announces establishment of the Stanford Humanities Center, which will support research and writing by humanities scholars from Stanford and elsewhere.

October 14 **BERG WINS NOBEL:** Biochemist Paul Berg wins a Nobel Prize. *(See page 154)*

November **CHICANO RESEARCH CENTER:** The Center for Chicano Research is created with history Prof. Albert Camarillo as its director.

November **TESTING EINSTEIN'S THEORY:** A team of scientists and engineers announce plans to test Einstein's General Theory of Relativity, which explains how gravity works. The elaborate project — now called Gravity Probe B — will culminate with 18 months of experiments in space. Prof. Francis Everett is principal investigator and Prof. Bradford Parkinson later joins as program manager and co-PI. The idea of a test of Einstein's general theory came out of a 1959 discussion at the Encina men's pool by three naked scientists — Profs. William M. Fairbank, Robert

*Donald Kennedy, center, is flanked by President Emeritus Richard W. Lyman, left, and Chancellor J.E. Wallace Sterling at his inauguration as eighth president in 1980. (Left) Kennedy takes a group of students birding in the baylands.*

*Lights burn brightly at Green Library, completed in 1980.*

Cannon, and Leonard Schiff. At the heart of the experiment are four superchilled gyroscopes, engineered to provide an almost perfect space-time reference system as they fly in polar orbit. If Einstein is right, the gyroscopes will tilt ever so slightly as they spin. The object of the test is to measure the tilt, if it occurs. Development of the spacecraft and its scientific package starts in January 1990. Liftoff is scheduled for fall 2002 from Vandenberg Air Force Base, using a Delta II rocket. NASA is paying for most of the $450 million cost.

December **HOOVER-REAGAN TIES:** A month after his election to the U.S. presidency, Ronald Reagan, an honorary fellow of the Hoover Institution, has named 21 Hoover scholars and Stanford professors to advisory committees.

December 8 **LAND USE PLAN:** Trustees approve Land Use Plan-1980, a document that illustrates possible land uses five and 30 years in the future. The plan includes a pioneering study of the environmental sensitivity of the Stanford foothills. University planners record 10 specific environmental features within four general categories. They also divide the land into 2.5-acre squares and give a numerical value to the features within each square. The computerized result is a detailed map showing the most and least suitable areas of possible growth.

# 1981

February **RONALD REAGAN PRESIDENTIAL LIBRARY:** Hoover Institution Director W. Glenn Campbell proposes that the Ronald Reagan Presidential Library be located at Stanford. It would be financed with private contributions and operated by the National Archives, and would include an independent public policy center. University trustees in February 1985 approve a site in the foothills overlooking Lagunita, after the White House drops plans for the policy center, which the university says must fall under normal academic governance. By 1986, the library plan is being criticized for location, traffic, size, conference facilities, presidential suite, movie theater, and a museum that is expected to attract 200,000 to 300,000 visitors annually. In December 1986 the Santa Clara County Planning Commission rules that the library would conform to low-intensity use regulations of the foothills. Opposition escalates when Campbell writes in the Hoover annual report that the university "can boast" of its connection to Reagan. The Faculty Senate condemns the statement in February 1987 as "counter to the non-partisan rationale offered by the Board of Trustees" when the board accepted the library proposal. During a three-hour meeting on April 2, 1987, the Faculty Senate adopts a resolution drafted by 12 of its former chairmen urging the Board of Trustees to scale down the facility or move it farther from campus. In an unprecedented appearance before the faculty representatives, Trustee President Warren Christopher says there is "little likelihood" the board will reconsider its commitments, but he promises to convey faculty concerns at the May 12 trustee meeting. But on April 23, the Reagan Presidential Foundation suddenly decides to build in Southern California, where it can merge the library and public policy center. Surprise, relief, and regret mark campus response to the news.

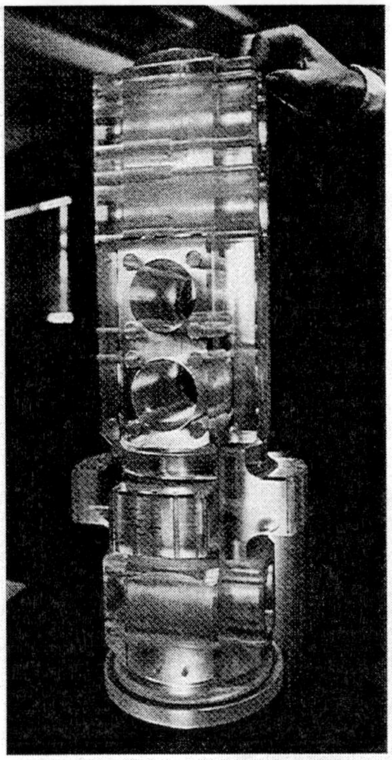

This perfectly round Ping-Pong-ball-sized gyro (right) will join three others in a housing (above) sent into space to test an Einstein theory.

*An architect's rendering of the Ronald Reagan Presidential Library, proposed in 1981 for a foothills site overlooking the university.*

*The Library Associates in 1983 presents this 15th century manuscript,* Dragmaticon, *as the library's 5 millionth volume.*

March 9 **HEART-LUNG TRANSPLANT:** At the Medical Center, the first combined heart-lung transplant in nearly 10 years is performed. The patient, Mary Gohlke of Mesa, Arizona, recovers successfully. Doctors use a new antirejection drug, Cyclosporin A, which had not been available earlier when operations brought only limited success.

October 19 **SCHAWLOW WINS NOBEL:** Physicist Arthur Schawlow wins a Nobel Prize. *(See page 154)*

Fall **FEMINIST STUDIES:** Students now can design an interdisciplinary major in feminist studies. One of the key organizers of the new major is Prof. Estelle Freedman, who wins a highly publicized fight for tenure in September 1983.

# 1982

January 8 **BAXTER AT JUSTICE DEPT.:** Law Prof. William F. Baxter, on leave as assistant attorney general in the U.S. Department of Justice, convinces AT&T to divest itself of 22 local Bell telephone companies, opening the door to widespread competition in the telecommunications industry. He also drops a 13-year antitrust suit against IBM. A pioneer scholar bridging law and economics, Baxter rewrites basic government guidelines for antitrust and does seminal work in pollution control.

March **HISTORY OF SCIENCE:** The Samuel I. and Cecile M. Barchas Collection in the History of Science and Ideas is donated to the University Libraries. It will support the academic program in the History of Science, founded in 1979. The Barchases have spent 35 years collecting the 2,000 rare volumes valued at $5 million, one of the largest private collections on the subject in the United States. In January 1985, the Barchas Room is dedicated in the Department of Special Collections.

May **HODGKIN'S DISEASE:** Twenty years of treatment for Hodgkin's disease are celebrated on campus by more than 500 former patients of Dr. Henry Kaplan. The Stanford radiologist changed Hodgkin's disease from a hopeless illness to one that is more than 90 percent curable when treated early. In no other malignancy has gains been more dramatic. Kaplan dies of lung cancer in February 1984.

November 20 **THE PLAY:** In a bizarre ending to the Big Game, the Cal Bears toss five laterals in one play and zip into the end zone, bowling over members of the Stanford Band, who had spilled onto the field as the clock runs out. Trombone player Gary Tyrell and his instrument are both trashed. Officials declare Cal the winner 25-20, although Stanfordites will forever claim that one official had earlier signaled the play dead. Four days after the game, the *Stanford Daily* distributes in Berkeley a bogus edition of the *Daily Californian,* falsely reporting that the NCAA has ruled the controversial play dead and awarded the game to Stanford. Eight years later, Stanford gets retribution when, in a lengthy cliffhanger, it scores twice in the last 17 seconds to defeat Cal 27-25.

December 19 **FRED TERMAN DIES:** Frederick E. Terman, retired provost and "father" of Silicon Valley, dies at 82.

*Graduate student Chuck Machlin, from the stands, caught this image of The Play. The disputed last play of the 1982 Big Game involves five laterals that take Cal through the Stanford Band as the clock runs out. Here, one official apparently is signaling the play dead (right circle), in the area where the second lateral's forward motion was stopped. Nevertheless, Kevin Moen (left circle) makes his way toward the end zone.*

# 1983

February **DOCTORAL PROGRAM RANKINGS:** Results of a 1982 national faculty survey, Assessment of Research Doctorate Programs in the U.S., ranks Stanford among the top 10 in 25 different fields, a record exceeded only by Berkeley, which finishes in the top 10 in 30 of the 32 fields surveyed. Stanford ranks first in four fields: biochemistry, computer science, psychology, and statistics-biostatistics. The faculty is among the top five in seven additional fields: economics, chemistry, geoscience, chemical engineering, civil engineering, electrical engineering, and mechanical engineering. Fourteen more departments rank among the top 10: anthropology, art history, English, German, history, linguistics, mathematics, microbiology, philosophy, physics, political science, Spanish, sociology, and zoology.

February 24 **ANTHROPOLOGY STUDENT DISMISSED:** The anthropology faculty votes to terminate Steven Mosher as a Ph.D. candidate, after an investigation of charges relating to Mosher's field research on a Chinese commune in 1979-80. Mosher claims his dismissal is in response to pressure from Chinese officials upset over his writing about forced abortions. After two years of publicity and formal appeals, the decision is upheld by President Kennedy on Sept. 30, 1985.

March 3 **QUEEN ELIZABETH VISITS:** Britain's Queen Elizabeth II and Prince Philip stop by for lunch at Lou Henry Hoover House with 92 guests, including students, faculty, and staff. The Stanford Band serenades the queen as hundreds mill about, hoping for a glimpse of her.

May 10 **NEW CLOCK TOWER:** A new 45-foot bell tower is dedicated near the Quad and the Education Building to house the bells and clockworks from the original steeple of Memorial Church. Placed in storage after the steeple fell in the 1906 earthquake, the bells and 1901 Seth Thomas clock were installed in a wooden tower behind the church in 1915, then went into storage again when the tower was removed in 1967. Hundreds of volunteer hours went into refurbishing the hand-wound clockworks. Westminster chimes play each quarter hour from 8 a.m. to 7:45 p.m. The tower is a gift of Board of Trustees' President William Kimball.

May 19 **CENTER FOR INTEGRATED SYSTEMS:** Ground is broken for the Center for Integrated Systems, a joint venture between the university and 20 industry sponsors. A major goal of the center is to bring together faculty and graduate students from engineering, computer science, and applied physics to work on a variety of projects of fundamental interest to the microelectronics and computer science industries. An addition, called the Paul Allen Center for Integrated Systems, is built in 1995. Paul Allen is cofounder of Microsoft.

July **HIV BLOOD SCREENING:** Stanford Blood Bank becomes the first in the nation to begin screening blood to prevent transmission of AIDS, at a time when it is still unclear that AIDS is transmitted by blood transfusion. Work by Profs. Carl Grumet and Edgar Engleman demonstrates that AIDS high-risk groups could be identified and excluded from the donor pool.

September 4 **SOCRATES, ONLINE:** A computerized cata-

Students from Stanford in Britain with a message from the Tower of London in 1982. (Below left) The Stanford Daily's bogus issue of the Daily Californian.

On morning of the 1983 dedication of a new clock tower, the campus awoke to a charming Mickey Mouse on one of the faces.

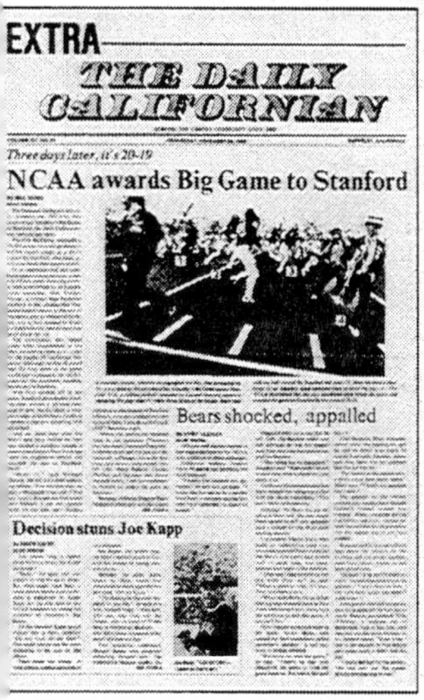
EXTRA

THE DAILY CALIFORNIAN

Three days later, it's 20-19

NCAA awards Big Game to Stanford

Bears shocked, appalled

Decision stuns Joe Kapp

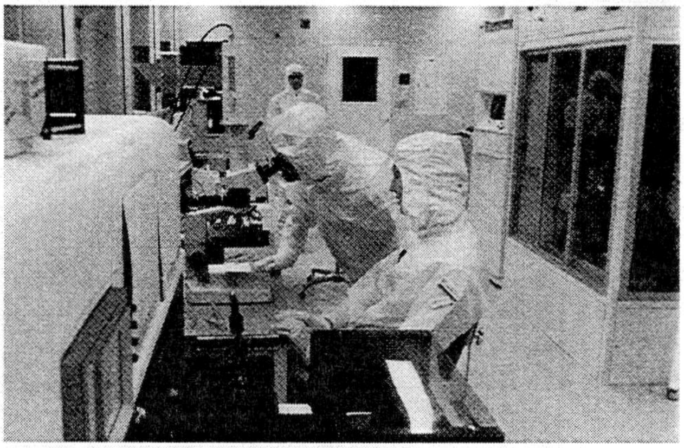

Researchers wear moonsuits in the clean room of the Center for Integrated Systems. Ground is broken for the center in 1983.

og of nearly 20 percent of the library's holdings becomes available online. Named Socrates for its "Socratic" form of questioning the user, the database includes more than 20,000 catalog entries, particularly those of items acquired since 1972. Socrates is available from any terminal inked to the university's IBM 3081 mainframe.

)ctober 9 **LIBRARY AT 5 MILLION:** University Libraries acquires its 5 millionth volume, a 15th-century manuscript of the *Dragmaticon* by William of Conches, presented by the Associates of the Stanford University Libraries.

)ctober 19 **TAUBE WINS NOBEL:** Chemist Henry Taube wins a Nobel Prize. *(See page 154)*

Iovember 1 **LINEAR COLLIDER:** Ground is broken for the tanford Linear Collider (SLC) at SLAC. SLC construction nvolves, in part, boring a 9,000-foot tunnel under the EP tunnel, and extensively upgrading the existing two-nile linear accelerator. After it goes into operation in 1987, LC proves that head-to-head linear accelerators can chieve very high energy electron-positron collisions vithout the energy loss to synchrotron radiation that lims circular machines. Tuned to produce Z-particles, this nachine demonstrates that there are no more than three ypes of light neutrinos, thus reinforcing the three-family orm of the Standard Model theory of particle physics.

Iovember **CENTER FOR THE STUDY OF LANGUAGE AND INFORMATION:** Inspired by a faculty profile in the *Stanford Observer*, System Development Foundation of Palo lto announces gifts of $21 million to the Center for the Study of Language and Information. The center, begun informally in 1981, now will become a major institute for the development of integrated theories of language, information, and computation, drawing researchers from linguistics, psychology, computer science, and philosophy.

## 1984

January **MEMORIAL CHURCH GETS SECOND ORGAN:** The Fisk-Nanney organ, considered one of the finest organs in the world, is completed in the center of the choir loft, joining the 1901 romantic-style Murray Harris organ. The new Baroque-style instrument, with 73 ranks and 4,422 pipes, can be switched easily from mean-tone to well-tempered tuning. Sadly, its builder, Charles Fisk, dies in December, a month before six experts from his Gloucester, Mass., workshop complete the installation. The organ is tuned from January through April; three dedicatory concerts begin in May. Its name also honors Herbert Nanney, university organist from 1947 to 1985. A small third organ, built by Paul Fritts of Tacoma, Wash., is added in 1995 in the side chapel. The Potter-Brinegar organ is a Renaissance-style instrument of 8 stops and 429 pipes.

March 4 **STANFORD STRING QUARTET:** The Stanford String Quartet, a new resident music ensemble, debuts during the dedication of the new Braun Music Center building. Formed by Prof. Andor Toth, the quartet garners immediate critical acclaim. On an international tour in 1988, it premieres a piece commissioned for the Stanford Centennial from alumnus and Pulitzer Prize-winning

The library's Socrates computerized catalog goes online Sept. 4, 1983, foreshadowing the end of the old-fashioned card catalog.

King Carl XVI Gustaf of Sweden, center, visits with Stanford's 10 Nobel laureates. From left: Henry Taube, Arthur Schawlow, Robert Hofstadter, Paul Flory, Paul Berg, the King, Burton Richter, William Shockley, Kenneth Arrow, Linus Pauling, and Arthur Kornberg.

President Kennedy introduces Queen Elizabeth to students Garin Veris, right, and Raga Elim. Her lunchtime visit on March 3, 1983, rivets the campus.

composer William Bolcom. The quartet is succeeded in fall 1998 by the St. Lawrence String Quartet of Eastern Canada.

March 6 ***GAY LIBERATION* STATUES VANDALIZED:** A lone vandal wielding a hammer severely damages four life-size statues by artist George Segal titled *Gay Liberation.* The sculpture of two males standing next to each other and two women seated on a park bench was installed in February on Lomita Mall. In May 1994, the white-painted bronze sculpture is again vandalized, this time by seven varsity athletes, who are disciplined.

March 14 **KING GUSTAV OF SWEDEN VISITS:** King Gustav XVI of Sweden drops by for breakfast at Hanna House with the university's 10 Nobel laureates and 20 Stanford students from Sweden.

March 26 **FRENCH PRESIDENT VISITS:** French President Francois Mitterrand visits the new Center for Integrated Systems, where he is greeted by numerous Silicon Valley leaders, then attends a reception at Lou Henry Hoover House.

May 2 **HISTORIC RED BARN RENOVATED:** Renovation is complete and horses begin moving back into the 27-stall Red Barn, the century-old stable that is the last significant building remaining from Leland Stanford's Palo Alto Stock Farm. The Red Barn had been the trotting department's training stable. L.W. "Bill" Lane Jr. headed a campaign to raise more than half the cost of the project, and surpassed his goal in just six weeks. The university sets aside 13 acres around the barn for support facilities, including paddocks and riding rings. In December 1985, the barn is added to the National Register of Historic Places.

June 18 **INNER QUAD COURTYARD RENOVATED:** Work begins on a $1 million renovation of the Inner Quad courtyard. Broken asphalt in the three-and-a-half acre courtyard is replaced with terra-cotta colored concrete interlocking paving blocks. Trees in the eight planted circles are pruned up and most eye-level shrubs removed to provide unobstructed views. A seat-height wall is built around each circle. The initial design for the renovation called for nearly doubling the diameter of each planted circle, but preservationists objected, saying the design should be consistent with university planner Frederick Law Olmsted's 19th-century conception of the space. They prevailed. The renovation is dedicated with a tea dance in front of Memorial Church on May 17, 1985.

July 29 **OLYMPIC SOCCER:** The Stadium is decked out for opening ceremonies of 1984 Olympic Games soccer trials and quarter-finals.

September **OXFORD PROGRAM OPENS:** Stanford-in-England reopens with a strengthened academic program at a site in Oxford, where higher education goes back to the 12th century. The previous center at the Cliveden estate was closed in August 1983.

October **WIRED CAMPUS:** Miles of trenches are dug around campus for the Stanford University Network (SUNet), a system of cables that will link almost every building and every computer on campus with every other building and computer. SUNet is an expansion and exten-

*The Red Barn, the last significant building from Leland Stanford's Palo Alto Stock Farm, is renovated in 1984.*

*The Baroque-style Fisk-Nanney organ, installed in Memorial Church in January 1984.*

*The Inner Quad Courtyard gets a $1 million makeover in 1984.*

sion of Ethernet, a commercial system developed by Xerox. In June 1988, the university is connected directly to the government-sponsored national computer network — now known as the Internet — allowing high-speed communication with other network members around the world.

December 5 **HOOVER-STANFORD RELATIONS:** Following months of contentious campus debate about political partisanship at the Hoover Institution, a six-member committee headed by political science Prof. Robert Ward issues a report saying systematic, cooperative relations between Hoover and the university offer "dazzling" opportunities for national leadership in the social sciences. The Faculty Senate, wanting its own study of Hoover, appoints an ad hoc committee chaired by sociology Prof. Sanford Dornbusch. In May 1985, that group concludes that "governance [is] the key to reduction of ideological concerns" in building better relations between the faculty and Hoover. Trustees in September reaffirm their intent to work toward "a systematically cooperative relationship" between Hoover and the university, "despite the very real difficulties that exist at present."

# 1985

January 20 **SUPER BOWL:** Professional football comes to Stanford, as Super Bowl XIX is played at the stadium. The 49ers beat the Miami Dolphins, 38-16.

March 9 **CENTENNIAL OF ENABLING ACT:** Stanford launches the celebration of its Centennial Years, 1985-1991, with a program commemorating the 100th anniversary of the Enabling Act, California legislation that provided the legal basis for the university's founding in November 1885. A centennial flag, designed by Eric Hutchinson, professor of chemistry emeritus, is unveiled, and former Board of Trustees' President Morris M. Doyle, class of 1929, provides a history lesson on the legal foundation of the university.

April **SOUTH AFRICA DIVESTMENT:** The South Africa divestment issue resurfaces when several hundred students protest the university's investment policy at a White Plaza rally, followed by Inner Quad sit-ins. Students ask the Board of Trustees to divest stocks in companies doing business in South Africa. When trustees fail to act at their May meeting, two dozen students block their cars by lying in the road. In June 1986, 206 faculty members petition trustees for total divestment. The university continues its policy of selective divestment.

May 16 **MARTIN LUTHER KING JR. PAPERS PROJECT:** History Prof. Clayborne Carson is selected by Coretta Scott King to edit the papers of her late husband, Martin Luther King Jr. The project moves to campus, opening up opportunities for faculty and students to work on an important American scholarly resource. Volume 1 of a projected 14 volume work on the Collected Papers of Martin Luther King Jr. is published in 1992. As of 2000, four volumes are complete.

July 1 **PRESIDENT STERLING DIES:** J.E. Wallace Sterling,

Lucile and David Packard, in 1986, pledge $70 million toward a new Children's Hospital. When it opens five years later, it is named in memory of Mrs. Packard.

In April 1985, students protesting university investments in South Africa block trustees' cars. At right is police chief Marvin Herrington.

History Prof. Clayborne Carson, left, selected in 1985 to edit the Martin Luther King Jr. papers.

chancellor and fifth president of the university (1949-68), dies of cancer at age 78.

November 11 **CENTENNIAL OF FOUNDING:** The university celebrates the centennial of its founding. The original calligraphed 100-year-old Founding Grant is put on public display. Cornell President Frank H.T. Rhodes, in his keynote address in Memorial Church, discusses the 100-year-old Stanford-Cornell axis.

Fall **HONOR CODE CASE:** In the largest disciplinary case in at least a decade, 12 undergraduates are charged with Honor Code violations in Prof. Philip Zimbardo's spring-quarter Psychology 1 class. The investigation of two dozen students in the introductory course of more than 700 students stems in part from computer-scored tests that suggest patterns of unpermitted collaboration. Most receive year-long suspensions. All receive a grade of No Credit.

# 1986

February **JEWISH STUDIES:** The University Libraries acquires a large collection on Jewish culture, history, and religion. The 20,000 volumes were collected by Salo Wittmayer Baron, professor emeritus at Columbia University and purchased with funds from several groups and Stanford alumnus Tad Taube. It becomes known as the Taube-Baron collection. The acquisition supports the establishment of the Jewish Studies Program, which is inaugurated in October with a series of lectures and receptions. About one-third of the faculty and 15 percent of the student body are Jewish.

February 6 **FIGURE SKATING CHAMPION:** Freshman premed student Debi Thomas wins the ladies' United States Figure Skating Championship, then follows up by winning the world title on March 21 in Geneva, Switzerland. She earns a bronze medal at the 1988 Winter Olympics. After graduating in 1991, she attends Northwestern University Medical School, studying to be an orthopedic surgeon.

May 7 **PACKARD CHILDREN'S HOSPITAL:** Lucile and David Packard pledge $70 million to finance construction of a new Children's Hospital at Stanford, a facility that will be integrated with the Medical Center, but governed separately. The $100 million, 300,000-square-foot Lucile Packard Children's Hospital, large on the outside but scaled for children on the inside, is dedicated April 14, 1991, and opens for patients two months later. Children's Hospital at Stanford evolved from the Stanford Home for Convalescent Children, opened in 1920.

September **GENDER, WOMEN'S RESEARCH:** The Center for Research on Women, founded in 1974, changes its name to the Institute for Research on Women and Gender to more accurately reflect the work of many scholars associated with it. In addition to supporting research, the institute organizes educational programs and conferences.

November 5 **STANFORD BAND IN TROUBLE (AGAIN):** Citing "an accumulation of problems," Athletics Director Andy Geiger bans the Incomparable Leland Stanford Ju-

Band members haul their "Geiger counter" onto the field at Big Game, 1986, at a halftime formation about Athletics Director Andy Geiger's recent short-lived ban of the Band. Homemade halo adorns a trombonist as the Band behaves at Big Game.

Students move back into Roble Hall nearly two years after it was suddenly closed in December 1987 for seismic bracing. The Loma Prieta quake hits less than a month after the reopening.

nior University Marching Band from playing at the UCLA game. Sins include spelling out a four-letter word and dropping pants during half-time shows. After proposing new behavioral standards and agreeing not to consume liquor on game days, the Incomparables are allowed to play again. At Big Game, they sport homemade halos. In October 1990, the Band offends fans at the University of Oregon doing a parody of the spotted owl vs. lumber industry controversy, and is suspended for one game. In 1997, the Band is prohibited from performing at games against Notre Dame until 2000 because of pre-game and half-time shows that included a parody of the Irish potato famine and a band member dressed as a Catholic nun.

November 28 **JAPAN PROGRAMS:** At a press conference in Japan, President Kennedy announces two cooperative programs with Kyoto University. The Stanford Center for Technology and Innovation will allow engineering and science students to combine study at Kyoto with internships in Japanese businesses. The Kyoto Center for Japanese Studies is designed for students studying Japanese language and culture. It is a consortium of several universities.

# 1987

February 10 **CENTENNIAL CAMPAIGN:** Trustees launch a five-year, $1.1 billion Centennial Campaign, the largest fundraising campaign to date in higher education. A nucleus fund of $307 million already has been raised. Goals include 100 endowed professorships. In early 1992, the final tally of $1.269 billion is $169 million over the original target.

March 10 **FORMER PRESIDENT CARTER VISITS:** Former U.S. President Jimmy Carter, at the Law School to accept its Jackson H. Ralston prize in international law, tells an overflow crowd at Kresge Auditorium that President Ronald Reagan has abandoned the president's role as world mediator and negotiator for peace.

May **CHEERLEADERS MAKE A COMEBACK:** With support from the Athletics Department, sophomore Kristin Jessen organizes a coed cheerleading squad that will perform stunts at football and basketball games. The 10-member team will practice fall quarter and start performing during the 1988 basketball season. Student reaction is divided. Stanford cheerleading fell on hard times in the 1970s.

May 14 **CENTENNIAL OF CORNERSTONE:** The university celebrates the centennial of the laying of the cornerstone on the anniversary of Leland Jr.'s birth. With temperatures hovering close to 100 degrees, 8,000 spectators in the Inner Quad listen to Secretary of State George P. Shultz and his counterparts from Canada and Mexico talk about the future of trilateral cooperation. History Prof. David Kennedy says that California of 1887 was an implausible spot for a Gilded Age university. Stanford Historical Society President H. Donald Winbigler presents the university with a commemorative bronze plaque to be installed near the cornerstone on Building 60. Other festivities include a banquet for 2,000 under a giant tent on the football field, and a big-band dance in the Inner Quad, capped by fire-

Math Prof. Emerita Mary Sunseri shades herself during the sun-drenched May 1987 celebration of the laying of the university's cornerstone.

A centennial time capsule is set in place before installation of the cornerstone centennial bronze plate, next to the original cornerstone, in May 1987.

works in the Oval. On May 31, the Historical Society's bronze plate is installed over a time capsule containing 7,000 signatures of individuals at the May 14 event.

June 7 **College World Series victors:** Coming from behind three times in life-or-death games, the baseball team wins the College World Series, a first for Stanford. The team is coached by Mark Marquess. Stanford wins again in 1988.

June 22 **Argentine President visits:** Argentine President Raul Alfonsin dons a sterile suit to visit the clean room at the Center for Integrated Systems.

September **Prostate cancer detection:** Dr. Thomas Stamey, chair of the Department of Urology, announces development of a new ultrasound probe, which, when combined with a special bioptic needle, permits near-painless biopsies for prostate cancer detection. Stamey's team also developes a more reliable chemical PSA (protein specific antigen) test and standards for its use, now adopted worldwide.

October **College rankings:** By a margin of one percentage point, Stanford finishes first for the third straight time in *U.S. News and World Report*'s rankings of undergraduate institutions. President Donald Kennedy calls the result a "beauty contest, not a serious analysis of quality."

November **Molecular and genetic medicine:** The $55 million Center for Molecular and Genetic Medicine, now under construction, is named for philanthropists Arnold and Mabel Beckman. Under the direction of Nobelist Paul Berg, the research center is an innovative effort to bridge the gap between basic science and clinical medicine. By bringing together scientists with molecular techniques and physicians who deal with problems of human health, the program seeks new ways to diagnose, prevent, and cure diseases now beyond medicine's grasp. The high-tech building is completed in early 1989. Beckman, founder of Beckman Instruments, donated $12 million toward construction. Ongoing program support from his foundation puts the total at more than $21 million of as 2000.

December 19 **Roble Hall seismic fears:** Roble Hall, home to 294 students, is abruptly closed and students forced to move out when it fails a seismic study. Experts fear the building could collapse in an earthquake of 20 seconds or more because its walls were constructed of hollow clay tile in 1918. Similar studies of Lou Henry Hoover House show that it is likewise threatened, forcing President Donald Kennedy, in January, to move out for a year. Both structures are seismically braced. Students start moving back into Roble on Sept. 21, 1989. Less than a month later — on Oct. 17 — both buildings ride through the Loma Prieta earthquake unscathed.

December **Jazz:** The Music Department grants permanent status to its two-year-old pilot program in jazz. The Jazz Program has grown to three instructors, a jazz band director, a fund for visiting artists, an extensive jazz combo program, and jazz great Stan Getz, who serves as artist-in-residence. Since 1972, the university has been hosting a summer jazz workshop.

*The university in 1988 acquires the Connecticut Avenue Club, in Woodley Park, as headquarters for the new Stanford in Washington program.*

*Students cast ballots in April 1989 in what may be the nation's first totally computerized election.*

*Student Gretchen Carlson wins the Miss America pagent in 1988.*

*Prof. Andor Toth leads the Stanford Symphony Orchestra in Beethoven's Ninth Symphony at Victoria Concert Hall in Singapore, part of the orchestra's summer 1988 tour. The chorus is local.*

# 1988

January **Stanford in Washington:** The university acquires the Connecticut Avenue Club, a residential hotel in the Woodley Park area, as headquarters for its new Washington, D.C., program. Named the Robert M. and Anne T. Bass Center in honor of its patrons, the new satellite campus is dedicated May 16 with 400 alumni, faculty, students, and dignitaries. In addition to providing students with rooms and meals, the former hotel becomes a gathering place for alumni and a forum for Stanford-sponsored public events. Through internships, the program offers students an opportunity to combine academic interests with practical government experience.

March 4-5 **National Centennial Celebration:** A rousing multimedia musical cabaret with student performers, covering highlights of Stanford's first century, premieres before 1,000 guests at a formal dinner in a San Francisco hotel ballroom, transformed into a replica of the Quad. The second day, faculty and alumni experts speak at a conference on the theme "2020 Vision: As Far as the Eye Can See." The show travels to a series of Centennial celebrations coast-to-coast.

March 31 **Cultures, Ideas, and Values:** After three months of debate, the Faculty Senate approves by 39-4, with 5 abstentions, new freshman requirements in Cultures, Ideas, and Values (CIV). The new program replaces the Western Culture requirement adopted in 1980, and requires freshmen to take courses that cover both European and non-European cultures. CIV will have "a substantial historical dimension" and will include works by women and minorities. The program generates much contentious debate, including a *Wall Street Journal* editorial in opposition and sharp criticism of the Faculty Senate in a campus talk by U.S. Education Secretary William Bennett. In May 1997, the Faculty Senate approves a new year-long Introduction to the Humanities course, which will replace Cultures, Ideas, and Values as a freshman requirement.

May 14 **Jesse Jackson Visits:** Civil rights leader Jesse Jackson, running for the Democratic nomination for president, tells 6,000 in White Plaza that whenever America has made progress toward social justice, "it has almost always been student-led or student-inspired."

May 25 **American Indian Archaeological Sites:** University officials adopt a policy calling for preservation and study of native American archaeological sites found on university lands. Some of the oldest and best preserved sites in the Bay Area are at Stanford, including a number of prehistoric villages and burial grounds. Many have been discovered in recent years along San Francisquito Creek.

May 26 **Land Use Plans:** Plans to build approximately 2.2 million square feet of new academic space and 1.6 million square feet of other facilities (shopping center expansion, Stanford West housing, and a proposed hotel, never built) by the year 2000 are announced by the university, as it seeks its next 10-year General Use Permit from Santa Clara County. Virtually all the new growth will take place in areas already developed. Provost James Rosse says that the university currently has no plans for development in

*The newly organized Students of Color Coalition in October 1988 leads a "rally against racism" from White Plaza to the Quad to present a platform for multicultural education.*

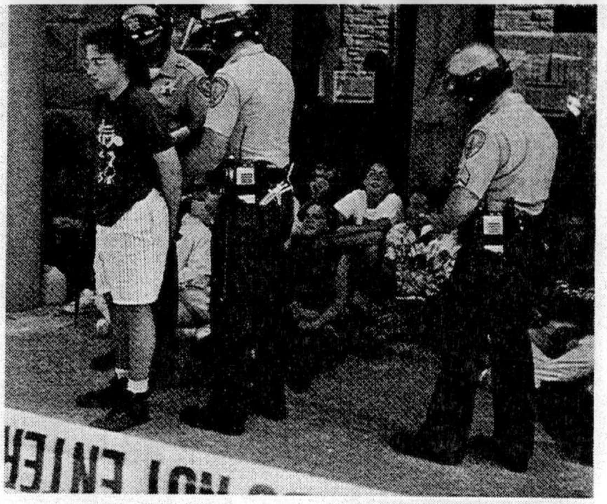

*Student is one of 21 arrested in May 1989 after an eight-hour takeover of the President's Office by a coalition of groups demanding faster progress on minority issues.*

*The 50-year-old boathouse, condemned in May 1989, is demolished in September. It has not been replaced.*

the foothills beyond a few small artists' studios.

June-July **SYMPHONY ORCHESTRA TOUR:** The Stanford Symphony Orchestra, under the direction of Prof. Andor Toth, tours Japan, Singapore, and Korea for 19 days with 87 musicians and four vocalists. In Japan, they share music stands with students from the Kyoto University Orchestra. In summer 1991, the symphony is again on the road, this time making a centennial tour to Vienna, Budapest, Prague, Leipzig, and Berlin, under the direction of Peter Jaffe. In summer 1995, the orchestra tours China, with Karla Lemon conducting.

September 10 **MISS AMERICA:** Senior sociology major Gretchen Carlson is named Miss America. Without telling professors what she is up to, she leaves for two quarters to prepare for the contest. She earns her degree in 1990.

September **INSTITUTE FOR INTERNATIONAL STUDIES:** Richard W. Lyman, president emeritus of Stanford and president of the Rockefeller Foundation for the past eight years, returns to campus to head the new Institute for International Studies. IIS will bring together many campus organizations working on international studies, and will conduct international conferences and policy-oriented interdisciplinary work.

September **ADULT EDUCATION PROGRAM LAUNCHED:** Six evening courses, ranging from the history of ancient athletics to modern molecular neurobiology, are offered during the inaugural quarter of the Continuing Studies program. Endorsed by the Faculty Senate in May, the program enables local community members to take courses from Stanford professors. In May 1991, the senate approves a Continuing Studies' proposal for a degree-granting program, starting in fall. Qualified students will complete a 36-unit interdisciplinary course of study for the Master of Liberal Arts degree. By 1999, 2,000 students are attending 80 courses, and 10 to 15 a year are earning degrees.

September 23 **MICE WITH HUMAN IMMUNE CELLS:** School of Medicine scientists, led by Dr. Irving Weissman, announce that they have developed a colony of experimental mice that possess human blood-forming and immune cells, an advance expected to pave the way for new studies of AIDS, leukemias, hepatitis, and a host of other human diseases.

October **RACIAL TENSIONS LEAD TO FREE SPEECH DEBATE:** Fueled by incidents in two undergraduate residences that raise serious issues of racial insensitivity, the campus begins an 18-month debate about the sensitive area where the right of free expression conflicts with the right to be free of discriminatory harassment. In 1990, the Student Conduct Legislative Council ratifies an interpretation — the so-called Grey Interpretation, named after law Prof. Thomas Grey, who drafted the language — to the Fundamental Standard of Student Conduct. The interpretation subsequently loses a legal challenge as being "overbroad" and is removed from the student conduct code in 1995. *(See also April 1896)*

October 19 **SCHWARTZ WINS NOBEL:** Consulting Prof. Melvin Schwartz wins a Nobel Prize. *(See page 154)*

*At 5:04 on Oct. 17, 1989, the university experiences its second major earthquake of the century.*

*Minutes before the quake, a student left his car next to the Old Chemistry Building.*

*The rotunda of Green Library's West Wing is dangerously cracked and the pillars knocked loose. It is one of many buildings closed.*

# 1989

January **NEW HOSPITAL WING:** A new $153 million wing of Stanford Hospital is completed and more than 200 patients are transferred from other sections of the 30-year-old hospital. Planned for 10 years and under construction for the last four, the four-story 440,000-square-foot structure can hold 276 of the hospital's total licensed capacity of 663 patients, and includes 20 operating rooms.

April 5 **STUDY OF MINORITY ISSUES:** An 18-month study by the University Committee on Minority Issues (UCMI) finds that, despite substantial interracial contact in close and casual friends and dating, undergraduates still perceive racial tensions and feel social distance from each other. Among 100 recommendations, the report urges adding 30 minority faculty over the next decade, doubling minority Ph.D. enrollment, doubling undergraduate courses focused on minorities, and establishing an ethnic studies requirement for graduation. Albert Camarillo, associate professor of history, headed the study, one of the most comprehensive of its kind.

April 18 **COMPUTER VOTING:** Students cast ballots by Macintosh computers, in perhaps the nation's first totally computerized election. The two-day event is widely watched by local and state election officials, as well as the news media. Students vote on a council of presidents, senate representatives, and fees for student organizations.

May **BOATHOUSE CLOSES:** Officials close the 50-year-old Lagunita boathouse when it is found to be in danger of collapse. It is demolished Sept. 25, less than a month before the Loma Prieta earthquake. Students have had a lakeside boathouse since 1892.

May 15 **STUDENT PROTEST:** A broad coalition of student groups stages an eight-hour takeover of the President's Office, barricading themselves inside the building to demand faster progress on minority issues and a stronger student voice in decision making. The demonstration ends with 56 arrests.

June **AMERICAN INDIAN REMAINS TO BE RETURNED:** University officials announce they will return skeletal remains and associated artifacts of about 550 prehistoric native Americans from the Stanford Museum to Ohlone-Costanoan tribal representatives for reburial. Most of the remains, acquired by Stanford scholars as far back as the turn of the century, are from Bay Area sites. The first set of 300 remains is presented in April 1990, and a second set a year later.

August 31 **HOOVER DIRECTOR RETIRES; HOOVER-STANFORD RELATIONS IMPROVE:** W. Glenn Campbell, outspoken director of the Hoover Institution for 29 years, retires, though not without a fight. In April 1988, he calls opponents on the faculty who were seeking to bring Hoover under tighter university control "very left-wing and very undistinguished." On May 10, 1988, the Board of Trustees present Campbell with what it calls a "generous" retirement package if he agrees to retire at 65. The board also announces formation of a search committee to pick Campbell's successor. When the university makes no fur-

*(Lower left) Prof. Haresh Shah, an expert in earthquake engineering, climbs over a fallen cabinet as he works around the clock checking buildings for damage. Campus libraries are hard hit, and the Stanford Museum (lower right) has numerous severe cracks. Students at the Beta house spend the first night sleeping outside.*

ther offers, Campbell accepts the terms. He is succeeded by John Raisian, former deputy director, who is appointed acting director, and later director. At the Sept. 28, 1989, Faculty Senate meeting, President Donald Kennedy says he is pleased with progress made in resolving long-standing Hoover governance issues since Raisian took over. By a vote of 18-15, the senate rejects a proposal tabled a year earlier to create the third group in the 1980s to study the Hoover-Stanford relationship.

October 5 **Nobelist Oscar Arias visits:** President Oscar Arias Sanchez of Costa Rica, at the Law School to accept the Jackson H. Ralston prize in international law, tells his audience that "underdevelopment and widespread poverty breed violence." Arias was recipient of the 1987 Nobel Peace Prize.

October 17 **Loma Prieta earthquake:** At 5:04 p.m. the campus and greater San Francisco Bay Area are hit with the second major earthquake of the century. Initially calculated at 7.1 on the Richter scale, but later revised downward to 6.9, the 10- to 12-second Loma Prieta quake, unlike the 1906 quake, causes no deaths or serious injuries on campus. About 1,600 students camp out the first night on lawns, basketball courts, and friends' floors. The university is shut down Oct. 18, as professors from the Civil Engineering Department and the John A. Blume Earthquake Engineering Center lead teams that begin inspecting all campus buildings. They red-tag 26 structures, and limit access to another 34. Property damage, initially estimated at about $160 million, is significant, especially to the Green Library West Wing, Building 260 (Language Corner), Building 320 (Geology Corner), the Museum, Memorial Church, the Graduate School of Business, and Hanna House. Also, 15 row houses are seriously damaged; some are repaired and reopen within two weeks. A group from Roth House takes up temporary residence with President Kennedy in Hoover House; 160 students are displaced for the remainder of the academic year. More than 400 student volunteers reshelve books that went flying in the university's hard-hit libraries. During the next 10 years, the university spends approximately $250 million on quake repair, improvements, and retrofitting, with the Federal Emergency Management Agency providing $50 million and donors contributing $90 million.

October 17 **VA Hospital damage:** The Medical School's affiliated Palo Alto Veterans Medical Center also is hard hit by the Loma Prieta earthquake. The VA center is a base for teaching, clinical care, and research for more than 50 faculty members, as well as residents in training. Faculty research is disrupted for months, until temporary laboratories are constructed in leased space in the Stanford Research Park. The Veterans Administration replaces the damaged structure eight years later with a new $150 million, 500-bed hospital.

# 1990

**STATISTICS:**

Undergraduate enrollment: 6,555

Graduate enrollment: 6,886

Faculty: 1,383

Tuition: $14,280 per year

Endowment: $2 billion

February **BUDGET CRISIS:** In the face of a projected budget shortfall, Provost James Rosse launches a $22 million "repositioning" program to cut nearly 6 percent from the university's $388 million operating budget. But the problem turns severe as cutbacks in government reimbursements of indirect costs, lower than expected research volume, the 1989 earthquake, and the general state of the national economy take their toll. In 1991, Rosse initiates a campus-wide process that produces a two-year $43 million program to cut budgets and increase income for fiscal years 1993 and 1994. In fall 1993, Provost Condoleezza Rice finds it necessary to keep cutting — she starts a new three-year effort, ending in fiscal year 1997, to reduce costs by another $18 million to $20 million.

April 1 **WOMEN'S BASKETBALL ON TOP:** The women's basketball team wins its first-ever NCAA crown, beating Auburn, 88-81. On the season, Stanford won 32 games, while losing just once (by three points). Along the way, the team breaks 100 school, conference, and national records. Jennifer Azzi is named to the All-American team a second time and wins both the Naismith Award and the Margaret Wade Trophy, the two most prestigious awards in the sport. Coach Tara VanDerveer is named Pac-10 Coach of the Year and the Naismith National Coach of the Year. In April 1992, the women again win the NCAA title, this time defeating Western Kentucky, 78-62. In 1995-96, VanDerveer takes a leave of absence to coach the American women's basketball team to its Olympic gold medal victory.

June **BIOETHICS CENTER:** The university establishes a new center to study ethics in the medical environment. The center's faculty includes scholars from medicine, religion, law, philosophy, and economics.

June 4 **SOVIET PRESIDENT VISITS:** Mikhail Gorbachev, president of the Soviet Union, briefly visits campus to make a major address in Memorial Auditorium in which he declares "the cold war has been left behind." Business on campus comes to a standstill as thousands turn out to greet Gorbachev and his 50-car motorcade. Community members line Palm Drive to cheer the motorcade, and stand behind barricades in the Inner Quad Courtyard yelling "Gor-bee, Gor-bee" as Gorbachev and his wife walk by, high-fiving and shaking hands with students.

Summer **INDIRECT COST CONTROVERSY:** Allegations that the university overcharged the federal government for several years for the indirect costs of federally sponsored research come to light, prompting separate reviews by the university and by two federal agencies. In addition, the House Subcommittee on Oversight and Investigations, chaired by Michigan Congressman John Dingell, starts its own investigation. President Donald Kennedy pledges Stanford's full cooperation and says he is "confident that the reviews in process will disclose nothing related to impropriety or fraud." The university announces the pending reviews on Sept. 12 and subsequent press accounts quote anonymous sources who allege that overcharges since 1981 by Stanford may be as high as $300 million. After initial public denials, the university confirms it has erroneously included in the indirect cost pool depreciation charges on a 72-foot yacht that had been donated to the Athletics Department. Thus begins the "indirect cost controversy," which suddenly pushes Stanford into a nationwide storm of criticism, including hostile congressional hearings and media attacks. In fall 1991, the Defense Contract Audit Agency says Stanford overcharged the government by $230 million between 1981 and 1988. Stanford denies the charge, saying it followed the rules. Paul Biddle, campus representative of the Office of Naval Research and the person who started the controversy, and who has pre-

*Soviet President Mikhail Gorbachev's motorcade rolls up Palm Drive, flanked by cheering well-wishers and shouting protesters, many waving flags in support of the Baltic republics.*

*Women's basketball team reacts emotionally to tributes after earning Stanford's first-ever NCAA crown in April 1990.*

viously sued the university personally, announces he is resigning his post to run for Congress. Biddle's campaign goes nowhere. This contentious controversy, which contributes to President Donald Kennedy's resignation, is finally settled by President Gerhard Casper in October 1994 for $1.2 million, with the government saying "it had no claims against Stanford for fraud, misrepresentations, or other wrong doing."

September **HUMAN GENOME PROJECT:** Gene research begins a new era of biomedical investigation on campus as researchers from the School of Medicine, biological sciences, and computer science assume key roles in the Human Genome Project. An international effort to decipher the entire genetic code of human beings, the project is expected to lead to discoveries that will improve diagnosis and therapy of human diseases. The role of computer science is important because after the human genome is completely sequenced, the challenges that remain will be analytical, requiring new generations of microprocessors and software designed for interpreting biological research results.

September 30 **CENTENNIAL YEAR LAUNCHED:** The university launches its Centennial Year with a convocation in Frost Amphitheater (complete with a high-tech "Centennial Fanfare"), the dedication of a U.S. Postal Service commemorative postal card, and a spectacular fireworks display over the Oval for a crowd of 5,000. *Stanford Daily* photographers Michael Topolovac and Ken Beer premiere a 15-minute slide show culled from 25,000 images before a crowd of thousands in the Inner Quad Courtyard. A centennial poster with a watercolor by art Prof. Nathan Oliveira is unveiled in October. The university sponsors three centennial symposia during the year: "The Information Age," "Beyond the Human Genome: Biological Nature and Social Opportunities," and "Ethnicity, Equity, and the Environment in an Interdependent World."

October 16 **SHARPE WINS NOBEL:** Business Prof. William F. Sharpe wins a Nobel Prize. *(See page 154)*

October 17 **TAYLOR WINS NOBEL:** SLAC physicist Richard W. Taylor wins a Nobel Prize. *(See page 155)*

## 1991

March 10 **CENTENNIAL YEAR FOUNDERS' DAY:** Wallace Stegner, professor emeritus of English, in an expanded centennial observance of Founders' Day, describes how the pioneer American West shaped the Stanfords' plans for their university. Other weekend activities include a Founders' Day Ball, unveiling of a centennial quilt hand-stitched by medical faculty wives and friends, premiere of a multimedia portrait about the Stanford family produced by the University Archives, and presentation by the Memorial Church Choir of the Gabriel Fauré Requiem. Other events leading up to the Grand Finale Weekend — Sept. 28 to Oct. 1 — include a series of multicultural celebrations, as well as special events at the 100th commencement on June 16.

May 23 **NEUROSURGEON CHARGES SEXISM:** Dr. Frances Conley, professor of neurosurgery, resigns her position,

*Thousands of students, faculty, and staff wait for hours behind police barricades in the Quad for a chance to see Mikhail Gorbachev. (Right) The Soviet leader greets George Shultz, former secretary of state. Raisa Gorbachev shakes hands with Shultz's wife, O'Bie, who is partially blocked from view.*

*The 72-foot yacht* Victoria *in 1990 becomes a symbol of allegations that the university overcharged the government for the costs of research.*

complaining of "pervasive sexism" at the Medical School. Three months later, she withdraws the resignation, citing positive steps taken by the administration to address the problem. Conley later chronicles her experiences in a book, *Walking Out on the Boys*. She is elected chair of the Faculty Senate for the 1997-98 academic year, and in 1998 is appointed chief of staff at the Stanford-affiliated Palo Alto Veterans Hospital.

June 13 **BASS GIFT:** Robert Bass and his wife, Anne, announce a $25 million gift celebrating the university's history of intellectual achievement. Bass, a 1974 graduate of the Business School, is a member of the Board of Trustees and later serves as its chairman.

July 28 **PRESIDENT DONALD KENNEDY TO STEP DOWN:** President Donald Kennedy announces that he will step down as president in August 1992, saying there is a "need to banish ambiguity and to look to the future as we resolve the problems of the past." His record has been overshadowed in recent months by the indirect cost controversy. In June 2000, Kennedy is named editor-in-chief of *Science,* the prestigious weekly peer-reviewed journal of the American Association for the Advancement of Science.

October **CLUES TO HIGH BLOOD PRESSURE:** A collaborative study provides clues of how heredity predisposes individuals to hypertension. Understanding the genetics of this complex disease, which affects 15 percent of the U.S. population, could help physicians detect it early and tailor better therapy. Researchers use a new technique known as internal analysis and total genome search to hone in on the trait responsible for hypertension. Researchers at Whitehead Institute, Cambridge, Mass., and the Stanford Department of Genetics have pioneered the technique.

October 1 **OPENING DAY CENTENNIAL:** The university observes the 100th anniversary of its opening day in a ceremony filled with music, speeches, and cheers that unexpectedly includes what President Donald Kennedy calls a "hard but successful test of Stanford's core values." A flag-bedecked re-creation of the opening day platform is the site of a planned stately culmination of four days of centennial festivities that draws more than 11,000 well-wishers to campus. It also turns out to be the venue for several hundred gay-rights protesters, who drown out keynote speaker Governor Pete Wilson because of his veto the previous day of a bill that would have strengthened homosexual rights.

December 12 **FIRST AMERICAN WEB SITE:** SLAC installs the first World Wide Web server outside Europe. Work on it began shortly after SLAC physicist Paul Kunz brought word of the brand-new "web" when he returned in September from a meeting at CERN, the European particle physics center where it was invented. Originally developed as a tool for world-wide high-energy physics collaborations, it remains a tool of physicists until 1994, when user-friendly browsers are developed and use of the web explodes.

# 1992

February 5 **BOOKSTORE CONTROVERSY:** The Bookstore's board of directors hires outside experts to review business

*Centennial Finale Weekend, Sept. 28 to Oct. 1, 1991, features panel discussions in big tents.*

*The Centennial Year is launched with confetti on Sept. 30, 1990.*

*Canadian Prime Minister Brian Mulroney is keynote speaker at a centennial convocation on Sept. 29, 1991. The Stanford Chamber Chorale performs at another convocation the next day that features Mexican President Carlos Salinas de Gortari.*

practices after the *Stanford Daily* raises questions about excessive perquisites for Stanford Bookstore managers, including a vacation home and eight leased cars. The newspaper also reports that the Bookstore — an independent nonprofit organization governed by a board of faculty, staff, and students — lost $1.8 million through bad investments in 1990. The review finds no evidence of fraud, but criticizes the directors and senior management for lax oversight and poor judgment. In 1993, the top two managers resign, the vacation home is sold, and the board is reorganized and strengthened. In June 1999, the Bookstore board selects Follett Higher Education Group to operate its stores. This includes the main campus bookstore, Tresidder Express, the Track House, the Book Shop at the museum, University Shop at Stanford Shopping Center, and Stanford Bookstore Palo Alto.

March 18 **GERHARD CASPER NAMED PRESIDENT:** Gerhard Casper, provost of the University of Chicago, is appointed Stanford's ninth president, succeeding Donald Kennedy, effective Sept. 1. Casper, born in Hamburg, Germany, in 1937, and now a naturalized citizen, is former dean of Chicago's Law School and an expert on constitutional law. At his inauguration on Oct. 2, he says he will be guided by Stanford's unofficial motto, *Die Luft der Freiheit weht* (the wind of freedom blows).

April 17 **SOVIET ARCHIVES:** The Hoover Institution and Russian officials agree to join in a $3 million program to preserve on microfilm part of the archives of the former Communist Party and the Soviet state. Several million pages of documents will be microfilmed, with Hoover paying the expenses. Other institutions had been vying for the deal, but Hoover officials trump the competition by offering the Russians microfilms of Hoover's unique collection of documents from the late Czarist and early Soviet periods.

May 27 **MAGNETIC RESONANCE IMAGING:** The School of Medicine dedicates the Richard M. Lucas Center for Magnetic Resonance Imaging (MRI). The opening paves the way for Stanford to reclaim a position of prominence in the field. Stanford's late physicist Felix Bloch won a Nobel Prize for discovering MRI.

Summer **STANFORD OLYMPIANS:** Current and former Stanford athletes win 19 medals, 17 in swimming events and two in volleyball, at the 1992 summer Olympics in Barcelona, Spain.

November 1 **MEMORIAL CHURCH REDEDICATED:** A repaired, strengthened, and improved Memorial Church is rededicated, three years after earthquake damage forced its closure. The Oct. 17, 1989, Loma Prieta earthquake damaged the dome and central arches — the area not rebuilt after the 1906 quake. Several arch stones shifted, and an 8-foot section of mosaic angel fell five stories, splintering wooden pews below. Though visible damage is relatively modest, there are serious structural problems. Engineers devise a method to brace the area around the dome using 469 tons of concrete and 22 tons of structural steel. Conservators direct repair of mosaics, sandstone arches, and the mosaic-like paint in the dome. Gold leaf is applied to the 80-foot dome ceiling, the stained glass windows (not

Patricia Ryan and Charles Lyons of the Drama Department recreate the roles of Jane and Leland Stanford in a reenactment of the university's 1891 opening ceremony.

*The centennial of Stanford's Oct. 1, 1891, opening includes three yell leaders from the first half century, leading a cheer used 100 years earlier: "Wah-hoo! Wah-hoo! L-S-J-U! STAN-ford!"*

*Staff members Kenneth Down and Linda Kovach, winners of a Leland and Jane look-alike contest.*

*Gay rights activists protesting the polices of California Gov. Pete Wilson drown out his keynote speech on Oct. 1, 1991.*

damaged by the quake) are thoroughly cleaned, the roof is strengthened and 30,000 red clay tiles are reattached. The west transept is turned into a small chapel for intimate events, and the balconies reopened with the addition of emergency exits. Former university trustee Melvin B. Lane leads the $10 million fundraising campaign, of which $1.5 million is set aside for an endowed maintenance fund. Many of the men and women who worked on the repair project attend the rededication ceremony.

December 8 **DOMESTIC PARTNERS' BENEFITS:** The university agrees to extend benefits — including health plans — to employees' long-term same-sex domestic partners.

# 1993

March 30 **WOMEN'S ATHLETICS:** In a move to achieve parity between the men's and women's sports programs, the university announces a four-year plan to add three varsity women's sports, extend 29 new scholarships to women athletes, and increase staff, funding, and facilities for women's programs. With the addition of synchronized swimming, lacrosse, and water polo, women will have 17 varsity programs. The men's program will continue with 15.

April 29 **STUDY OF UNDERGRADUATE EDUCATION:** President Casper announces formation of a commission to make a study of undergraduate education "more thorough and radical than any of the past 25 years." In fall 1994, the Commission on Undergraduate Education proposes stiffer academic requirements and calls for increased faculty involvement with undergraduates. It also calls for more undergraduate courses in science and culture, and discourages graduation in three years.

August 25 **GRADUATE KILLED IN SOUTH AFRICA:** Graduate Amy Biehl, 26, is killed in South Africa. She is the first American to die in the violence associated with the country's transition from apartheid to democracy, a transition she has been studying on a Fulbright scholarship. Biehl, who is white, is ambushed by a group of youths while driving black friends home from a party in her honor. She was drawn into study of African democratic movements while writing her honors thesis. Biehl's family sets up a scholarship and summer fellowship program at Stanford in her memory. In June 2000, the *a cappella* group Talisman, which sang at her memorial service, celebrates its 10th anniversary by performing in the South Africa townships where Biehl had registered black voters. It also sings in Gugulethu, where Biehl died and where her parents now operate a foundation to benefit local residents.

August 30 **DYING MAUSOLEUM OAK REMOVED:** The campus loses one of its most significant trees when the 300-year-old coast live oak *(Quercus agrifolia)* that has guarded the mausoleum dies from bacterial diseases. Until Leland Jr.'s death in 1884, the Stanfords had expected this tree to shade the site of their planned Palo Alto mansion. At its peak, the oak was 70-feet tall, with a branch spread of 120 feet and a trunk diameter, at breast height, of 55 inches. The tree was scheduled for removal a year earlier, but was given a reprieve when a nesting pair of starlings was discovered. Removal was again delayed by discovery of

*Gerhard Casper dons a Stanford sweatshirt in March 1992 after President Kennedy introduces him to a basketball crowd as the university's next president.*

*The mausoleum's dying guardian oak. It is removed in 1993.*

*Predecessors Richard W. Lyman, left, and Donald Kennedy celebrate Gerhard Casper's Oct. 2, 1992, inauguration as Stanford's ninth president, along with Board of Trustees Chairman John Freidenrich, right.*

a woodpecker nest. Wood from the giant tree is made available to local woodworkers. Later, a 20-foot-tall replacement oak is moved to the site from the Stanford Research Park, where it grew on a Hetch Hetchy right of way.

September 1 **FIRST WOMAN PROVOST:** Political science Prof. Condoleezza Rice, 38, becomes provost, the first woman and first African American to hold the No. 2 job. She steps down in June 1999. In December 2000, President-elect George W. Bush appoints her national security adviser.

October 6 **SEXUAL HARASSMENT POLICY:** After three years of debate and rewriting, a new policy prohibiting sexual harassment goes into effect. It creates a more extensive informal means of resolving complaints, while retaining existing formal grievance procedures, and applies to faculty, students, and staff. Stanford's sexual harassment policies date to May 1978, when informal procedures were established. The new policy replaces one that was formalized in 1981.

December **OVARIAN CANCER RESEARCH:** An analysis based on 12 studies of women with ovarian cancer confirms that a woman's likelihood of developing the most common form of this cancer is reduced with each pregnancy and with use of oral contraceptives. In addition, breast feeding after pregnancy appears to have a protective effect.

# 1994

April 6 **TERMAN FELLOWSHIPS PROGRAM:** William Hewlett and David Packard donate $25 million to establish a fellowship program in honor of their late mentor, former Provost Frederick Terman. It will provide funding for junior faculty in the natural sciences and engineering to launch research projects.

April 19 **DALAI LAMA VISITS:** The Dalai Lama, winner of the 1989 Nobel Peace Prize, speaks to a capacity crowd at Memorial Church. In his talk, he emphasizes the need for a "global community and universal responsibility." His two-day visit includes two long discussion sessions with faculty groups — one representing the physical and biological sciences and the other humanities and social sciences.

April 28 **GRADING POLICY:** The Faculty Senate approves a tougher grading policy, the most significant overhaul in 24 years. The new policy shifts the add-course and drop-course deadlines to an earlier date; it reinstates the "F"; and it limits students' ability to repeat classes for higher grades.

May 6 **CHICANA STUDENTS HUNGER STRIKE:** Four Chicana students end a three-day fast at midnight. They and their fellow protesters (at times as many as 300) leave the Inner Quad the next morning, after accepting a statement by President Casper and Provost Rice promising to study their issues. The statement calls for three committees to 1) examine demands for a grape boycott on campus, 2) enhance collaborations with East Palo Alto, and 3) add a Chicano studies program. It also says that the School of Humanities and Sciences will examine pending requests con-

*Conservator Lesley Bone (far left) gets help from Tony Holley gluing into place chunks of angel wing mosaic that fell in Memorial Church.*

*The 1992 restoration of Memorial Church following the Loma Prieta earthquake puts workers up high: They gain access to the building's framework from the roof and the inner dome skylight (right).*

cerning Asian American studies. The Chicana hunger strike was largely triggered by the dismissal of Cecilia Burciaga, the university's highest-ranking Latina administrator. Although the students initially also demanded a new high-level job for Burciaga, they were told nothing could be done because it "was part of budget cutting in the Office of Student Affairs."

May 12 **ASIAN AMERICAN STUDENTS DISRUPT FACULTY SENATE:** A group of two dozen students advocating establishment of a full Asian American studies program disrupts the Faculty Senate meeting, seeking faculty support, but instead causes an abrupt adjournment. This is apparently the first such adjournment in the senate's 26-year history. Before the meeting started, an ethnically mixed crowd of 75 greet arriving faculty with chants of "Asian American studies now — not another 20 years," a reference to the first attempts, in 1972, to establish such a program.

June 23 **JAPANESE EMPEROR VISITS:** Emperor Akihito and Empress Michiko of Japan visit SLAC and tour the klystron gallery and the SLAC Large Detector (SLD).

July 13 **STANFORD AT THE SMITHSONIAN:** A researchers' laboratory bench and equipment become a permanent part of a Smithsonian exhibit on "Science in American Life." The donated items were used by Stanford geneticist Stanley N. Cohen to conduct research in collaboration with UCSF biochemist Herbert Boyer that led to the invention of genetic engineering and the launching of the biotechnology industry. The original U.S. patent, which covers Cohen's and Boyer's discoveries and proved to be the most lucrative in Stanford's history, is also on display.

July-August **PALM DRIVE RECONSTRUCTION:** Palm Drive, the university's 3,750-foot-long ceremonial entry road, is completely rebuilt and resurfaced. The project, which finally incorporates granite curbs, as specified in Frederick Law Olmsted's original 1888 campus plan, is completed 20 days early and $100,000 under the $3.5 million budget. It later earns a Merit Award in Design from the American Society of Landscape Architects, an unusual honor for a road project.

September **TIGER WOODS REGISTERS:** Future golf star Eldrick "Tiger" Woods registers as a freshman. He completes two years before leaving to earn millions as a professional golfer.

September 29 **CZECH PRESIDENT VISITS:** Czech President Václav Havel visits the Law School to give a speech and accept the school's Jackson H. Ralston Prize. He calls for a "renaissance of spirituality" that in time would lead to "a new civic behavior."

October **SCIENCE AND ENGINEERING QUAD:** William Hewlett and David Packard together give $77.4 million toward completion of the 41-acre Science and Engineering Quad west of the Main Quad. Plans to redevelop Stanford's "industrial slum" began in the 1980s, and several buildings already have been completed. The final component will cost $140 million and requires removal of several postwar science and engineering buildings, including the often-criticized Physics Tank. James Ingo Freed of Pei

*Dean of the Chapel Robert Gregg escorts the Dalai Lama to a meeting with faculty scientists, part of a two-day campus visit in 1994.*

*Amy Biehl's parents at the campus memorial service for their daughter, right, killed in South Africa in 1993.*

Cobb Freed & Partners designs the mix of sleek modern architecture, traditional red-tiled roofs, and linking landscape features, which takes six years to complete and includes four new buildings: David Packard Electrical Engineering Building, the Teaching Center, Sequoia Hall (replacing an earlier building of the same name), and the Gordon and Betty Moore Materials Research Building. The project also includes renovation of the Jack McCullough Building and minor changes to Varian Physics Building.

# 1995

Winter **FAILED HOSPITAL MERGER:** It starts with a chance conversation on health care costs between Stanford President Gerhard Casper and Dr. Joseph Martin, chancellor of the University of California at San Francisco, at a conference in Palm Springs. Soon they ask their staffs to explore the pros and cons of merging their hospitals. Many meetings and arguments later, on Nov. 1, 1997, a new entity — called "UCSF Stanford Health Care" — comes into being. It includes the Stanford Hospital and Clinic, Lucile Packard Children's Hospital, UCSF Medical Center, and UCSF/Mount Zion Hospital. The goal of the merger is to provide cost-effective health services, improve community access to the latest advances in medical science, and maintain strong medical training programs in a changing medical world. Problems, especially with cost control, integration, and management, as well as declining reimbursements from Medicare and large health maintenance organizations, plague the venture from the start. Also, the lack of adequate faculty consultation helps prevent the development of a cooperative culture. After a rocky 1998, a surprise first-quarter 1999 loss prompts 2,000 job cuts. Projections of large, continuing losses force Casper and UC system President Richard Atkinson to begin a review of the merger on Aug. 5, 1999. Four days later, the two top officers of UCSF Stanford Health Care resign, paving the way for a cost-cutting consultant to take over. On Oct. 28, Casper advises Atkinson that because the merger has failed, the two partners must "begin the process of unraveling the current venture." Casper also writes that "I have concluded that we have taken on too much. We have failed to achieve a new common UCSF Stanford Health Care culture that could provide the whole-hearted support needed." Later that day, Casper tells the Stanford Faculty Senate that the decision to dissolve UCSF Stanford Health Care is the most anguishing of his eight-year presidency. The failed merger costs $176 million in combined losses for the 29 months of its existence, according to audited financial results released in December 2000. The two universities agree to split the losses 50-50.

January **PUBLISHING SCHOLARLY JOURNALS ONLINE:** University Libraries launches HighWire Press to provide online publication and access services to publishers and societies owning many of the world's leading peer-review scholarly journals in science and medicine. The effort begins with online production of the weekly *Journal of Biological Chemistry,* the most highly cited of any peer-review journal. By January 2001, HighWire Press provides access to 221 journal sites, with many more planned. While most of the journals require subscriptions to recent issues, all provide free access to abstracts, and many offer free access

President Gerhard Casper and Provost Condoleezza Rice in May 1994 meet with students staging a hunger strike to press for a Chicano studies program and other demands.

*Students who took part in a hunger strike celebrate what they call a partial victory.*

*Proponents of an Asian American studies program wait outside a May 1994 Faculty Senate meeting, which is adjourned prematurely when other students disrupt the meeting.*

to issues more than a year old. Rather than simply mounting electronic images of printed pages, HighWire adds links among authors, articles, and citations. It also provides multimedia, and interactive capabilities, as well as advanced searching abilities and high-resolution images. In February 2000, HighWire announces a comprehensive archiving plan involving redundancy and geographic dispersion to ensure the safety and preservation of the distributed database. HighWire Press is often referred to as the Silicon Valley version of a university press.

June **NCAA CHAMPS:** Stanford is crowned the NCAA's champion of champions for the ninth time in 10 years. The university wins five team championships: men's tennis, gymnastics, and water polo, and women's volleyball, and swimming and diving. This ties the all-time record first set by UCLA in 1981.

August **LIBRARY ACQUISITION:** University Libraries acquires the Black Panther Party collection. The organization was founded in Oakland in the 1960s to work for the advancement of African Americans, often by militant means.

August 1 **GENE THERAPY:** A study led by biological sciences Prof. Robert Sapolsky shows for the first time that gene therapy can protect some brain cells from severe damage after seizures, strokes, or other sudden brain injuries. By using an altered form of herpes simplex virus to deliver a key gene to the brain cells of rats, researchers demonstrate that they can reduce significantly the number of neurons that are killed, even when treatment is administered after brain trauma has begun. The study is published in the *Proceedings of the National Academy of Sciences*.

September **SOPHOMORE COLLEGE:** Designed to combat "sophomore slump," a new program is inaugurated with 50 students divided into five faculty-led seminars, including one led by Provost Condoleezza Rice on "The Fall of Communism and the New World Order." The two-week program of intensive study held just before the start of fall quarter expands to eight seminars for 80 students the second year. By fall 1999, it has expanded to 35 seminars for 420 sophomores. The seminars meet five mornings a week for two weeks. In the afternoons, students attend workshops to learn about undergraduate research and other opportunities.

September **ACADEMIC RANKINGS:** The National Research Council ranking of doctoral programs, done once a decade, reports improvement at Stanford in 16 programs, declines in eight, and no change in the rankings of three. Progress is noted in the humanities, notably in English, French, and linguistics. Art history, music, classics, religious studies, and Spanish and Portuguese receive lower rankings. UC-Berkeley had the highest percentage of top-ranked doctoral programs, followed by Stanford, then Harvard. The rankings are based on a survey of 8,000 faculty members at 274 institutions.

September 27 **CABLE TV LAUNCHED:** Stanford's cable television station, Channel 51, is launched. It broadcasts lectures, interviews, university job listings, sports scores, and more.

The electrical engineering building, part of the Science and Engineering Quad (right and below), is named in honor of David Packard, who dies in 1996.

Norwegian King Harald V and Queen Sonja visit the university in 1995.

Emperor Akihito and Empress Michiko of Japan talk with Dr. Regina Casper, wife of President Casper, during their 1994 visit.

October 11 **PERL WINS NOBEL:** SLAC physicist Martin Perl wins a Nobel Prize. *(See page 155)*

October 23 **NORWAY'S KING VISITS:** King Harald V and Queen Sonja of Norway tour campus and have lunch at Lou Henry Hoover House with President Gerhard Casper, Dr. Regina Casper, and community members of Norwegian descent.

## 1996

January 30 **GATES COMPUTER SCIENCE BUILDING:** Microsoft founder Bill Gates and his wife, Melinda, attend the dedication of the $38 million William Gates Computer Science Building. In 1992, Gates donated $6 million for the building, which provides unified working space for one of the nation's leading computer science departments. Gates, who briefly attended Harvard, notes that he was a college drop-out who "didn't even drop out of the right college."

February 13 **FOOD RESEARCH INSTITUTE TO CLOSE:** Trustees accept President Gerhard Casper's recommendation to close the Food Research Institute (FRI), effective June 1998 — the first closing of an academic unit in 20 years. FRI, which has 13 professors and 71 graduate students, was founded in 1921 by Herbert Hoover to study the world's production, consumption, and distribution of food. Once independent, it has a separate endowment of $12 million plus four endowed chairs. In recent years FRI has focused on food and economic development issues in Third World countries. Many graduates work in international organizations, such as the World Bank and International Monetary Fund, and in Third World governments.

March 26 **DAVID PACKARD DIES:** Former president of the Board of Trustees David Packard, one of the founders of Hewlett-Packard Co. and of Silicon Valley, dies of pneumonia at 83 at Stanford Medical Center. Packard earned a bachelor's degree in engineering in 1934 and the advanced degree of Engineer in 1939. In 1938, he and William Hewlett started their legendary company. The two donate more than $300 million to various university projects over the years. While he was alive, Packard repeatedly declined to have his name placed on buildings, but after his death his family agrees to an exception. The David Packard Electrical Engineering Building, completed in 1999, is located in the new Science and Engineering Quad.

Spring **EARLY DECISION ON ADMISSIONS:** Under a new early decision program, high school seniors commit to enroll at Stanford if they are admitted early in the admissions process. Of 3,047 who apply in the program's first year, 568 are admitted.

May **QUAD CORNERS RENAMED:** In recognition of three large donations to Stanford's Restoration Fund, a decision is made to rename three of the Quad corners. History Corner will be Lane Corner, honoring L.W. "Bill" Lane, former publisher of *Sunset* magazine and former ambassador to Australia, and his family. Language Corner (formerly Engineering Corner) will be renamed Pigott Corner, in honor of Charles Pigott, former university trustee, and his family. And Geology Corner will be called Braun Corner, in honor

Food Research Institute students hang a "Save FRI" sign in White Plaza, but to no avail. Trustees in 1996 accept a proposal to close the institute, started by Herbert Hoover in 1921.

The university's ceremonial entry road, Palm Drive, gets a long-overdue overhaul in summer 1994. Granite curbs are added, and the drainage system improved (right).

of Henry Braun, retired business executive, and his family.

May 1 **WEB SITE:** The university launches its official World Wide Web site (www.stanford.edu), designed by an East Coast firm and quickly criticized for inappropriate typography and colors (e.g., extensive use of blue). It is redesigned with classic-style typography and extensive use of red, and relaunched on Jan. 7, 1999. Stanford's first site was put up by computer science student Don Geddis around 1994 and modified by the university's computer unit, Information Technology Systems & Services (ITSS), in 1995.

May 9 **FRESHMAN SEMINARS PROGRAM:** President Gerhard Casper calls for a new Freshman Seminars Program — a major part of his Stanford Introductory Studies Initiative. Students may chose from more than 70 seminars taught by a regular faculty members. Casper notes that "students should be challenged and their minds stretched from their first year onward. The first year sets the tone." The seminars start in September 1997. The university had also operated a freshman seminars program from the 1960s through the 1980s.

May 22 **LIBRARY ACQUISITION:** University Libraries acquires, as a gift, the papers and documents of American author and playwright William Saroyan. Stanford, working in partnership with the Saroyan Foundation, will establish an annual writers prize in Saroyan's name. More than 900 boxes of manuscripts, diaries, personal effects, contracts, and letters are transported to Stanford, and more are to come.

October 9 **OSHEROFF WINS NOBEL:** Physicist Douglas Osheroff wins a Nobel Prize. *(See page 155)*

November 21 **PROGRAM ON RACE AND ETHNICITY:** The Faculty Senate approves a new interdisciplinary program in Comparative Studies in Race and Ethnicity. By 2000, more than 100 faculty are involved.

# 1997

January **NEW METHOD TO IDENTIFY CANCER GENES:** Stanford researchers isolate cancer genes through an innovative strategy called homozygous knockout (RHKO) devised by Stanley N. Cohen, professor of genetics, and postdoctoral fellow Limin Li. Using this method, researchers can simultaneously inactivate, or "knock out," copies of a gene in a cell without knowing the gene's identity or function. By identifying cells containing mutations that cause the loss of a particular trait, it is possible to find the gene responsible for that trait — in this case individual cells that are capable of forming cancers. The new strategy has enabled researchers to isolate a key gene involved in human breast cancer. The gene, called TSG101, was defective in almost half of the breast cancers the researchers studied.

February **SILICON CHIPS TO SCAN GENES:** Scientists develop a new technique, using silicon chips, to allow them to gather information about the functions of thousands of genes at once. Techniques developed independently by Stanford and Affymetrix, a biotechnology company in Santa Clara, use thumbnail-size silicon chips carrying

The traditional Big Game bonfire in the Lagunita lakebed is declared dead in 1997; it last burned there in 1992. The lakebed is habitat for the rare yellow-and-black California tiger salamander. The bonfire, seen here in 1910 and 1990, has burned in various campus locations. Smaller fires continue.

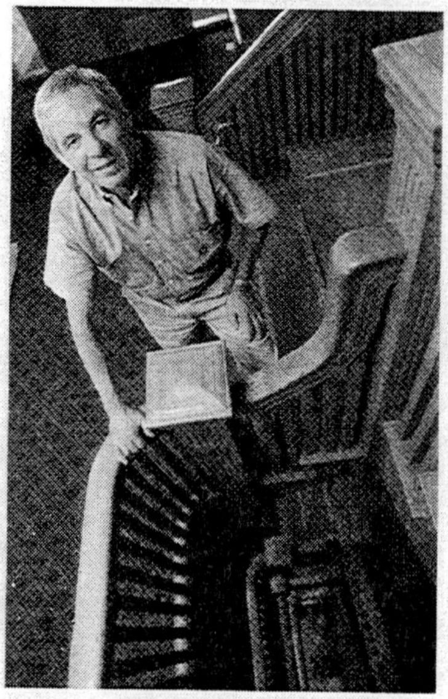

Master stairbuilder Michael Urge with the historic five-story staircase he restores in 1998 in the east wing of Encina Hall.

DNA fragments. They are created through the use of photolithography methods pioneered by the semiconductor industry to make silicon chips, and standard DNA-making techniques perfected by genetic researchers. Chip-based technology is expected to increase the pace and reduce the cost of several important efforts, including disease diagnosis, basic biological research, and the search for new pharmaceuticals.

April 9 **RAKOVE WINS PULITZER:** History Prof. Jack Rakove is awarded a Pulitzer Prize for his book *Original Meanings: Politics and Ideas in the Making of the Constitution.*

May **ENCINA HALL RENOVATION:** Work begins on a major renovation of Encina Hall as home for the Institute for International Studies, the Department of Political Science, and several related programs. The east wing, closed since the Encina fire of 1972, is seismically braced and its fire-damaged fifth floor rebuilt. The central wing is refurbished and the two-story dining room off the main lobby — from Encina's early days as a men's dormitory — is remodeled into the Bechtel Conference Center to accommodate meetings of up to 230 people. The room's grand fireplace is restored and most of the original windows and wainscoting are salvaged and reused. The lobby is restored to the style of its original 1891 appearance. The building reopens in fall 1998. During the next two years, the west wing and top floor of the central wing are renovated for Political Science and related programs. Total cost of the renovations is approximately $35 million.

May 21 **LEARNING LAB:** The university establishes the Stanford Learning Lab, which will explore ways to enrich learning by using multimedia software, digital video, and other educational technology innovations. In March 1999, the Wallenberg family of Sweden donates $15 million to the lab to establish the Wallenberg Global Learning Center. Building 160 on the Quad is remodeled for the center and named Wallenberg Hall. The center is part of an international network of labs supported by the Wallenbergs to improve formal and informal learning at all educational levels and disciplines, and across cultural and geographic boundaries.

September **CELEBRITY STUDENT:** Chelsea Clinton, daughter of President Bill Clinton, enrolls as a freshman. President Clinton and Hillary Rodham Clinton (plus Secret Service) attend freshman orientation. Campus media promise to respect her privacy, and they do.

October 1 **LAKEBED BIG GAME BONFIRE ENDS:** The administration officially ends the lakebed Big Game Bonfire — traditionally celebrated on the Thursday night before Big Game. The bonfire last burned in the lake in 1992. In 1993, the bonfire was canceled when it was discovered that Lagunita's dry lakebed was the last known breeding site of the threatened California tiger salamander. Studies since then have not found a way to have both the fire and the salamander. The Axe Committee experiments with smaller fires elsewhere. Students have used bonfires to stir up rallies or celebrate sports victories since the 1890s. For decades, the favorite site has been the dry lakebed, where scrap-wood pyres reaching 40 feet and flames of 200 feet were commonplace. The bonfires of 1976 through 1985

New student Chelsea Clinton shows her Dad the words of the Stanford hymn, printed on the back of fans distributed at 1997 freshman orientation.

University Librarian Michael Keller, right, shows flood damage to President Casper and Provost Rice on Feb. 3, 1998.

The Stanford Alumni Association merges into the university in 1998, and the university constructs for it a new $30 million building, completed in 2001, on Galvez Street.

were canceled because of crowd control and safety problems, and the fire of 1989 was canceled for lack of student funding.

October 14 **SCHOLES WINS NOBEL:** Business Prof. Myron S. Scholes wins a Nobel Prize. *(See page 155)*

October 15 **CHU WINS NOBEL:** Physicist Steven Chu wins a Nobel Prize. *(See page 155)*

November **LIBRARY ACQUIRES APPLE COMPUTER COLLECTION:** University Libraries acquires the museum and historical collections of Apple Computer as a gift. The documents, hardware, software, memorabilia, and artifacts encompass the business and technological history of the company, as well as its corporate culture.

November 4 **SAND HILL ROAD DEVELOPMENT:** After years of delay, Palo Alto voters approve a Stanford plan to develop Sand Hill Road and the area around it. The project includes widening the road from two to four lanes from Oak Creek Apartments to Arboretum Road, and connecting it to El Camino Real; constructing Stanford West, 628 rental apartments, mostly for staff and faculty, on a large vacant field between the road and San Francisquito Creek; constructing a large complex for seniors on the site of the old Children's Hospital; and expanding the Stanford Shopping Center by 80,000 square feet. Total cost of the projects is pegged at $342 million. Fifty-five percent of the voters favor the project. A superior court judge in September 1998 rejects a Menlo Park lawsuit challenging the adequacy of the project's environmental impact report.

December 26 **FORMER PRESIDENT PITZER DIES:** Kenneth S. Pitzer, a respected chemist and educator who served as Stanford's sixth president from Dec. 1, 1968, to Sept. 1, 1970, dies of heart failure at age 83. After Stanford, he taught at Berkeley until his 1984 retirement.

# 1998

February 3 **CAMPUS FLOOD:** After nearly four inches of rain falls in 24 hours, storm drains are overloaded and building basements start flooding. Soon up to four feet of mud fills basements at the School of Education, Braun Music Center, Green Library, and the Jonsson Government Documents Collection in Meyer Library. The flood causes power outages and forces some students from their dorms. Classes are canceled. Volunteers help library staff haul books and other materials from knee-high water to higher floors. More than 120,000 books and documents are sent to a special facility to be frozen before mildew can set in. Elsewhere, students enjoy the flooded center of campus, which turns into a water park. Losses are in the $3 million to $5 million range. The Archive of Recorded Sound eventually disposes of more than 10,000 damaged recordings. Several scholars lose computers and academic papers stored in their basement carrels.

April 7 **ALUMNI ASSOCIATION MERGER:** A proposal to merge the independent Alumni Association with the university clears its first hurdle when the Stanford Board of Trustees endorses a draft agreement outlining the plan. The board also approves the concept of building a new $30

Workers examine the interior of BaBar, the detector that tracks the brief lifetimes of B-mesons created in SLAC's latest particle collider, the Asymmetric B Factory.

*Stanford's seven Nobel physicists gather Oct. 13, 1998, to celebrate the life and work of Prof. Emeritus Arthur Schawlow, third from left. Schawlow is joined by, from left, Steven Chu, Martin Perl, Robert Laughlin, Burton Richter, Richard Taylor, and Douglas Osheroff. This is an especially exciting day for Laughlin. Very early this morning he received a phone call from Sweden telling him he has won a Nobel Prize. His is the fourth in four years for Stanford physicists.*

*Stanford Museum, seriously damaged in the 1989 earthquake, reopens in 1999 with an extensive addition. The two components form the Iris & B. Gerald Cantor Center for the Visual Arts.*

million facility for the Alumni Association and the Office of Development. In the summer, about 37 percent of the 67,000 eligible members of the Stanford Alumni Association vote overwhelmingly (92 percent) to make the association a division of the university, effective Sept. 1. Some opponents say that literature mailed to members only presented one side of the issue, and express concern that the association may lose its flexibility and independence. The association was founded as an independent group in 1892. In 2001, the new alumni and development building — the Frances C. Arrillaga Alumni Center — opens on Galvez Street.

June **LIBRARY AT 7 MILLION:** A colorful gift of 444 Victorian and Edwardian novels from the Associates of the Stanford University Libraries marks the acquisition of the library's 7 millionth volume.

June 12 **SOUTH KOREAN PRESIDENT VISITS:** South Korean President Kim Dae-Jung brings a message of democratic and economic reform. President Casper introduces Kim, 74, as "a man of heroic stature in the struggle for democracy." Kim calls for numerous reforms in South Korea and the end of "crony capitalism." Earlier in the week, Kim suggested to President Clinton that America end the sanctions against North Korea to help bring it out of its isolation.

September **ONLINE DEGREES:** The university offers its first completely online degree program — a master's in electrical engineering.

September 1 **ANTHROPOLOGY DEPARTMENT SPLIT:** The 50-year-old Department of Anthropology splits into the Department of Anthropological Sciences and the Department of Cultural and Social Anthropology. The decision to divide the department comes on the heels of a much-publicized disagreement over the tenure of one faculty member, but also reflects longer-term tensions in the field nationally that are rooted in diverging interests, methods, and theory.

October **ELECTRONIC NEWS:** Stanford News Service and the Alumni Association send out the inaugural issue of *@Stanford,* a monthly newsletter of campus news and research. By March 2001, approximately 65,000 recipients, mostly alumni, subscribe to the newsletter, which is distributed free via the Internet.

October 13 **LAUGHLIN WINS NOBEL:** Physicist Robert B. Laughlin wins a Nobel Prize. *(See page 155)*

October 26 **B FACTORY:** The newest particle collider, the Asymmetric B Factory, is dedicated at SLAC. The B Factory is designed to explore the differences in the laws of physics between matter and antimatter. What distinguishes the B Factory from previous colliders (and the reason it is called asymmetric) is that it has two rings, with different energies for the electrons and positrons. The produced pair of B mesons (particle and antiparticle) travel chiefly in the direction of the higher-energy electron beam. This allows scientists to pinpoint where each disintegrates, and hence to test predicted decay rates. Construction of the B Factory began in 1994. The detector for this facility, known as BaBar for its elephantine scale, is built and operated by a

*The old Main Library, known in the 1980s as Green West, reopens a decade after the Loma Prieta quake as the Bing Wing of Green Library. The Munger rotunda (left) is bathed in light, and the old reference room, now Lane Reading Room, has had its skylight uncovered.*

collaboration of more than 500 physicists from 10 nations, with funding from all over the world.

# 1999

January 24 **MUSEUM REOPENS:** An estimated 17,000 art lovers flock to the Stanford Museum, now part of the newly named Iris & B. Gerald Cantor Center for the Visual Arts, when it reopens a decade after damage from the Loma Prieta earthquake. A new 42,000-square-foot wing for modern and contemporary art and special exhibitions is built behind the 1891 neoclassical structure. Polshek & Partners of New York design the $37 million expansion and renovation. A $5 million gift from Carmen Christensen launches the rebuilding campaign and later The Christensen Fund gives $5 million in matching funds toward the center's endowment. The Cantors, who have given the university more than 200 works by Auguste Rodin, donate more than $10 million for the project.

April 15 **ONLINE NEWSPAPER:** *Stanford Report Online* begins publication five days a week. It began as a weekly online edition April 9, 1997. The address: news.stanford.edu.

July **LIBRARY ACQUISITION:** University Libraries acquires the R. Buckminster Fuller Archive. This huge collection contains the personal papers and working records of Fuller — architect, engineer, inventor, philosopher, author, cartographer, futurist, teacher, and poet — assembled during his lifetime and maintained since his death in July 1983.

August 2 **LIBRARY REOPENS:** The newly restored west wing of Green Library, closed since the 1989 Loma Prieta earthquake, reopens and is officially dedicated on Oct. 12. It is renamed Bing Wing to recognize Peter S. and Helen L. Bing for their support of the restoration. As part of the $49 million project, workers construct seismic-resistant interior concrete shear walls. Bing Wing houses the Humanities and Area Studies Resource Center, the Social Sciences Resource Center, the Jonsson Library of Government Documents, and the Department of Special Collections. The structure was built in 1919 as the Main Library.

September 1 **FIRST WOMAN SCHOOL DEAN:** Kathleen Sullivan, 44, a constitutional law expert, becomes the first woman to head a school at Stanford when she takes over as dean of law. She came to the Stanford law faculty in 1993 from Harvard.

September 14 **PRESIDENT GERHARD CASPER TO STEP DOWN:** President Gerhard Casper announces that he will step down as president in August 2000. He will have served for eight years.

September 20 **LAND USE PLANS:** The university submits to Santa Clara County the draft of a 10-year development plan. After months of negotiation and debate, the controversial plan wins approval of the county Board of Supervisors on Dec. 12, 2000. Under the plan, called the General Use Permit, the university will be allowed to build 2 million square feet of academic space — in addition to its current 12 million square feet — and build 3,000 new housing units, while preserving 2,000 acres of the foothills as open

Bio-X, started in 1999, acquires a supercomputer for 3-D images of complex biomedical processes.

Under terms of a 1999 agreement, Stanford will preserve 2,000 acres of foothills as open space for 25 years in exchange for permission from Santa Clara County to build 2 million square feet of additional academic space.

space for the next 25 years. Before completion of the first 1 million square feet of new academic space, the university must submit to the Board of Supervisors a satisfactory "sustainable development plan" — essentially a study of Stanford's ultimate capacity — in order to start on the second million square feet. The battle over the permit was mainly a fight over the foothills and what, if any, development restrictions should be placed on them. Environmental groups called for a permanent ban, while Stanford wanted no restrictions. The final compromise is to place a 25-year academic growth boundary along Junipero Serra Boulevard to keep future campus development from spilling into the foothills.

October 16 **SUPREME COURT JUSTICES:** Three members of the U.S. Supreme Court attend the Law School's "Convocation on Law" as part of the school's Alumni Weekend. Associate Justices Sandra Day O'Connor, Anthony Kennedy, and Stephen Breyer are all alumni. Chief Justice William Rehnquist, also an alumnus, does not attend. About 350 graduates serve in the nation's judiciary. A "Judiciary Atrium" is dedicated in the Crown Quadrangle, located on the first floor of the classroom building. In 1981, O'Connor became the first woman appointed to the Supreme Court.

October 26 **BIO-X:** Entrepreneur James Clark, a former Stanford professor, announces he will donate $150 million to jump-start a cross-disciplinary initiative in biomedical engineering and sciences. The James H. Clark Center for Biomedical Engineering and Sciences will house 50 scientists, physicians, and engineers who will work to increase understanding of biological systems. In addition to providing the building, the gift will fund equipment, endow faculty positions, and support graduate students. Clark says he feels indebted to the university because, as a professor in the early 1980s, he was allowed to develop technologies that brought him success in the private sector. Later, an anonymous gift of $60 million brings the total to $210 million. Clark co-founded Silicon Graphics, Netscape, Healtheon, and myCFO. The Program in Biomedical Engineering and Sciences is known informally as Bio-X.

October 27 **MEDICAL SCHOOL FACILITIES OVERHAUL:** Trustees endorse a $185-million, five-year plan to revitalize the 40-year-old Medical School facilities. A vocal group of students signed petitions seeking improvements, and the Liaison Committee on Medical School Accreditation criticized the inadequate facilities.

December 13 **E-COMMERCE:** The Graduate School of Business, which aims to be a world leader in research on e-commerce, announces it is creating the Center for Electronic Business and Commerce. The center will develop new research and education initiatives needed to understand the impact of information and communication technologies on firms, industries, and markets. The center will disseminate research to the business community through seminars and educational programs. Three e-commerce pioneers — Charles Schwab & Co., General Atlantic Partners, and eBay — provide most of the $20 million initial funding.

# 2000

**STATISTICS:**

Undergraduate enrollment: 6,548

Graduate enrollment: 7,700

Faculty: 1,672

Tuition: $24,441 per year

Endowment: $8.9 billion

January 1 **ROSE BOWL LOSS:** In its first trip to the Rose Bowl in 28 years, Stanford loses to Wisconsin, 17-9.

January **CARILLON BELLS TO BE REFURBISHED:** Twenty-three of the 35 carillon bells that hang in Hoover Tower are shipped to the Netherlands to be refurbished and retuned.

February 28 **SPACE TELESCOPE:** NASA announces award to the university for development of a space-based gamma ray telescope named GLAST. The telescope will be built as a collaboration of NASA, the Department of Energy, and five foreign countries. Management of the project will be centered at SLAC. Stanford physics Prof. Peter Michaelson is principal investigator.

April 3 **JOHN HENNESSY NAMED PRESIDENT:** John Hennessy is named Stanford's 10th president, effective Sept. 1. Hennessy, 47, came to Stanford in 1977 as an assistant professor of electrical engineering. He spent a decade as director of the Computer Systems Laboratory, then was named chair of the Computer Science Department in 1994. Two years later, he was appointed engineering dean. He became provost on July 1, 1999. In the early 1980s, Hennessy headed a project to develop a faster computer chip using an alternative computer architecture, RISC (reduced instruction set computers), that revolutionized the industry. Hennessy played a key role in transferring the technology to industry, co-founding MIPS Computer Systems (now MIPS Technologies), which specializes in production of microprocessors.

April 10 **DAVID KENNEDY WINS PULITZER:** History Prof. David Kennedy wins the Pulitzer Prize for *Freedom From Fear: The American People in Depression and War, 1929-1945.* The book, a comprehensive history of the Great Depression, the New Deal, and World War II, is the fourth volume in the Oxford University Press series on the history of the United States. Kennedy spent 11 years on the 858-page book.

April 18 **GRADUATE FELLOWSHIPS:** Stanford Graduate Fellowships, a first-of-its-kind program that allows students to engage in research based on intellectual curiosity alone, meets its target endowment by raising $200 million. The program will provide ongoing support to at least 300 of the university's most promising doctoral students per year. Stanford Graduate Fellows, who are nominated by their departments and selected by a senior faculty committee, are able to work in the lab or do research of their choice. Since President Gerhard Casper established the program in 1997, several other universities have emulated it.

April 13 **STANFORD BAND DIRECTOR ENDOWMENT:** The Stanford Band Alumni Board presents a check for $1.5 million to President Casper to fund the Dr. Arthur P. Barnes Endowment for the Stanford Director of Bands. The university now will be able to hire a full-time band director. The Band Alumni Board, composed of 18 former band members and Dollies, began the campaign in May 1999.

April **KEY PROTEIN STRUCTURE:** Researchers solve the structure of the RNA polymerase protein, one of the pivotal molecules in biology. The work conducted in the laboratory of Dr. Roger Kornberg, professor of structural biology at the School of Medicine, is an essential step in the transfer of information from gene to protein. Understanding this process becomes important as the human genome project nears completion and the DNA sequence of a human being is revealed.

May 2 **FOOTHILLS PRESERVATION:** The university announces that the foothills area known as "the Dish" will

*On April 3, 2000, John Hennessy is named Stanford's 10th president, effective Sept. 1. (Left) President Hennessy is framed by banners at his Oct. 20 inauguration. Afterward, pre-med student Kimeli Willson Naiyomah, a member of the Masai tribe, presents the new president with his own warrior leader beaded staff, as Hennessy's wife, Andrea, looks on.*

*In 1984, Hennessy, center, discusses the MIPS project with John Shott, left, and James Meindl. The faster computer chip revolutionizes the computer industry.*

become a special area for habitat conservation, as well as for continued academic use. Recreational use will be permitted, but limited to jogging or hiking on approved service roads. No pets or social events, such as picnics, will be permitted. The university also will explore an agreement with federal, state, and local agencies to assist with the preservation of several threatened animals species and will implement an environmental restoration program under the direction of the Stanford Center for Conservation Biology. The plan will be implemented by Sept. 1. The Dish refers to the radio telescope that is the most prominent landmark in the area.

May 5 **WOMEN IN SCIENCE AND ENGINEERING:** An anonymous donor gives $20 million to help boost the university's efforts at attracting and retaining women faculty and students in science and engineering.

May 9 **MED SCHOOL INTERNET START-UP:** The School of Medicine launches the first Stanford-branded commercial Internet spin-off, called e-SKOLAR. The company will, for a fee, give physicians anywhere in the world access to SKOLAR, MD, an Internet medical search service. Physicians who use this service also will have the opportunity to earn continuing medical education credits. The company e-SKOLAR has also established a similar service for nurses, called SKOLAR, RN.

May 18 **CLINICAL SCIENCES BUILDING:** The new Center for Clinical Sciences Research is dedicated. The four-story glass and concrete building next to the Beckman Center will house both basic scientists and clinical researchers in an effort to encourage a bench-to-bedside approach to medical research. It is designed by London-based architects Foster and Partners, known for designing the Hong Kong airport and the Century Tower in Tokyo. The building has 489 lab benches, 12 seminar rooms, and two auditoriums. Research specialties include molecular pharmacology, immunology, genetics, oncology, anatomy, dermatology, and bone marrow transplantation.

May 23 **NEW LAB BUILDING:** Lorry I. Lokey, class of 1949, gives $20 million for a new laboratory building for biological sciences and chemistry. It will be named after Lokey, the founder of Business Wire, and will open on Roth Way in September 2002.

June **STANFORD WINS SEARS CUP (AGAIN):** The university wins the Sears Directors Cup, awarded for the best overall collegiate athletic program, for the sixth straight year. The cup, given by the National Association of Collegiate Directors of Athletics, has been won by Stanford every year but one since it was established in 1994.

June 11 **UNITED NATIONS LEADER SPEAKS:** In his commencement address, U.N. Secretary-General Kofi Annan says he has been shocked not so much by the poor state of the environment as by the "state of the debate on the environment. In a nutshell, the need for sustainable development is failing to register on the political radar screen."

June **MEN'S TRACK TEAM IS TOPS:** The men's track and field team wins its first NCAA outdoor championship since 1934.

In May, the university announces limitations on recreational use of the hills immediately behind campus.

U.N. Secretary-General Kofi Annan talks at commencement in June about the need for better political understanding of environmental issues.

The Science and Engineering Quad's new Teaching Center has three lecture halls and two auditoriums with 360-degree revolving stages.

July 11 **CANCER TREATMENT BUILDING:** The Palo Alto City Council unanimously approves the proposed Center for Cancer Treatment and Prevention/Ambulatory Care Pavilion. The center will bring together all clinical cancer services. The 218,000-square-foot building will cost $117 million and will be located on Blake Wilbur Drive.

August 22 **HEART RESEARCH:** The Donald W. Reynolds Foundation awards $24 million to establish a Reynolds Cardiovascular Research Center. The center will enable heart specialists to use new genetic information to improve the diagnosis of coronary artery disease and the application of standard therapies.

August 31 **EXTRAORDINARY ENDOWMENT GAIN:** The combination of favorable investment returns — especially from venture capital projects — and gifts pushes the university's endowment to a record $8.9 billion at the end of fiscal year 2000. The $2.7 billion increase — 43 percent — over the prior year exceeds the total amount of the endowment eight years earlier.

October **DISTANCE LEARNING:** Stanford, Oxford, Princeton, and Yale announce that each will provide $3 million toward a "distance" learning venture for their combined 500,000 alumni. University Alliance for Life-Long Learning will provide online courses in the arts and sciences, interactive seminars, multimedia programs, and topical websites for the alumni. It is expected to be operational by late 2001.

October 20 **HENNESSY ANNOUNCES CAMPAIGN:** At his inauguration as university president, John Hennessy announces a five-year $1 billion Campaign for Undergraduate Education (CUE), which will provide permanent funding for recent innovations in undergraduate education — including Freshman Seminars, Sophomore College, and Sophomore Dialogues — and further improvements, especially focused on the junior and senior years. During his inauguration, which is broadcast live over the Internet, Hennessy also invites the community to engage in a dialogue on Stanford's future.

October 20 **TIMELY NEW ART:** Noted sculptor Maya Lin dedicates her latest outdoor artwork, *Timetable,* an eight-ton piece of black granite, steel, and stone, that features a water element and rotating parts that mark time. The work is 10½ feet in diameter and 21 inches high. A gift to the university from Helen Bing, *Timetable* is located in the courtyard in front of the David Packard Engineering Building, not far from the bold new three-story Teaching Center (a replacement for the Physics Tank). Lin notes that the artwork evolved from a concept she developed after consulting with Stanford professors. Lin, also an architect and artist, designed the Vietnam Memorial in Washington, D.C., and the Civil Rights Memorial in Montgomery, Ala.

November **HOOVER CAMPAIGN:** The Hoover Institution successfully completes a campaign launched in 1997 to raise $100 million. Of the total, $80 million was given to support Hoover's current research, with the balance, both deferred gifts and funds, earmarked for endowment. The campaign doubled Hoover's donor base.

*Sculptor Maya Lin tugs at the ribbon donor Helen Bing has just cut at the October 2000 dedication of Lin's black granite artwork in the Science and Engineering Quad.*

*Audio oscillator, Hewlett-Packard's first product. Co-inventor and co-founder William Hewlett dies in 2001.*

November 9 **FACULTY HOUSING SUBSIDIES:** Stanford announces a significantly improved program to help junior and senior faculty buy or rent houses or apartments. The program, projected to cost the university $85 million over the next five years, is an attempt to confront escalating Bay Area housing costs and faculty recruitment problems.

November 21 **CENTER FOR TEACHING AND LEARNING CELEBRATES:** More than 150 faculty, students, and staff help the Center for Teaching and Learning celebrate its 25th anniversary, at the Bechtel Conference Center. President Hennessy sets the tone when he notes "there is no higher calling than teaching. Teaching is at the heart of the university." The center focuses on helping faculty and teaching assistants become better instructors. Since course evaluations became mandatory in 1979, approximately 1,000 faculty and 10,000 teaching assistants have used the center's services.

December 12 **GENOME PROJECT:** Scientists at the Stanford Genome Technology Center complete the sequencing of the genome of the plant *Arabidopsis thaliana.* Together with researchers from the University of California and the University of Pennsylvania, the 17-member Stanford group has sequenced the plant's five chromosomes. Their decoding marks the first time a plant genome has been completely sequenced. *Arabidopsis,* a member of the mustard family, shares similar genes of food-producing crops. It is expected to make a useful model organism to enable biologists and crop scientists track down genes that help plants fight off diseases or grow more efficiently. The Arabidopsis Genome Initiative, launched in 1996, has involved researchers from the United States, several nations from Europe, and Japan.

December 13 **PHOTONICS RESEARCH:** High-tech entrepreneur Michael J. Fitzpatrick and his wife, Patty, announce they will donate $25 million to both Stanford and Duke universities to establish new centers for advanced photonics. Engineers say photonics, a technology that blends light with electronics, is at a stage of development similar to where electronics was in the 1950s. It promises high-speed, broadband fiberoptic Internet communications for use in future applications in education, medicine, entertainment, and commerce.

## 2001

January 12 **WILLIAM HEWLETT DIES:** William R. Hewlett, co-founder of Hewlett-Packard Co. and one of the founders of Silicon Valley, dies of natural causes at 87 at his Portola Valley home. Hewlett earned a bachelor's degree in engineering at Stanford in 1934 and the advanced degree of Engineer in electrical engineering in 1939. At the urging of their mentor, Prof. Frederick Terman, Hewlett and his friend David Packard launched their engineering company in 1938. They pulled together $538 in capital and started in a rented garage at 367 Addison Avenue, Palo Alto. Their first product was an audio-oscillator, modeled after one Hewlett developed in Terman's graduate electronics course. Walt Disney bought eight of the machines to use in production of the movie "Fantasia." They cost $71.50 each.

# Awards

**STATISTICS** (as of Dec. 31, 2000):

American Academy of Arts and Sciences: 222

National Academy of Sciences: 126

National Academy of Engineering: 79

American Philosophical Society: 41

National Academy of Education: 26

## Nobel laureates

### STANFORD PROFESSORS

1952 **FELIX BLOCH:** Stanford's first Nobel laureate. Co-winner of the physics prize for work on nuclear magnetic resonance. He discovered that when atoms are exposed to a strong magnetic field, the atoms would absorb certain radiowave frequencies and their core would "resonate" or vibrate. The discovery leads to magnetic resonance imaging, a widely used diagnostic tool in medicine. The term "nuclear" is dropped in a successful public relations move. He dies in 1983 at age 77. *(See also April 1934)*

1954 **LINUS PAULING:** Winner in chemistry for work at Cal Tech on the nature of chemical bonds, the force that gives atoms the cohesiveness to form molecules. In 1962, he wins the Nobel Peace Prize for his efforts to bring about an international ban on nuclear testing. He joins the faculty in 1969 for two years. He creates a stir in 1970 with his book *Vitamin C and the Common Cold,* in which he proposes massive doses of vitamin C to prevent colds. He dies in 1994 at age 93.

1955 **WILLIS E. LAMB JR.:** Co-winner in physics for his discovery at Columbia of a phenomenon called the "Lamb shift," which establishes a deviation from the previously accepted formula for the structure of the hydrogen atom. This work becomes one of the foundations of quantum electrodynamics, a key aspect of modern elementary particle physics. He is a member of the Stanford faculty during 1951-56.

1956 **WILLIAM SHOCKLEY:** Co-winner in physics for research conducted at Bell Laboratories on semiconductors and the transistor effect. In 1955, he returns to Palo Alto, where he grew up, and launches a company, Shockley Semiconductor Laboratory. Scientists that Shockley recruits to his firm quit in a management dispute, eventually spawning scores of Silicon Valley firms. Shockley joins Stanford as a lecturer in electrical engineering several months before receiving the Nobel Prize, and is elevated to professorial rank in 1963. In the 1970s, he becomes a highly controversial figure for his theory that African Americans are genetically inferior to whites. He dies in 1989 at age 79.

1958 **JOSHUA LEDERBERG, GEORGE BEADLE, AND EDWARD TATUM:** Co-winners in physiology/medicine. Lederberg, at Wisconsin, is cited for discoveries concerning genetic recombination and organization of the genetic material of bacteria. He is recruited to Stanford in 1959, then leaves in 1978 to become president of Rockefeller University in New York. Beadle and Tatum are cited for their discovery that genes act by regulating definite chemical events, work carried out in the basement of the Department of Biological Sciences (Jordan Hall), using the common bread mold, *Neurospora.* Beadle was at Stanford during 1937-47, then at Cal Tech. He later becomes president of the University of Chicago. He dies in 1989. Tatum was at Stanford during 1937-45 and 1948-57, and then goes to Rockefeller Institute. He dies in 1975.

1959 **ARTHUR KORNBERG:** Co-winner in physiology/medicine while at Washington University in St. Louis for his work in synthesizing DNA, the chemical that controls growth and heredity. He joins the Stanford faculty in 1960. *(See also December 1967)*

1961 **ROBERT HOFSTADTER:** Co-winner in physics for research on the structure of atomic nuclei. He joins the faculty in 1950. Using Stanford's Mark III linear accelerator, he obtains extremely accurate measurements of the densi-

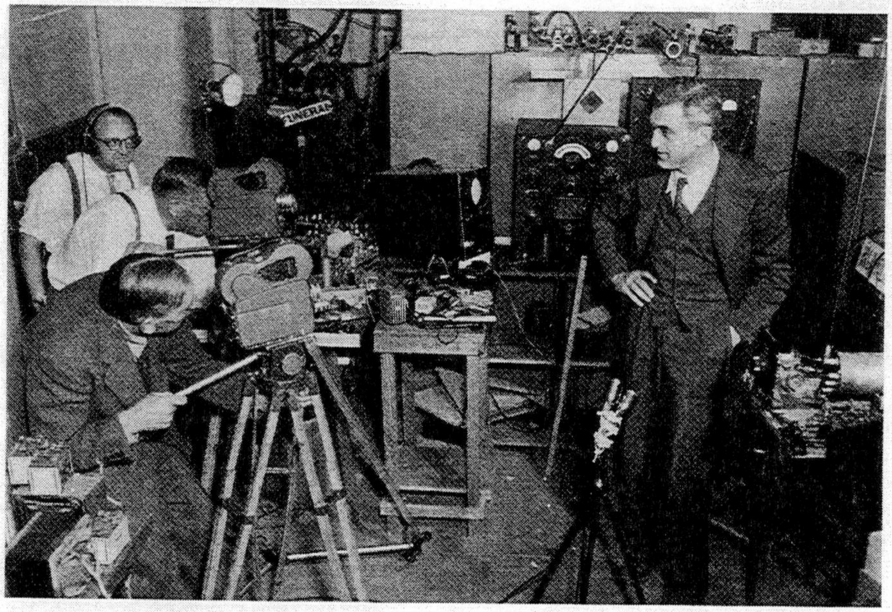

Stanford's first Nobel laureate, physics Prof. Felix Bloch, faces newsreel cameras in 1952.

ty distributions of electric charge within protons and neutrons, the constituents of atomic nuclei. His success stimulates interest in building the Stanford Linear Accelerator Center (SLAC) and its two-mile long accelerator. He dies in 1990 at age 75.

1972 **KENNETH ARROW:** Co-winner in economic sciences for his pioneering work on general equilibrium theory and the concept of social choice. He also makes major contributions to the theory of decision making under uncertainty, leading to better understanding of business cycles and the workings of financial markets. Arrow teaches economics and statistics at Stanford from 1949 to 1968, moves to Harvard for 10 years, then returns to Stanford in 1979.

1974 **PAUL J. FLORY:** Winner in chemistry for research at Stanford and Cornell on the chemistry and physics of giant molecules, or polymers, which make up such materials as natural and synthetic rubber, fibers, and plastics. The plastics used in many popular products are derived from principles first explained by Flory. He comes to Stanford in 1961. He dies in 1985 at age 75.

1976 **BURTON RICHTER:** Co-winner in physics for directing a team of Stanford and Lawrence Berkeley Lab physicists who discover an elementary particle — the psi particle — containing a fourth kind of quark, the charm quark, in November 1974 using the Stanford Positron Electron Asymmetric Ring (SPEAR) at SLAC. Twelve days after its initial discovery, the SLAC team discovers a second member of this family of new subatomic particles. Richter joins the Physics Department in 1956.

1980 **PAUL BERG:** Co-winner in chemistry for his fundamental studies of the biochemistry of nucleic acids, particularly recombinant DNA, which set the stage for subsequent development of genetic engineering techniques. He joins Stanford in 1959.

1981 **ARTHUR SCHAWLOW:** Co-winner in physics for work done earlier at Bell Laboratories that led directly to creation of the first laser. He comes to Stanford in 1961 to work in laser spectroscopy — advancing laser techniques and using them to probe the properties of matter. His research has wide impact in medicine, military, scientific research, communications, and entertainment. He dies in 1999 at age 77.

1983 **HENRY TAUBE:** Winner in chemistry for discovering basic mechanisms in chemical reactions, ranging from how enzymes and batteries work to the critical energy processes that maintain life. Taube, who comes to Stanford in 1961, determines how elements known as transition metals react. The work is important to industry because reactions determine how molecules will combine and change form, how complete the change will be, and how it can be controlled. One application of such research is improvement to the fuel cell, which combines oxygen with hydrogen to produce water and electricity.

1988 **MELVIN SCHWARTZ:** Co-winner in physics. Honored with two others for work at Columbia that finds an unexpected difference in certain kinds of neutrinos — subatomic particles that travel at the speed of light and have no mass when they are at rest and no electric charge. Schwartz is a member of the Stanford faculty during 1966-83, and a consulting professor for many years, including the year he wins the Nobel.

1990 **WILLIAM F. SHARPE:** Co-winner in economic sciences for his contributions to financial market theory. Sharpe's Capital Asset Pricing Model provides a way of matching potential gain from investment with potential

*Physics professor and 1981 Nobel Laureate Arthur Schawlow demonstrates his ability to tune a laser. He will pop the Mickey Mouse balloon inside the transparent balloon.*

risk. An associate describes the work "as a major innovation, of enduring practical and theoretical significance. No aspect of finance has been unaffected." Sharpe joins the Business School faculty in 1970.

1990 **RICHARD E. TAYLOR:** Co-winner in physics. Taylor, who joins Project M (later SLAC) in 1962, and his collaborators are honored for work on very inelastic collisions of electrons with protons and bound neutrons. These experiments, done in the late 1960s and early 1970s, provide the first direct evidence that protons and neutrons are composed of quarks, as had been theorized in the early 1960s.

1995 **MARTIN PERL:** Co-winner in physics. Perl, who joins SLAC in 1963, is honored for his discovery in experiments from 1974 to 1978 at SPEAR of the "tau" particle, a heavy electron-like particle that is the first one found in a new third family of elementary particles. This discovery requires the extension of the Standard Model theory of particle physics to its current three-family form.

1996 **DOUGLAS OSHEROFF:** Co-winner in physics for discovering the superfluid state of helium-3, while at Cornell in 1972. Previously it was thought that helium-3 had no superfluid state. This discovery opens the way to many important developments in low-temperature physics. Osheroff joins the faculty in 1987.

1997 **MYRON S. SCHOLES:** Co-winner in economic sciences for a new method to determine the value of financial derivatives, such as options. The method, developed while at MIT, becomes known in the financial world as the Black-Scholes Options Pricing Model, a benchmark formula for the valuation of stock options and other derivatives under conditions of uncertainty. He joins the Stanford Business School faculty in 1983.

1997 **STEVEN CHU:** Co-winner in physics for his work at Bell Laboratories on the fundamental interplay between light and atomic particles. One outcome is the development of methods to cool and trap atoms with laser light, thus providing new ways to study atoms and molecules. He joins the faculty in 1987.

1998 **ROBERT B. LAUGHLIN:** Co-winner in physics, the fourth Stanford professor to win the physics prize in as many years. He is honored for explaining the fractional quantum Hall effect, in which electrons flowing in a semiconductor subjected to strong electromagnetic fields act like a liquid made up of "particles" with an electrical charge that is a fraction of that of an electron. He joins the faculty in 1984.

## HOOVER INSTITUTION SCHOLARS

1976 **MILTON FRIEDMAN**: Winner in economic sciences, while at the University of Chicago, for his achievements in the field of consumption analysis and monetary history and theory. He joins the Hoover Institution as a senior research fellow in 1977.

1992 **GARY S. BECKER:** Winner in economic sciences for work at the University of Chicago extending the domain of microeconomic analysis to a wide range of human behavior and human interaction, including non-market behavior. He joins the Hoover Institution as a senior fellow in 1990.

1993 **DOUGLASS NORTH:** Winner in economic sciences for work in economic history that applied economic theory and quantitative methods to explain economic and institutional change. He joins Hoover Institution as a senior fellow in 1997.

*Chemistry Prof. Henry Taube, winner of both a Nobel Prize and a National Medal of Science, with posters of two of his favorites: Harpo Marx and Albert Einstein.*

# National Medal of Science winners

*The National Medal of Science is nation's highest award for distinguished achievement in science, mathematics, and engineering. Anyone can submit nominations; a presidential commission selects recipients, who receive the award from the president at a White House ceremony, sometimes many months after the official award year.*

1963 **CORNELIS B. VAN NIEL,** microbiology: "For his fundamental investigations of the comparative biochemistry of microorganisms, for his studies of the basic mechanisms of photosynthesis, and for his excellence as a teacher of many scientists." Presented January 1964.

1967 **PAUL J. COHEN,** mathematics: "For epoch-making results in mathematical logic which have enlivened and broadened investigations in the foundation of mathematics." Presented February 1968.

1969 **WOLFGANG K.H. PANOFSKY,** SLAC: "For classic experiments probing the elementary particles of matter and for contributions to advancing the means of experimentation in this challenging field." Presented February 1970.

1973 **CARL DJERASSI,** chemistry: "In recognition of his major contributions to the elucidation of the complex chemistry of the steroid hormones and to the application of these compounds to medicinal chemistry and population control by means of oral contraceptives." Presented October 1973.

1974 **PAUL FLORY,** chemistry: "For his outstanding contributions to our understanding of the modes of formation and structure of polymeric substances." Presented September 1975.

1974 **RUDOLF KOMPFNER,** applied physics: "For his invention of the traveling-wave tube and for major contributions to communication satellites and to optical communications." Presented September 1975.

1974 **LINUS PAULING,** chemistry: "For the extraordinary scope and power of his imagination, which has led to basic contributions in such diverse fields as structural chemistry and the nature of chemical bonding, molecular biology, immunology, and the nature of genetic diseases." Presented September 1975.

1975 **GEORGE B. DANTZIG,** operations research and computer science: "For inventing linear programming and discovering methods that led to wide-scale scientific and technical applications to important problems in logistics, scheduling, and network optimization, and to the use of computers in making efficient use of the mathematical theory." Presented October 1976.

1975 **FREDERICK E. TERMAN,** provost emeritus: "For his principal role in creating modern electronics and his ability to document his knowledge so that it could be effectively communicated to his many students who now populate the worlds of industry, academia, and public service." Presented October 1976.

1976 **HENRY TAUBE,** chemistry: "In recognition of contributions to the understanding of reactivity and reaction mechanisms in inorganic chemistry." Presented November 1977.

1979 **ARTHUR KORNBERG,** biochemistry: "For accomplishments providing the conceptual and experimental framework for much of our current understanding of the manner in which DNA, the genetic substance, is replicated." Presented February 1980.

1979 **DONALD KNUTH,** computer science: "For his significant research into the mathematical analysis and design of efficient computer algorithms and for his profoundly influential books which have codified fundamental knowledge at the core of computer programming." Presented February 1980.

1982 **EDWARD TELLER,** Hoover Institution: "For his outstanding contribution to molecular physics, understanding the origin of stellar energy, the theory and application of fusion reaction, the field of nuclear safety, and for his continued leadership in science and technology." Presented May 1983.

1983 **PAUL BERG,** biochemistry: "For fundamental contributions to understanding the mechanisms of gene expression, for the development of recombinant DNA, and for a deep concern for its safe and humane application to medicine." Presented February 1985.

1983 **RICHARD N. ZARE,** chemistry: "For his seminal contributions to molecular spectroscopy, photochemistry, and chemical reaction dynamics, especially for his incisive theoretical methods and the development of the experimental technique of laser induced fluorescence." Presented February 1985.

1986 **ROBERT HOFSTADTER,** physics: "For his discovery and development of the sodium iodide scintillation counter, leading to its application to spectroscopy in virtually all branches of science and technology, including imaging in medicine, and for his contributions to the understanding of the structure of elementary particles and atomic nuclei stemming from the development of the electron scattering method." Presented March 1986.

1987 **WILLIAM S. JOHNSON,** chemistry: "For his outstanding achievements in organic synthesis, notably in the stereoselective total synthesis of steroids by classical and biomimetic pressures." Presented June 1987.

1988 **STANLEY N. COHEN,** genetics: "For his discovery of methods for propagating and expressing the hereditary information of DNA introduced into living cells, thereby enabling the cloning of individual genes and the study of their structure and function." Presented July 1988.

1988 **MILTON FRIEDMAN,** Hoover Institution: "For his theoretical contributions, and for application, of the principles of scientific empirical and statistical methods to the field of economics and the social sciences, and to problems critical to the nation in general." Presented July 1988.

1988 **JOSEPH B. KELLER,** mathematics and mechanical engineering: "For his outstanding contribution to the geometrical theory of diffraction. This is a major extension of geometrical optics which succeeds, after many centuries, in adding the physics of diffraction to the simple ray concepts of optics and of other wave motions." Presented July 1988.

1989 **SAMUEL KARLIN,** mathematics: "For his broad and remarkable researches in mathematical analysis, probability theory and mathematical statistics, and in the application of these ideas to mathematical economics, mechanics, and population genetics." Presented October 1989.

1989 **HARDEN M. MCCONNELL,** chemistry: "For his seminal contributions in developing the power of nuclear and electron magnetic resonance spectroscopy; the introduction of the spin labelling technique; and for original discoveries of the structures, properties, and functioning of cell membranes." Presented October 1989.

1990 **JOHN MCCARTHY,** computer science: "For his fundamental contributions to computer science and artificial intelligence, including the development of the LISP programming language; the mathematical theory of computation; the concept and development of time-sharing; the application of mathematical logic to computer programs that use commonsense knowledge and reasoning; and the naming and thus the definition of the field of artificial intelligence itself." Presented November 1990.

1990 **PATRICK SUPPES,** philosophy: "For his broad efforts to deepen the theoretical and empirical understanding of four major areas: the measurement of subjective probability and utility in uncertain situations; the development and testing of general learning theory; the semantics and syntax of natural language; and the use of interactive computer programs for instruction." Presented November 1990.

1991 **ARTHUR L. SCHAWLOW,** physics: "For his role in the conception of the laser and in advancing its applications, especially in laser spectroscopy." Presented September 1991.

1992 **CALVIN F. QUATE,** engineering & applied physics: "For his contributions to microscopy, particularly the scanning acoustic microscope and the atomic force microscope." Presented June 1992.

1995 **ROGER N. SHEPARD,** psychology: "For his theoretical and experimental work elucidating the human mind's perception of the physical world and why the human mind has evolved to represent objects as it does; and for giving purpose to the field of cognitive science and demonstrating the value of bringing the insights of many scientific disciplines to bear in scientific problem solving." Presented October 1995.

1999 **JOHN ROSS,** chemistry: "For his outstanding contributions and enormous impact in physical chemistry, in particular molecular studies, the kinetics and thermodynamics of nonlinear systems, and new approaches to the determination of complex chemical and biological reaction mechanisms." Presented March 2000.

# Index

*Pages may have more than one relevant entry.*

*Italic numbers indicate a photograph.*